THE OHIO RIVER VALLEY SERIES

Rita Kohn and William Lynwood Montell
Series Editors

THE
O·H·I·O
FRONTIER

An Anthology
of Early Writings

EMILY FOSTER

Editor

THE UNIVERSITY PRESS OF KENTUCKY

Copyright © 1996 by The University Press of Kentucky

Scholarly publisher for the Commonwealth,
serving Bellarmine College, Berea College, Centre
College of Kentucky, Eastern Kentucky University,
The Filson Club, Georgetown College, Kentucky
Historical Society, Kentucky State University,
Morehead State University, Murray State University,
Northern Kentucky University, Transylvania University,
University of Kentucky, University of Louisville,
and Western Kentucky University.

Editorial and Sales Offices: The University Press of Kentucky
663 South Limestone Street, Lexington, Kentucky 40508-4008

Library of Congress Cataloging-in-Publication Data
The Ohio frontier : an anthology of early writings / Emily Foster,
    editor.
       p.   cm.   —(The Ohio River Valley series)
    Includes bibliographical references (p.   ) and index.
    ISBN 0-8131-1957-X (alk. paper)
1. Ohio—History—To 1787—Sources. 2. Ohio—History—1787-1865
—Sources. 3. Frontier and pioneer life—Ohio—Sources. 4. Indians of
North America—Ohio—History—Sources. I. Foster, Emily, 1945- .
II. Series.
F495.O353 1996   95-45218
977.1—dc20

Contents

Part Two: The Tomahawk, the Sword, and the Plough, 1782-1815   68

Part Three: The Passing of the Frontier, 1816-1843   139

Illustrations and Maps

Illustrations

Maps

Series Foreword

The Ohio River Valley Series, conceived and published by the University Press of Kentucky, is an ongoing series of books that examine and illuminate the Ohio River and its tributaries, the lands drained by these streams, and the peoples who made this fertile and desirable area their place of residence, of refuge, of commerce and industry, of cultural development and, ultimately, of engagement with American democracy. In doing this, the series builds upon an earlier project, "Always a River: The Ohio River and the American Experience," which was sponsored by the National Endowment for the Humanities and the humanities councils of Illinois, Indiana, Kentucky, Ohio, Pennsylvania, and West Virginia, with a mix of private and public organizations.

The Always a River project directed widespread public attention to the place of the Ohio River in the context of the larger American story. This series expands on this significant role of the river in the growth of the American nation by presenting the varied history and folklife of the region. Each book's story is told through men and women acting within their particular place and time. Each reveals the rich resources for the history of the Ohio River and of the nation afforded by records, papers, and oral stories preserved by families and institutions. Each traces the impact the river and the land have had on individuals and cultures and, conversely, the changes these individuals and cultures have wrought on the valley with the passage of years.

As a force of nature and as a waterway into the American heartland, the Ohio and its tributaries have touched us individually and collectively. This series celebrates the story of that river and its valley through multiple voices and visions.

Emily Foster's *The Ohio Frontier*, through first-person accounts, illuminates life in the region from the initial encounters of Europeans and Native Americans to the growing settlement of the Northwest Territory and, finally, to the 1840s removal of major tribal influence. Foster shows that the dispossession of the Natives by white settlement is a major defining theme in the history of Ohio—the state as well as the valley as a whole. This is a part of the story that has been neglected. The uniqueness of Foster's book is her willingness to allow these voices, from roughly 1750 to 1843, to speak directly to us without imposing her interpretation.

This gathering allows the reader to experience the Ohio country as a frontier, to be part of life as it was lived, to feel how people felt and hear what they thought about coming to the very fringes of the frontier, and to learn the thoughts and deeds of the people who saw them coming.

Removal of a significant part of the original population has resulted in loss and alienation by those who did the removing as well as by those who were forced to leave. We can no longer see or understand the landscapes that enticed hunters, squatters, traders, land speculators, missionaries, and eventually farmers and entrepreneurs to give up homes along the Atlantic seaboard or, in the case of direct immigration, to forge a new pattern of settlement. They changed the country beyond all recognition, as Foster shows, and few mementos remain of what the Ohio country was like before white people transformed it.

How could those who felt the need to cut down forests and drain swamps have known that some hundred and fifty years later the people now living on their "improved" land would be seeking ways to recapture a sense of the "original" place, or that those who were forcibly removed would be welcomed back as teachers? The words Foster brings to us help us visualize our past and prepare for the future. *The Ohio Frontier* joins the other titles of the Ohio River Valley Series to make history meaningful.

Rita Kohn
Lynwood Montell
Series Editors

Acknowledgments

My greatest debt is to the Ohio Humanities Council, without whose funding this book would not exist. Most particularly, I am grateful to Oliver Jones, executive director, who prodded me to write a grant proposal, gave encouragement and support throughout the long months of compiling the anthology, and participated in the search for a publisher.

I would like to thank also the staff of the Ohio Historical Society archives, especially Charles Arp. This wonderful repository of Ohio history put most of the contents of the anthology at my fingertips, and the patience and helpfulness of the staff were invaluable.

For the boundless enthusiasm and wisdom of Rita Kohn, co-editor of the Ohio River Valley Series, I am deeply grateful; she conveyed more confidence in my powers than I felt. I also would like to thank James O'Donnell and Charles Cole for reading the manuscript and pulling me back from the brink of many pitfalls. Whatever errors remain are mine alone. Also, to Charles Cole, for cheerfully taking time from his own projects to make suggestions about mine, and to Jack and Scott DeGroff, who drove me on a cold, wet day to find the grave of Daniel Diver, I extend my further thanks.

Mike Barber, who photographed a number of the illustrations, put his considerable photographic expertise at the disposal of a photo dunce. I am in his debt.

Finally, for more than two years of watching my evenings and weekends consumed by this project, and for not complaining most of the time, I am indebted to my husband, Lee Brown.

Introduction

Ohio. What images does that word bring to mind? To outsiders, perhaps not many. To some coastal dwellers, Ohio is another flyover state somewhere near, say, Chicago. To more sophisticated travelers, it's part of the great American heartland, with its feet firmly planted in the Midwest. Anything else? Hmmm. . . .

Even Ohioans often are vague about Ohio. Northern Ohioans look around and see old industrial cities, rich ethnic diversity, Lake Erie, and a few New England church spires. Southern Ohioans are more conscious of Appalachian culture, strip-mining, heavily logged hardwood forests, and the Ohio River. Western Ohioans look out across the flat farmland and the German brick church steeples toward the Great Plains; nowhere else does agriculture seem so much a part of the essence of Ohio. What is the glue that holds these assorted images together? What is Ohio?

It may be that present-day Ohioans do not have a clear sense of a place called Ohio because when white settlers came to the state they worked so hard and fast—and successfully—to change it. The story of the Ohio country is the story of its transformation. Only by understanding what Ohio was like two hundred and more years ago is it possible to grasp how much it has been changed by successive waves of immigrants, starting with the first European settlers. The taming of the wilderness and the building of European-style agrarian and manufacturing communities changed the landscape itself beyond anything those first awestruck European visitors or the native inhabitants would recognize today.

In the late eighteenth century, Ohio was a prize. For more than sixty years, whites and Native Americans fought to the death among themselves and with each other for possession of it. It was one of the Indians' best hunting grounds. It was a rich source of pelts for the lucrative fur trade. And, eventually, it became both the next frontier for land-hungry Americans and also a line drawn in the sand by Native Americans who said, "This far, and no farther." It is hard to appreciate now what an important role early Ohio played in the fantasies and ambitions of Europeans and in the political and cultural realities of Native Americans.

1

Before the mid-eighteenth century, very few Europeans had traveled through Ohio, and even fewer could or did write about their travels. And Indians had no written language. We know that Sieur de La Salle explored the Ohio Valley in the seventeenth century, but we know little about other early voyagers. In La Salle's time, Ohio had few native inhabitants. The Iroquois had wiped out the tribe of Erie Indians who had lived in northern Ohio in the mid-seventeenth century. Ohio was used as a hunting and trapping ground for many tribes. Indians began to settle in Ohio in significant numbers only as Europeans drove them out of their homes elsewhere.

The Miamis came from the west and northwest. The Wyandots came down from the northwest and Canada. The Shawnees migrated from the south and east at the invitation of the Miamis. And the Delawares came via Pennsylvania, where white settlement had encroached on their hunting grounds. These major tribal groups who lived in Ohio in the eighteenth century tended to settle in the area of the state where they had entered. The Shawnees filtered up the Scioto River valley from the south; the Miamis (also called Twigtwees) lived in western Ohio, along the Maumee and Miami Rivers; the Wyandots settled in northwestern and north-central Ohio and the Delawares concentrated mostly on the Muskingum and Tuscarawas Rivers in eastern Ohio. They overlapped with each other (Delawares settled along the Scioto, for example), and tribes also shared space among themselves, such as the Ottawas, who lived along Sandusky Bay.

The tribes lived roughly in these areas when the English and French first cast a covetous eye on the land. In 1749, the French sent Celeron de Bienville down the Ohio River to claim the Ohio River valley for France. Bienville buried lead plates along the way declaring the land to be French. He traveled into the interior as well, where he met some of the English traders who already had set up shop to compete for the fur trade. In 1750 the Ohio Company, a group of mostly Virginian speculators, sent Christopher Gist to scout the country in the British-American interest. It wouldn't be long before the fierce competition between these two powers for control of Ohio, its resources, and the important Ohio River waterway to New Orleans would become a war.

Besides being wary of each other, early European travelers and traders also had to deal with suspicious and often hostile Indians, who already had much to fear and loathe in Europeans, but who also had become almost completely dependent on European trade. By the mid-eighteenth century, Indians considered as necessities such things as blankets, guns and ammunition, and iron tools. They themselves did not manufacture such things, so they traded furs for them. Unfortunately, they also had become enamored of alcoholic beverages, a theme that will recur throughout the readings in this book.

Whenever the whites fought each other, Indians found they had to choose sides, for the outcome of such quarrels usually affected their trading rights and the course of white settlement. By the middle of the century, Indians were feeling the stress of the constant encroachments on their territory. They had been cheated by the whites, who sometimes also pitted tribes against each another. As Indian tribes moved into Ohio, they tried to divorce themselves from the intertribal quarrels between the Iroquois and other eastern nations and to establish themselves as independent spokespersons for their own tribal interests.

Accordingly, they usually didn't work together. They considered themselves Delawares or Shawnees rather than Indians. Bear in mind they were no more alike as individuals or tribes than were groups of Europeans. While some tribes were warlike, others prided themselves on diplomacy. While some, such as Ottawas, seemed to be rather free and easy about sexual relationships, others, such as the Shawnees, were restrained to the point of prudishness. While some Indians practiced cannibalism and torture, others disapproved.

Like European nations, the various Indian nations had a long history of fighting one another, so when unity against the white interlopers would have been an advantage to them, they had trouble working together. Only exceptional Indian leaders, such as Pontiac and Tecumseh, were able to ally some of them successfully for a short time.

After the middle of the eighteenth century, it became more and more apparent to the Ohio natives that Ohio might be a final testing ground for their ability to live on their own land without interference. To the west lay hostile tribes; to the east and south, growing outposts of white civilization. When the Six Nations tribes signed the Treaty of Fort Stanwix in 1768 ceding much of present West Virginia, Kentucky, and western Pennsylvania to the whites, Ohio Indians felt betrayed; thereafter they considered themselves independent of their brothers in New York and disregarded the treaties made on their behalf. That didn't stop whites such as Daniel Boone from moving into Kentucky, but they did so at their peril.

It was clear to the Indians that white people respected no bound-

aries except their own. Long before the whites actually moved across
the Ohio River and began to farm the Indians' land, they hunted on
it and, in effect, stole the Indians' food and furs.

The story of early Ohio is the story of the dispossession of the
Indians. In fact, that single struggle so dominates the history of frontier Ohio that it sets the theme of this book. Accounts of how the
Indians fought to keep their land, how they lost it, and the dire effect of this loss are found throughout this anthology. On the other
hand, the stories of how the white settlers fought to win Ohio, and
how hard and bitter their struggle was are also found here.

Today, except for place names, hardly a single reminder is left of
the native Ohioans. They left no monuments to their civilization.
(The Indians of the eighteenth and nineteenth centuries knew as little
of the prehistoric mound-builder Indians as we do.) They have no
reservations in Ohio. They left no written accounts of their history
in the state. Perhaps that is one of the reasons Ohioans have forgotten an important part of Ohio--because reminders of that history were
swept out like the dust a long time ago. The last groups of natives
were forced to emigrate to Kansas and Oklahoma in 1838 and 1843.

In their place, white settlers flooded the state. The land rush
started with the Ohio River villages of Marietta, Belpre and others
in the 1780s, and became a tidal wave after the Indians relinquished
two-thirds of the state by the 1795 Treaty of Greenville. European
Americans grabbed up the cheap new land of the "west." They cut,
cleared, milled, and mined, slaughtering predators and prey as fast
as they could, occupying the land for white civilization. It was tre-
mendously hard work. They were far away from the amenities of
eighteenth-century European life. They suffered from heat, cold, fever, accidents, and, for years, from the attacks of hostile Indians.
Many of them died prematurely. Some died horribly.

But they kept coming. Ohio was reputed to be a magical place. It
was a land of unbelievable beauty and plenty. Settlers recorded the
biggest fish, the thickest trees, the largest flocks of birds, and the
fattest game anyone had ever seen. The land was covered with immense forests. Huge wild grapevines festooned the ancient hard-
woods. Bears, elk, and wolves roamed the forests, which were broken by vast cane brakes. Buffalo browsed on the prairie and along
the rivers. To settlers from New England, even the milder climate of
Ohio was a siren's call.

While most of the people who traveled to Ohio came away deeply
awed and impressed by its natural beauties, the European travelers
also frequently saw past the landscape as it was to the landscape as

also frequently saw past the landscape as it was to the landscape as it could be with the help of the plow, the saw, and the ax. From the portage at "Camp Sandusky" where he was negotiating with the Indians, Lieutenant Colonel Israel Putnam wrote to a fellow officer in Connecticut in 1764: "I suppose you will think it strange that in many places in this country there are 10,000 to 20,000 acres of land without a bush or a twig, all covered with grass so big and high that it is very difficult to travel; and all as good plow land as you ever saw, any of it fit for hemp." In the selections in this book by Reverend David Jones and Christopher Gist, both writers express similar sentiments, as if to say, "Isn't this country wonderful? It only needs a bit of work to make it perfect"—that is, fit for civilization.

The Europeans came to Ohio in many guises. They came first as hardy traders, such as George Croghan, who often acted as a liaison, interpreter, and scout between the British (later the American) government on the one hand and the Indians on the other. They came as missionaries, such as David Zeisberger, David Jones, and John Heckewelder, and as adventurers and woodsmen, such as Daniel Boone and Simon Kenton, who competed with the Indians for the same game and often were admired by them for their proficiency in forest craft. They came as speculators or the agents of speculators, such as Christopher Gist, who surveyed tracts of land for later development, and as squatters, who hoped to stay on the land long enough to make improvements and be paid for their trouble. They came as military men with the awesome task of making war in a strange land by strange rules. They came as decent farmers and small traders, who bought the speculators' lands. They came as doctors, lawyers, and criminals. They even came as captives of the Indians, such as James Smith and Jonathan Alder, whose loyalties sometimes were divided between their natural and adopted peoples.

As they arrived in Ohio they had to overcome the challenge of the environment. And they also had to live with the fear of the frontier. For years, their lives were on the line, especially if they lived on the fringes of the white settlements, where they were easy targets for attacking Indians. Even after Indians were no longer a threat, white settlers complained of the sheer loneliness of the forest, where the trees cast a permanent shadow and one might not see another white face for months on end.

The new settlers brought with them every imaginable bias, including religious and racial. Some hated Indians; others wanted to convert them. A few were sympathetic to the Indians' plight and, of course, those who had been captured and adopted by Indians often and self-interest. Some European settlers who came to Ohio had little sympathy for the land and people around them. Some were not interested in civilized life at all. As the French tourist Francois Michaux noticed, some stayed in a place only as long as it was unsettled; as soon as a few neighbors moved in, they sold their land, picked up, and moved farther away.

The accounts in this book are colored by the status, motives, and prior experiences of the observers, so the tone is variously patronizing, romantic, or businesslike. The writer may take a place's military or agricultural measure. The stories they tell may not even be literally true. The rescue of Mrs. Stoops from the Indians, of which three versions are included here, is an example of how a story gets distorted when told and retold.

As for the Indians' point of view, in 1759 an Englishman named Charles Thomson wrote "An Enquiry into the Causes of the Alienation of the Delaware and Shawanese Indians," regarding a disputed land purchase in Pennsylvania. He observed: "It is true, as the Indians have no Writings, nor Records among them, save their memories and belts of wampum, we can only have recourse to the minutes taken, and records kept, by one party, nay, oftentimes, by those who, if any advantage was taken of the Indians, must have been concerned in it, and consequently would not care, by minuting every thing truly, to perpetuate their own disgrace." True to Thomson's insight, it was impossible to eliminate the misunderstandings and exploitation that resulted from this communication gap.

All we know of the Indians during this period is what is recorded by whites. Not all accounts are unfriendly. Indeed, some, such as those of Jonathan Alder and James Smith, are by whites who had adopted Indian ways. It was not uncommon for white captives who were well treated by the Indians to prefer life with them to repatriation. Some of these adoptees remained "Indian" for the rest of their lives. Others re-entered the white community and left their memoirs of life among the Indians for their children and grandchildren. Did they necessarily tell the whole truth about their own role in Indian raids and hostilities against whites? It would be naive to think so.

Another marginalized people in early Ohio were the African-Americans, some of whom lived among the Indians. After white settlement began in earnest, others came with their former owners to work as laborers. One of the most remarkable early African-American personalities was James Stewart. Inspired by religious conviction, and speaking no Indian language, he spent years preaching among the Wyandots of Upper Sandusky.

As the distinction between slave states and free states became more pronounced in the nineteenth century, Ohio was a place of refuge for runaway slaves. Jumping ship in Cincinnati or swimming the Ohio River, however, was not a guarantee of their freedom. Slave owners or their agents often pursued their "property" to reclaim it. Anti-slavery supporters helped the runaways; some Ohio abolitionists established the Underground Railroad, a loose network of safe houses to escort runaways on their way to Canada. They acted out of human kindness or religious conviction, such as the Quaker Wells Brown, who saved the life of the escaped slave who took the name William Wells Brown. Unfortunately, few black Americans could read and write sufficiently to contribute personal recollections of this period in Ohio.

This book is history made of bits and pieces of the Ohio experience from as close up as possible. In that sense it is without the context a formal history would have. Each voice is as important as the next. Each writer cares only about what is in front of him or her. Few of the writers know or care how their experiences fit into a larger story about Ohio, America, or the world.

What this book may offer is a better sense of the place called Ohio. Each of the people whose words form this book came to that place and experienced it. They may not have known how their experiences fit into a larger historical picture, but they knew as well as any of us what they felt and saw and did. They were not historians, but they witnessed and made the history of Ohio. They saw the passenger pigeons overhead, they cut down the trees, they feared for their lives, they shot the game, they slogged over the muddy roads, they made war, they plowed and planted, they built cities.

They were so successful that in fifty years Ohio was almost unrecognizable. The prize was won. Later generations transformed the state into the diverse, urban society it is today without retaining a collective memory of its roots or a sense of how the Ohio community was formed. This book is a partial restoration of that loss.

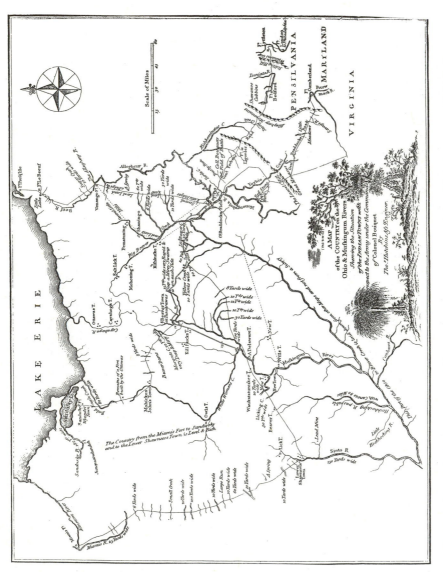

Thomas Hutchins's early map of Western Pennsylvania and the Ohio Country. Although a facsimile of this was inserted into the 1870 edition of Col. James Smith's account of his captivity in the 1750s, the map dates from the mid-1760s.

PART ONE

Europeans Discover Ohio
1750-1782

What Sort of People Are the Whites?
—Tontileaugo

Before this book opens, in the middle of the eighteenth century, Ohio was a busy place, crisscrossed with Indian trading routes, but it was not home to large numbers of people. By mid-century, however, Indian tribes began drifting into Ohio to take up residence, mainly because they were being crowded out of their homes elsewhere by white settlement. The Delawares moved west from their homes in western Pennsylvania, and the Wyandots drifted south around Lake Erie from their homes on the north shore. The Shawnees were invited to move into the Scioto River valley by the Miamis, or Twigtwees, partly because the Miamis hoped to use the Shawnees as a buffer between themselves, in western Ohio, and troublesome whites on the east.

As the Indians came, a few white traders came with them. Some of them married into tribes and lived in Ohio. Others came and went on business. But whites were few and scattered. As far as most American colonists were concerned, Ohio was virtually unexplored wilderness.

Naturally, several trading posts sprang up, such as the Miami trading post of Pickawillany on the Great Miami River. One of the major problems for the Indians who came to Ohio with the fur trade was alcohol. The unregulated flow of spirits was a longstanding grievance of Indian leaders. In 1744, Governor George Thomas of Pennsylvania wrote: "I cannot but be apprehensive that the Indian Trade as it is now carry'd on will involve us in some fatal Quarrel with the Indians. Our Traders in Defiance of the Law carry Spirituous Liquors amongst them, and take the Advantage of their inordinate Appetite for it to cheat them of their Skins and their Wampum, which is their Money, and often to debauch their Wives into the Bargain."

For years Indian leaders tried to stop or regulate the trade, but they were never successful. In the stories of James Smith and the Reverend David Jones the subject arises again and again. It was a problem that was never resolved while the Indians remained in Ohio.

The French and English, so often at war in Europe, translated their international rivalry into fierce competition over the lucrative North American fur trade and came to blows on the frontier, too. Each side worked hard to win over the Indian tribes. While the Wyandots, Delawares, and Shawnees usually supported the British, the Miamis often allied themselves with the French. But the situation was always fluid. Often British diplomatic failures alienated those tribes that were usually friendly. At other times, the Indians became disgusted with the French and tried to make their peace with the British.

So the Indians seesawed back and forth, depending on who treated them better, who kept promises, who gave the best prices for goods—and who they thought would come out on top. In the 1750s, they were less happy with the British. They thought them incompetent warriors, especially after General Edward Braddock's defeat in 1755, which James Smith mentions in his memoirs. But later, after inflicting a terrible scourge on the British settlements in western Pennsylvania, the Indians turned around and made peace with the British.

But peace never seemed to last. All sorts of grievances, such as broken treaties and cheating traders, kept the frontier a dangerous place. The murder of Chief Logan's family on Yellow Creek in 1774 touched off what was called Lord Dunmore's War. And scarcely was that skirmish settled, when another event threw everything into turmoil again.

After the French lost their Canadian empire at the close of the French and Indian War, the British and American colonists turned on each other. Once again, the native tribes were in the middle, trying to choose sides with an eye to their own best interests. Mostly, they preferred the British. The weak, young, American government made promises it couldn't keep, and it had virtually no control over the hunters, traders, and speculators who did as they pleased on the frontier.

In 1768 the Iroquois had signed the first Treaty of Fort Stanwix, making the Ohio River a boundary water and giving up most of Kentucky and western Pennsylvania and some of present-day West Virginia. Unfortunately, the Ohio Indians received none of the proceeds of the sale and refused to recognize the treaty. The Shawnees in particular had long regarded Kentucky as their special hunting preserve and did not consider themselves bound by anything the Iroquois agreed to. They defended their claim to Kentucky strenuously. But the treaty was a signal to adventurers such as Daniel Boone to head west. He and his fellows thought they had as much right as the Indians to hunt there. And where they hunted they soon brought their families and settled.

At best, when the Indians caught white hunters in Kentucky, they confiscated their furs and guns and sent them packing with a warning. Later, as whites came in greater numbers to establish settlements, the confrontations turned violent. The Indians raided settlements and blockhouses, stole horses, killed whites, and tried to drive them off. But it was a losing battle. Irate colonists raised militias and struck back in kind—usually, if not always, with the blessings of the new American government.

As long as the whites were caught up in the Revolutionary War, however, the Indians mostly were secure in their Ohio home. They still had reason to believe that they owned Ohio and, with a show of force, might retain Kentucky. That situation changed abruptly with the end of the Revolutionary War, as we shall see in Part Two.

The writers represented in Part One are not literary men. Nor did they write for the purpose of entertainment, with the possible exception of the Englishman Nicholas Cresswell. Most wrote the equivalent of business reports, or they kept journals for their own and their friends' edification. Some were plainly better writers (and spellers) than others. That must be taken into account when reading their observations.

Second, place names and proper names had no standardized spelling, nor even necessarily standardized names. The Shawnees were Shannoahs, Shawanes or Shanaws. The Scioto River was called Sciota or Sciodoe. White Woman's Creek is now the Walhonding River. Some places have disappeared altogether, such as the Indian villages of Tuscarawa or Pickawillany. And the Shawnees had several villages they called Chillicothe, only one of which was on the site of present-day Chillicothe.

For all these reasons, the first section is the hardest to read and has the most explanatory notes. Only one entry, that of Colonel Richard Butler, has been altered to make it more readable.

The First English Journal of the Ohio Country: Christopher Gist's Journals, 1750-1751

The very first European travelers in Ohio were not tourists. They came on business, primarily the fur trade. Christopher Gist was the first Englishman to travel to what is now Ohio and write about his trip afterward. He was a fur trader, surveyor, ranger, and man of means. In the late 1740s he associated himself with the Ohio Company, a trading and land development company.

In 1750 the Ohio Company asked him to travel to Ohio. His orders stated: "You are particularly to observe the Ways & Passes thro all the Mountains you cross, & take an exact Account of the Soil, Quality, & Product of the Land, and the Wideness and Deepness of the Rivers. . . . You are also to observe what Nations of Indians inhabit there, their Strength & Numbers, who they trade with, & in what Comodities they deal." Gist was also to survey the largest piece of good land he found and describe it so it could be found again.

The English already had a busy fur trade with the Ohio Indians, but it was threatened by the French traders. So Gist was to try to win the Indians over to the English. His orders suggest he also was to look over the countryside with an idea of developing it. So Gist looked about him at the wonderful landscape and imagined European-style improvements. The Indians he met would not have been happy to read his mind.

Gist's three-month trip to Ohio took him from present Beaver, Pennsylvania, to Lisbon, Ohio, and to the Ottawas' town at the junction of the Big Sandy and Tuscarawas Rivers just above present Bolivar. Then he went to Old Wyandot Town within a mile of present-day Coshocton. He arrived there in mid-December, 1750, and celebrated Christmas by witnessing a horrible murder.

Wednesday Dec. 26.—This Day a Woman, who had been a long Time a Prisoner, and had deserted, & been retaken, and brought into the Town on Christmass Eve, was put to Death in the following manner: They carried her without the Town, and let her loose, and when she attempted to run away, the Persons appointed for that Purpose pursued her, & struck Her on the Ear, on the right Side of her Head, which beat her flat on her Face on the Ground; they then stuck her several Times, thro the Back with a Dart, to the Heart, scalped Her, & threw the Scalp in the Air, and another cut off her Head: There the dismal Spectacle lay till the Evening, & then Barny Curran desired Leave to bury Her, which He, and his Men, and some of the Indians did just at Dark.

Wednesday [January] 9.—The Wind Southerly, and the Weather something warmer: this Day came into Town two Traders from among the Pickwaylinees (these are a Tribe of the Twigtwees [Miamis]) and brought News that another English Trader was taken prisoner by the French, and that three French Soldiers had deserted and come over to the English, and surrendered themselves to some of the Traders of the Pick Town [Pickawillany, a Miami trading town near present-day Fort Loramie], that the Indians woud have put them to Death, to revenge their taking our traders, but as the French Prisoners had surrendered themselves, the English woud not let the Indians hurt them. . . .

Tuesday 15.—We left Muskingum [Coshocton], and went W 5 M, to the White Woman's Creek, on which is a small Town; this White Woman was taken away from New England, when she was not above ten Years old, by the French Indians; She is now upwards of fifty, and has an Indian Husband and several Children—Her name is Mary Harris, she still remembers they used to be very religious in new England, and wonders how the White Men can be so wicked as she has seen them in these Woods.

Wednesday 16.—Set out SW 25 M, to Licking Creek—The Land from Muskingum to this Place rich but broken—Upon the N Side of Licking Creek about 6 M from the Mouth, are several Salt Licks, or Ponds, formed by little Streams or Dreins of Water, clear but of a blueish Colour, & salt Taste[.] [T]he Traders and Indians boil their Meat in this Water, which (if proper Care be not taken) will sometimes make it too salt to eat.

Gist traveled from Hockhocking, now Lancaster, southwest to a Delaware Indian town in present Pickaway County on the Scioto River, which he calls Sciodoe Creek.

Sunday 27. . . . We lodged at the House of an Indian whose Name was Windaughalah, a great Man and Chief of this Town, & much in the English Interest. He entertained Us very kindly, and ordered a Negro man that belonged to him to feed our Horses well. . . .

Then Gist and his group went to the big Shawnee Town at the mouth of the Scioto River, west of the present city of Portsmouth. For many years, this was the most important Shawnee village in Ohio. There he attended an unusual ritual, a sort of mate-swapping dance. In early published editions of Gist's journal, his description of the dance, which he promised to describe "at the end of my journal," was expurgated.

Tuesday 29.—Set out SW 5 M, S 5 M, to the Mouth of Sciodoe Creek opposite to the Shannoah [Shawnee] Town. . . . The Shannoah Town is situate[d] upon both Sides [of] the River Ohio, just below the Mouth of Sciodoe Creek, and contains about 300 Men, there are about 40 Houses on the S Side of the River and about 100 on the N Side, with a Kind of State-House of about 90 Feet long, with a light Cover of Bark in which they hold their councils. . . .

Thursday 31st, to Monday February 11th. Stayed in the Shawane [Shawnee] town. While I was here the Indians had a very extraordinary festival, at which I was present, and which I have exactly described at the end of my journal [inserted here as follows]. In the evening a proper officer made a public proclamation, that all the Indian marriages were dissolved, and a public feast was to be held for the three succeeding days after, in which the women (as their custom was) were again to choose their husbands.

The next morning early the Indians breakfasted, and after spent the day in dancing, till the evening, when a plentiful feast was prepared; after feasting, they spend the night in dancing.

The same way they passed the two next days till the evening, the men dancing by themselves, and then the women in turns round fires, and dancing in their manner in the form of the figure 8, about 60 or 70 of them at a time. The women, the whole time they danced, sung a song in their language, the chorus of which was,

> I am not afraid of my husband;
> I will choose what man I please.

Singing those lines alternately.

The third day, in the evening, the men, being about 100 in number, danced in a long string, following one another, sometimes at length, at other times in a figure of 8 quite round the fort, and in and out of the long house, where they held their councils, the women standing together as the men danced by them; and as any of the women liked a man passing by, she stepped in, and joined in the dance, taking hold of the man's stroud, whom she chose, and then continued in the dance, till the rest of the women stepped in, and made their choice in the same manner; after which the dance ended, and they all retired to consummate.

Gist then went to the Miami town, Pickawillany, more or less to spy out the number of Indians living there.

Sunday [February] 17.—. . . . All the Way from the Shannoah Town to this Place (except the first 20 M which is broken) is fine, rich level Land, well timbered with large Walnut, Ash, Sugar Trees, Cherry Trees &c, it is well watered with a great Number of little Streams or Rivulets, and full of beautiful natural Meadows, covered with wild Rye, blue Grass and Clover, and abounds with Turkeys, Deer, Elks and most Sorts of Game particularly Buffaloes, thirty or forty of which are frequently seen feeding in one Meadow: In short it wants Nothing but Cultivation to make it a most delightfull Country. . . . This town [Pickawillany] is situate on the NW Side of the Big Miamee River about 150 M from the Mouth thereof; it consists of about 400 Families, & daily encreasing, it is accounted one of the strongest Indian Towns upon this Part of the Continent. . . .

While he was there, some Indians came from the French, bringing brandy and tobacco, and tried to woo back the Miamis to trade with them. Gist and his party were doing the same on behalf of the English. Gist won the war of words. The Miamis dismissed the French representatives, saying they would never trade with them again, and gave presents and made a friendly speech to the English.

Friday March 1.—We received the following Speech from the Twigtwees the Speaker stood up and addressing himself as to the Governor of Pennsylvania with two Strings of Wampum in his Hand, He said—"Brothers our Hearts are glad that You have taken Notice of Us, and surely Brothers We hope that You will order a Smith to settle here to mend our Guns and Hatchets, Your Kindness makes Us so bold to ask this Request. You told Us our Friendship should last as long, and be as the greatest Mountain, We have considered well, and all our great Kings & Warriors are come to a Resolution never to give Heed to what the French say to Us, but always to hear & believe what You our Brothers say to Us. . . .

Even as Gist signed a treaty of friendship with the Indians, he looked covetously on their land. "The Land upon the great Miamee River is very rich level and well timbered, some of the finest Meadows that can be."

Sunday [March] 3.—This Morning We parted, They for Hockhockin, and I for the Shannoah Town, and as I was quite alone and knew that the French Indians had threatened Us, and woud probably pursue or lye in Wait for Us, I left the Path, and went to the South Westward down the little Miamee River or Creek, where I had fine traveling thro rich Land and beautiful Meadows, in which I coud sometimes see forty or fifty Buffaloes feeding at once. . . .

Gist went down the Ohio River on his way to the falls at present Louisville. But hearing reports of a large number of French-aligned Indians being there, he went back to Virginia through Kentucky.

The Burning of Pickawillany: Captain William Trent's Journal of His Trip from Logstown to Pickawillany, 1752

A year after Christopher Gist went to Ohio in 1751, Captain William Trent was sent there by Virginia governor Robert Dinwiddie. He, too, went to the Miami trading post of Pickawillany and to Shawnee Town at the mouth of the Scioto. His mission was much the same as Gist's—to woo the Miamis away from the French and secure them as trading partners for the Ohio Company. But he arrived in Ohio to hear that Pickawillany had been burned to the ground by a group of French and their Indian allies. Some English traders there had been murdered. As Dinwiddie later reported to the Board of Trade: "[Y]ou'll please observe the risk he run, and the miserable condition he found these poor people in; their town taken, and many of their people killed by the French and Indians in amity with them, and many of the English traders ruined. . . ."

Trent was a Pennsylvania soldier and a brother-in-law of the well-known trader and Indian agent George Croghan, who had been on Gist's expedition. In 1750 Trent and Croghan formed a partnership to trade with the Indians. As a result Trent often was used by the government to act as a go-between with the Indians and even to go on military expeditions. His private and public interests therefore overlapped. Trent was made responsible for building a fort at the Forks of the Ohio, and was in the process of doing so when it was captured by the French, who promptly built Fort Duquesne (later Fort Pitt, then Pittsburgh).

In 1763 Trent was ruined when his storehouses near there were plundered and burned during the Indian uprising called Pontiac's Conspiracy. Later, he got a grant of land to make up for this misfortune, but he never was a friend to the Indians, as Croghan and some others were. At one point in his career, Trent participated in a scheme to send blankets infected with smallpox to the Indians.

In 1752, when Trent went on the journey he describes below, the major trading center in western Pennsylvania was a place called Logstown (now Ambridge, Pennsylvania). That was Trent's starting point.

[June] 29th. We got to [the] Muskingum, 150 miles from the Logstown, where we met some white men from Hockhocken [present-day Lancaster], who told us the town [Pickawillany] was taken and all the white men killed, the young Shawanees king having made his escape and brought the news.

July the 2d. We reached Hockhocken where we met with William Ives, who passed by the Twightwee town [Pickawillany] in the night. He informed us that the white men's houses were all on fire, and that he heard no noise in the fort, only one gun fired, and two or three hollows.

6th. We arrived at the lower Shawanees town [near present-day Portsmouth], where the Indians received us very kindly, with the firing of guns, and whooping and hollowing, according to their custom, and conducted us to the long house (the council house), where, after they had given us victuals, they inquired the news; we told them the next day we would let them know everything.

Then Thomas Burney and Andrew McBryer, the only two men that escaped, when the town was attacked, came to us and told us that 240 French and Indians, on the 21st of June, about nine o'clock in the morning, surprised the Indians in the cornfields, and that they came so suddenly on them that the white men, who were in their houses, had the utmost difficulty to reach the fort. Three not being able to get to the fort shut themselves up in one of the houses. At this time there were but twenty men and boys in the fort, including the white men.

The French and Indians having taken possession of the white men's houses, some of which were within ten yards of the fort, they kept a smart fire on the fort till the afternoon, and had taken the three white men who had shut themselves up in one of the houses. Though they had plenty of arms and ammunition in the house, they could not be prevailed upon by the white men and Indians in the fort to fire a gun, though they encouraged them as much as possible, but as soon as they were taken told how many white men were in the fort.

The French and Indians in the afternoon let the Twightwees [Miamis] know that if they would deliver up the white men that were in the fort, they would break up the siege and go home. After a consultation it was agreed by the Indians and whites that as there were so few men and no water in the fort, it was better to deliver up the white men, with beaver and wampum, to the Indians not to hurt them, than for the fort to be taken, and all to be at their mercy. The white men were delivered up accordingly, except Burney and Andrew, whom the Indians hid. One of the white men that was wounded in the belly, as soon as they got him they stabbed and scalped, and took out his heart and eat it. Upon receiving the white men they delivered up all the Indian women they had prisoners, and set off with the plunder they got out of the white men's houses, amounting to about three thousand pounds. They killed one Englishman and took six prisoners, one Mingoe [Iroquois] and one Shawanees killed, and three Twightwees; one of them, the old Pianguisha [Piankashaw] king, called by the English Old Britain, who, for his attachment to the English, they boiled, and eat him all up. . . .

Trent, his men, and some Indians went to Pickawillany, which was deserted. They lowered the French flag and raised the British, took what furs had been left behind and returned to the Shawnee town.

29th. We reached the Shawanees town after a very tiresome and tedious journey, having then carried the goods between six and seven hundred miles, the weather the hottest that ever was known in these parts, many of the Indian dogs dropping dead as they were hunting;

the runs and creeks were so dry, that we were almost perished for want of water, having traveled one day two and twenty miles without a drop. . . .

After a brief quarrel about which flag to fly, French or English, they got down to the business of negotiating. The Indians gave a number of speeches, accompanied with belts of wampum for emphasis.

The Twightwees made the following speech to the English, with a green belt and pipe:

"Brothers: when we first went to see you, we made a road which reached to your country, which road the French and Indians have made bloody; now we make a new road, which reaches all the way to the sun-rising, one end of which we will hold fast, which road shall remain open and clear forever, that we and our brothers may travel backwards and forwards to one another with safety; and if we live till the Spring, our brothers may expect to see us, and we send this pipe that our brothers may smoke out of, and think upon what we say, and they may depend upon seeing us in the Spring, at which time we will give a full answer." (Gave the belt and pipe.) . . .

When we found that Old Britain was killed, we gave the cloths, by advice of the Six Nations [the eastern Iroquois federation], in the following manner: The scarlet cloak to Old Britain's son, a young lad; the hat and jacket, with the shirt and stockings, to the young Pianguisha king; we clothed Old Britain's wife; and gave the rest of the goods to the young Pianguisha king, the Turtle, and two more men of the nation, for the use of the Twightwees; and I persuaded an Indian trader to carry the goods for them, who promised to do it, and he set off with horses for the lower Shawanees town for that purpose.

James Smith's Captivity among the Indians: The Memoirs of James Smith, 1755-1759

There was another side to the Indians besides that described by William Trent. When the Indians weren't killing their white opponents, they often were adopting them to replace members of their tribe who had died or been killed in war. It was not uncommon for a war party to descend on a farmhouse, wipe out most of the family, and take one or two into captivity, where they were treated with great tenderness and accepted fully into the tribe. Many white captives later wrote about the kind treatment they received. A few stayed by choice with their

Indian families for the rest of their lives. James Smith's story is not unusual in this respect. In the five years he lived among them, he learned to love and respect his Delaware family and came to appreciate their way of life.

In May, 1755, Smith, age eighteen, traveled with a party of three hundred road-cutters to make a wagon road for General Edward Braddock's troops, who were marching against the French in Pennsylvania. During this work, young Smith and another man, Arnold Vigoras, were sent on an errand. "About four or five miles above Bedford," he wrote, they were set upon by three Indians. Vigoras was shot and killed, while Smith was taken as a captive to Fort Duquesne, then a French stronghold. Just outside the fort, he was beaten unconscious while running the gauntlet. One of his Indian captors later told him that the gauntlet implied no malice, but "was like how do you do."

On July 9, Smith watched a large party of Indians and French march off; later that day they returned in triumph bearing scalps and British booty. They had just routed Braddock's forces in one of the more humiliating defeats of the English soldiers by the Indians.

A few days later, the Caughnewaga Indians, who were Mohawks and therefore part of the Iroquois nation, took Smith west to their town on the west branch of the Muskingum River. There they plucked out most of his hair and readied him for an adoption ceremony.

As I at that time knew nothing of their mode of adoption, and had seen them put to death all they had taken, and as I never could find that they saved a man alive at Braddock's defeat, I made no doubt but they were about putting me to death in some cruel manner. The old chief holding me by the hand made a long speech very loud, and when he had done he handed me to three young squaws, who led me by the hand down the bank into the river until the water was up to our middle. The squaws then made signs to me to plunge myself into the water, but I did not understand them; I thought that the result of the council was that I should be drowned, and that these young ladies were to be the executioners.

They all three laid violent hold of me, and I for some time opposed them with all my might, which occasioned loud laughter by the multitude that were on the bank of the river. At length one of the squaws made out to speak a little English (for I believe they began to be afraid of me) and said, *no hurt you;* on this I gave myself up to their ladyships, who were as good as their word; for though they plunged me under water, and washed and rubbed me severely, yet I could not say they hurt me much.

These young women then led me up to the council house, where some of the tribe were ready with new cloths for me. They gave me a new ruffled shirt, which I put on, also a pair of leggins done off with ribbons and beads, likewise a pair of mockasons, and garters dressed with beads, Porcupine-quills, and red hair—also a tinsel laced cappo. They again painted my head and face with various colors, and tied a bunch of red feathers to one of these locks they had left on the crown of my head, which stood up five or six inches. They seated me on a bear skin, and gave me a pipe, tomahawk, and polecat skin pouch, which had been skined pocket fashion, and contained tobacco, killegenico, or dry sumach leaves, which they mix with their to-bacco—also spunk, flint and steel.

. . . —At length one of the chiefs made a speech which was deliv-ered to me by an interpreter,—and was as followeth:—"My son, you are now flesh of our flesh, and bone of our bone. By the ceremony which was performed this day, every drop of white blood was washed out of your veins; . . . —My son, you have now nothing to fear, we are now under the same obligations to love, support and defend you that we are to love and defend one another, therefore you are to con-sider yourself as one of our people."

This ceremony took place in Tecanyaterighto's, or Pluggy's, town. That night there was a war dance with battle songs. The next morning Pluggy and a party of warriors left for the east.

Smith was entrusted with a rifle for a short time, but when he got lost in the woods during a hunting trip, the Indians took it back and demoted him to bow and arrow. When Pluggy and his warriors returned, they brought some scalps from their raid along the Potomac and an English Bible, which they gave to Smith.

He then went hunting with his adopted brother, Tontileaugo. They traveled up the Muskingum and overland to Lake Erie, then walked along the shore until they came to a Wyandot town at the mouth of the Canesadooharie, or Black, River, where Tontileaugo's Wyandot wife was staying. They and the Wyandots hunted up the Black River to the falls at what is now Elyria. There Smith's Bible mysteriously disappeared.

After this I was again out after nuts, and on my return beheld a new erection, which were two white oak saplings, that were forked about twelve feet high, and stood about fifteen feet apart. They had cut these saplings at the forks and laid a strong pole across which ap-peared in the form of a gallows, and the posts they had shaved very smooth and painted in places with vermilion. I could not conceive the use of this piece of work, and at length concluded it was a gal-lows, I thought that I had displeased them by reading my books, and that they were about putting me to death.—The next morning I observed them bringing their skins all to this place and hanging them over this pole, so as to preserve them from being injured by the weather, this removed my fears. They also buried their large canoe in the ground, which is the way they took to preserve this sort of a canoe in the winter season.

They made a winter camp with the Wyandots along "a large creek that empties in Lake Erie betwixt Canesadooharie, and Cayahaga [Rocky River]." There they built a log house with a bark roof and a bearskin covering the doorway. Then they had to hunt for food. At first, they killed only two turkeys, which were divided equally among twenty-one men, women, and children. Smith was struck by the Indians' cooperative way of life. When they needed horses to improve their chances at hunting, the men went on a raid and stole some. In the spring, they tapped maple trees for sugar. Then they planned to move into town and plant corn. The women rendered the rest of the bears' fat and put it into deer skins to transport it.

On our arrival at the falls, (as we had brought with us on horse back, about two hundred weight of sugar, a large quantity of bears oil, skins, &c.) the canoe we had buried was not sufficient to carry all; therefore we were obliged to make another one of elm bark. While we lay here a young Wiandot found my books: on this they collected together; I was a little way from the camp, and saw the collection, but did not know what it meant. They called me by my Indian name, which was Scoouwa, repeatedly. I ran to see what was the matter, they shewed me my books, and said they were glad they had been found, for they knew I was grieved at the loss of them, and that they now rejoiced with me because they were found. . . . —This was the first time that I felt my heart warm towards the Indians. Though they had been exceeding kind to me, I still before detested them, on account of the barbarity I beheld after Braddock's defeat. Neither had I ever before pretended kindness, or expressed my[s]elf in a friendly manner; but I began now to excuse the Indians on account of their want of information.

Instead of going to town, Smith and Tontileaugo went on another hunt along Lake Erie, and once again Smith learned something about the Indian way of sharing.

After some time the wind arose, and we went into the mouth of a small creek and encamped. Here we staid several days on account of

high wind, which raised the lake in great billows. While we were
here Tontileaugo went out to hunt, and when he was gone a Wiandot
came to our camp; I gave him a shoulder of venison which I had by
the fire well roasted, and he received it gladly, told me he was hungry, and thanked me for my kindness. When Tontileaugo came home,
I told him that a Wiandot had been at camp, and that I gave him a
shoulder of roasted venison: he said that was very well, and I suppose you gave him also sugar and bears oil, to eat with his venison. I
told him I did not; as the sugar and bears oil was down in the canoe I
did not go for it. He replied you have behaved just like a Dutchman.
Do you not know that when strangers come to our camp, we ought
always to give them the best that we have? I acknowledged that I
was wrong. He said that he could excuse this, as I was but young;
but I must learn to behave like a warrior, and do great things, and
never be found in any such little actions.

Smith and Tontileaugo rejoined the tribe at the village at Sunyendeand, on a
creek (either Cold or Pipe Creek) at the bottom of Sandusky Bay. There they
traded their skins with French traders for clothes, paint, tobacco, and other necessities. In June, 1756, the men of the tribe all marched off to war. Once again
those left in camp were reduced to near starvation before the warriors returned
with food, along with scalps, horses, and white prisoners.

One John Savage was brought in, a middle-aged man, or about forty
years old. He was to run the gauntlet. I told him what he had to do;
and after this I fell into one of the ranks with the Indians, shouting
and yelling like them; and as they were not very severe on him, as
he passed me, I hit him with a piece of pumpkin—which pleased the
Indians much, but hurt my feelings.

The tribe lived a lazy life of plenty the rest of the summer, with much singing,
dancing, and gaming on Sandusky Bay. In October, Tontileaugo's older brother,
a chief named Tecaughretanego, asked Smith to go on a hunt. They joined a
larger party from other tribes and camped and hunted all over northeastern Ohio
until the first of December. Then the group wintered in their tepees in present-
day Mahoning County and hunted beaver. There Smith and Tecaughretanego
both showed a little ignorance about the world around them.

It is a received opinion among the Indians, that the geese turn to
beavers and the snakes to raccoons; and though Tecaughretanego,
who was a wise man, was not fully persuaded that this was true; yet

he seemed in some measure to be carried away with this whimsical notion. He said that this pond had been always a plentiful place of beaver. Though he said he knew them to be frequently all killed, (as he thought;) yet the next winter they would be as plenty as ever. And as the beaver was an animal that did not travel by land, and there being no water communication, to, or from this pond—how could such a number of beavers get there year after year? But as this pond was also a considerable place for geese, when they came in the fall from the north, and alighted in this pond, they turned beavers, all but the feet, which remained nearly the same. . . .

In conversation with Tecaughretanego, I happened to be talking of the beavers' catching fish. He asked me why I thought that the beaver caught fish? I told him that I had read of the beaver making dams for the conveniency of fishing. He laughed, and made game of me and my book. He said the man that wrote that book knew nothing about the beaver. The beaver never did eat flesh of any kind; but lived on the bark of trees, roots, and other vegetables.

In order to know certainly how this was, when we killed a beaver I carefully examined the intestines, but found no appearance of fish; I afterwards made an experiment on a pet beaver which we had, and found that it would neither eat fish or flesh; therefore I acknowledged that the book I had read was wrong.

In March, 1757, the group headed the forty or fifty miles back to the forks of the Cuyahoga, carrying hundreds of pounds of skins with them. They stopped briefly at a pond to hunt waterfowl.

While we remained here I went in company with a young Caughnewaga, who was about fifteen or seventeen years of age, Chinnohete by name, in order to gather crannberries. As he was gathering berries at some distance from me, three Jibewa [Chippewa] squaws crept up undiscovered and made at him speedily, but he nimbly escaped, and came to me apparently terrified. I asked him what he was afraid of? He replied did you not see those squaws? I told him I did, and they appeared to be in a very good humor. I asked him wherefore then he was afraid of them? He said the Jibewa squaws were very bad women, and had a very ugly custom among them. I asked him what that custom was? [H]e said that when two or three of them could catch a young lad, that was betwixt a man and a boy, out by himself, if they could overpower him, they would strip him by force in order to see whether he was coming on to be a man or not. He said that was what they intended when they crawled up, and ran so violently at him, but said he, I am very glad that I so narrowly escaped. . . .

When we came to the forks, we found that the skins we had scaffolded were all safe. Though this was a public place, and Indians frequently passing, and our skins hanging up in view, yet there was none stolen; and it is seldom that Indians do steal anything from one another; and they say they never did, until the white people came among them, and learned some of them to lie, cheat and steal,—but be that as it may, they never did curse or swear, until the whites learned them; some think their language will not admit of it, but I am not of that opinion; if I was so disposed, I could find language to curse or swear, in the Indian tongue.

I remember that Tecaughretanego, when something displeased him, said, God damn it.—I asked him if he knew what he then said? he said he did; and mentioned one of their degrading expressions, which he supposed to be the meaning or something like the meaning of what he had said. I told him that it did not bear the least resemblance to it; that what he said, was calling upon the great spirit to punish the object he was displeased with. He stood for sometime amazed, and then said, if this be the meaning of these words, what sort of people are the whites? . . . He said he remembered once of a trader's accidentally breaking his gun lock, and on that occasion calling out aloud God damn it—surely said he the gun lock was not an object worthy of punishment for Owaneeyo, or the Great Spirit; he also observed the traders often used this expression, when they were in a good humor and not displeased with anything. . . .

Smith and Tecaughretanego dug up their canoes, built yet another, and paddled and sailed along the shore of Lake Erie to the Wyandot town opposite Fort Detroit, where they traded some of their skins for provisions. Smith got a new gun. Then a French trader arrived with brandy.

We purchased a keg of it, and held a council about who was to get drunk, and who was to keep sober. I was invited to get drunk, but I refused the proposal—then they told me that I must be one of those who were to take care of the drunken people. I did not like this; but of two evils I chose that which I thought was the least—and fell in with those who were to conceal the arms, and keep every dangerous weapon we could, out of their way, and endeavor, if possible to keep the drinking club from killing each other, which was a very hard task. Several times we hazarded our own lives, and got ourselves hurt, in preventing them from slaying each other. . . .

When the trader had got all our beaver, he moved off to the Ottawa town, about a mile above the Wiandot town.

When the brandy was gone, and the drinking club sober, they appeared much dejected. Some of them were crippled, others badly wounded, a number of their fine new shirts tore, and several blankets were burned:—a number of squaws were also in this club, and neglected their corn planting.

We could now hear the effects of the brandy in the Ottawa town. They were singing and yelling in the most hideous manner, both night and day; but their frolic ended worse than ours; five Ottawas were killed and a great many wounded.

In late fall, 1757, Smith and his group went back into Ohio for their winter hunt. The party split in two at Cedar Point, and Smith went south to the Sandusky plains between the Scioto and Sandusky with Tecaughretanego, Tontileaugo, and two families of Wyandots. Already they were regretting the profligate spending of their beaver pelts on liquor.

The little family group then crossed the Scioto and made their camp by what Smith referred to as Olentangy Creek, but which was probably Big Darby Creek. There Tontileaugo and his wife quarreled, and she packed up the children and left. Saying he was afraid some harm might befall the children, Tontileaugo went after her. Smith, Tecaughretanego, crippled by rheumatism, and his young son were left behind. For a while, Smith was able to provide for the three of them, but then game disappeared and soon they were facing starvation. The nearest people were at least forty miles away. Smith despaired. Tecaughretanego ordered his son to boil up some bones for the weary hunter, then made a speech.

"Brother,
As you have lived with the white people, you have not had the same advantage of knowing that the great being above feeds his people, and gives them their meat in due season, as we Indians have, who are frequently out of provisions, and yet are wonderfully supplied, and that so frequently that it is evidently the hand of the great Owaneeyo that doth this: whereas the white people have commonly large stocks of tame cattle, that they can kill when they please, and also their barns and cribs filled with grain, and therefore have not the same opportunity of seeing and knowing that they are supported by the ruler of Heaven and Earth. . . .

Brother,

Owaneeyo some times suffers us to be in want, in order to teach us our dependance upon him, and to let us know that we are to love and serve him: and likewise to know the worth of the favors that we receive, and to make us more thankful.

Brother,

Be assured that you will be supplied with food, and that just in the right time; but you must continue diligent in the use of means—go to sleep, and rise early in the morning and go a hunting—be strong and exert yourself like a man, and the great spirit will direct your way."

The next morning I went out, and steered about an east course, I proceeded on slowly for about five miles, and saw deer frequently, but as the crust on the snow made a great noise, they were always running before I spied them, so that I could not get a shoot. A violent appetite returned, and I became intolerably hungry;—it was now that I concluded I would run off to Pennsylvania, my native country. As the snow was on the ground, and Indian hunters almost the whole of the way before me, I had but a poor prospect of making my escape; but my case appeared desperate. If I staid here I thought I would perish with hunger, and if I met with Indians, they could but kill me.

I then proceeded on as fast as I could walk, and when I got about ten or twelve miles from our hut, I came upon fresh buffaloe tracks,—I pursued after, and in a short time came in sight of them, as they were passing through a small glade—I ran with all my might, and headed them, where I lay in ambush, and killed a very large cow. I immediately kindled a fire and began to roast meat, but could not wait till it was done—I ate it almost raw. When hunger was abated I began to be tenderly concerned for my old Indian brother, and the little boy I had left in a perishing condition. I made haste and packed up what meat I could carry, secured what I left from the wolves, and returned homewards.

I scarcely thought on the old man's speech while I was almost distracted with hunger, but on my return was much affected with it, reflected on myself for my hard-heartedness and ingratitude, in attempting to run off and leave the venerable old man and little boy to perish with hunger. . . .

As it was moon-light, I got home to our hut and found the old man in his usual good humor. He thanked me for my exertion, and bid me sit down, as I must certainly be fatigued, and he commanded Nunganey to make haste and cook. I told him I would cook for him, and let the boy lay some meat on the coals, for himself which he did, but ate it almost raw, as I had done. I immediately hung on the kettle with some water, and cut the beef in thin slices, and put them in:—when it had boiled awhile, I proposed taking it off the fire, but the old man replied, "let it be done enough." This he said in as patient and unconcerned a manner, as if he had not wanted one single meal. He commanded Nunganey to eat no more beef at that time, least he might hurt himself; but told him to sit down, and after some time he might sup some broth—this command he reluctantly obeyed.

When we were all refreshed, Tecaughretanego delivered a speech upon the necessity and pleasure of receiving the necessary supports of life with thankfulness, knowing that Owaneeyo is the great giver.

They ended the winter there with plenty of food. In spring, 1759, the three canoed from Detroit to Montreal, where Smith heard of a ship at anchor there with English prisoners aboard to be exchanged. Smith quietly joined them and eventually made his way back to his family in Pennsylvania in 1760. "They received me with great joy, but were surprised to see me so much like an Indian, both in my gait and gesture."

Although Smith had many more adventures in his life, and distinguished himself in the Revolutionary War, he never returned to the land where he had lived with the Indians.

The Indians Preach to the Preacher: Charles Beatty's Missionary Trip to the Ohio Indians, 1766

In 1766, Charles Beatty was appointed by the Presbyterian synod of New York and Philadelphia to preach to the Indians in Ohio. He spent two months among them. At what was then called Tuscarawa town (which he calls Tuscalawa), a Delaware town on the site of present Bolivar, he was welcomed warmly, once the Indians found he was not from the Moravian sect of Protestant missionary, for they were not friendly toward Moravians at that time. He met with the chief and head men and requested permission to preach. They allowed him to do so, but they also had a few things to say to him about the rum trade, which was sapping the natives' morale and health; it is a recurring theme in their dealings with the traders and settlers. Beatty recorded the speech of one chief in his journal.

Brothers, you have spoken to us against getting drunk—What you have said is very agreeable to our minds.—We see it is a thing which is very bad; and it is a great grief to us, that rum, or any kind of strong liquor, should be brought among us, as we with the chain of friendship, which now unites us and our brethren, (meaning the English) together, may remain strong. But,

Brothers, the fault is not all with us, but begins with our brothers, the white people; for if they will bring out rum some of our people will buy it; they must buy it; it is for that purpose it is brought; but, if none was brought, then they could not buy it. And, now,

Brothers, we beseech you, be faithful, and desire our brothers, the white people, to bring no more of it [to] us. Shew this belt to them for this purpose, (at the same time holding forth a large belt of wampum) shew it to the great man of the fort (meaning the commanding officer of Fort Pitt) and to our brothers on the way as you return; and to the great men in Philadelphia (meaning the principal men in the government) and in other places, from which rum might be brought, and intreat them to bring no more. And, now,

Brothers, there is another thing we do not like, and complain of very much. There are some (meaning white people) who do at times, hire some of our Squaws, (that is their women) to let them lie with them; and give them rum for it. This thing is very bad. The Squaws then sell the rum to our people, and make them drunk.

We beseech you, advise our brothers against this thing, and do what you can to have it stopped."

After having delivered their speech, they gave the belt of wampum, and desired us to take down in writing what they had said, that we might not forget any part of it; for that it was a matter about which they were much concerned.

A Would-Be Missionary: The Journal of the Reverend David Jones, 1772-1773

As a missionary, the Reverend David Jones had serious drawbacks. He didn't speak any Indian language and he never gained the trust of the Ohio Indians. Having traveled to Ohio to preach, he stayed only two months before leaving in frustration. His account of his trip during the winter of 1772-73 is highly colored by his prejudices and naivete. It wasn't that he disliked Indians; he just had no imagination about their point of view. Many of the Delawares and Shawnees he dealt with didn't like the idea of white religion. Nevertheless, they mostly were kind, if firm, in their dealings with him. In fact, he might not have survived the trip without the charity of both the Indians and whites he met on the frontier.

Jones kept a travel diary of the trip that tells us a lot about him, the hardship of travel, the lay of the land, and the habits of the natives. It records how he journeyed down the Ohio River in December, 1772. A minister who traveled with him died on the way and was buried near Grave Creek, in present-day West Virginia, but Jones pressed on. He caught a ride with a trader in a sixty-foot canoe.

Monday [December] 28, . . . This night was severely cold—the canoe was loaded near eighteen inches above its sides; on this was my lodging. Though well furnished with blankets, was afraid my feet would have been frozen. It may be well supposed that thoughts of sleep in such apparent danger were not the most pleasing; for moving a few inches in sleep, would have made the bottom of Ohio to be my bed. . . .

Monday [January] 4, set out for the river Siota, and about the middle of the day came to the mouth of it. —the Shawannee Indians formerly lived near the mouth of this river, but finding that their enemies had too easy access, they moved their habitation up the stream. . . . The name which the Shawannees give Siota, has slipt my memory, but it signified Hairy River. The Indians tell us that when they came first to live here, deers were so plenty, that in the vernal season, when they came to drink, the stream would be thick of hairs; hence they gave it the name. . . .

Was informed that this river has its sources towards Lake Erie, and that there is but a very small land passage between this river and the streams that empty into that Lake. This will afford a communication with this western world not much thought of; for it is said goods from New-York can be afforded much cheaper at Fort Detroit, than from Philadelphia by land carriage. . . .

Thursday 7, as the canoe was poled up the stream for the advantage of killing game, chose to walk on land; but mistaking the way that the river turned, lost myself on the largest walnut bottom that ever I met with before. After some time, found myself mistaken— what added to my surprise, night approached, and the sun did not shine.

After ruminating on my case, and recollecting the courses I came, concluded that I knew which way the west lay; therefore set off and run over several bad places, till at last the top of a very high hill appeared. Exhilarated with the view, with not a little speed to this my course was bent; but before it was ascended far, had the pleasing prospect of the river, yet was at a loss to determine whether the canoe was below or above me. Went first up the stream, some times whistling, and at other times hollowing till discouraged—then returned down the stream for some miles, till I was satisfied that they were above me—thence returning up again, expecting little else than to be left in this solitary wilderness, with no provisions, and little amunition to kill any: but while musing thus, heard them fire at their camp for me. Returned the report, firing as I went; but as the wind blew towards me, they heard me not, though happily their guns were always heard. With as much speed as the darkness of the night would permit, being directed by their continual firing, at last arrived safe at the camp, and was received joyfully; for their distress seemed greater than mine, lest some evil had befallen me, and they should bear the blame. . . .

Having met up with a trader named William Butlar, Jones decided to go with him overland toward the Indian town of Pickaweeke near Deer Creek. There Jones met two traders, Joseph Nicholas and John Irwine.

Mr. Irwine's chief habitation is a small town, situated W. N. W. of Pickaweeke about three miles. By the English it is called Bluejackets Town, an Indian of that name residing there.

Before this is described, it is proper to take notice of Pickaweeke—it is situated south of a brook that, east of the town, empties into Deer Creek. . . . Now it consists of about one hundred souls, being a mixture of Shawannees and other nations, so that it is called a Shawannee town. It is the most remarkable town for robbers and vilains, yet it pretends to have its chief men, who are indeed very scoundrels guilty of theft and robbery without any apology or redress. Some of these took four or five mares from Mr. McMechen on Ohio, nor was there any prospect of redress. . . .

Wednesday 13, Mr. Irwine invited the king [Kishshinottisthee, or Hardman] and some of his friends to take breakfast with me, having previously informed him that I was no trader, but was a good man, whose employment among white people was to speak of GOD and heavenly matters, and came with that view to see my brothers the Indians. . . . Kishshinottisthee is indeed a man of good sense, and by all that appeared was my hearty friend. . . . He may be said to possess some degree of hospitality—being much indisposed one day, the king's wife came with what was thought might suit a weak stomach as a present to me; the dish consisted of pumkins which had been dried, but were now boiled, and with it some bears oil to eat with the pumkin. As it was a demonstration of benevolence, tho' my appetite was poor, yet I eat a little. . . .

It was with reluctance this town was left, before an opportunity

was obtained to instruct the Indians; but being destitute of an interpreter, concluded to move to the chief town.

Friday 22, in company with Mr. Irwine, set out for Chillicaathee,
and arrived there in the afternoon. . . . Chillacaathee is the chief
town of the Shawannee Indians—it is situated north of a large plain
adjacent to a branch of Paint Creek. This plain is their corn-field,
which supplies [a] great part of their town. Their houses are made of
logs, nor is there any more regularity observed in this particular than
in their morals, for any man erects his house as fancy directs. . . .

Monday 25, made a further inquiry about the person recommended for my interpreter, was informed that he was hunting bears,
and would not be in till spring. This news blasted all my prospects
of making an useful visit, and having no other remedy, applied to
one James Gerty,[1] who was well acquainted with their language, but
a stranger to religion; neither had he any inclination to engage in
such solemn matters, so contrary to the tenor of his life. . . ; yet he
was civil, and, after much persuasion, engaged to assist me. . . .

Jones tried to preach to the white men in town, but the Indians were so suspicious that the whites, fearing the Indians' anger, refused to assemble.

February 1, an Indian lately returned named Othaawaapeelethee, in
English the Yellow Hawk, came with some others to Mr. [Moses]
Henry's to converse with me. . . . After common formalities were
past, he told me that he wanted to know my business among them
for he understood that I was no trader. First, informed him from
whence I came, and that my chief business was to instruct them
from GOD. . . . Then he proceeded to make a long *speech*, not with a
very pleasant countenance, nor the most agreeable tone of voice, and
replied to this effect, viz. "When GOD, who at first made us all, prescribed our way of living, he allowed white people to live one way,
and Indians another way"; and as he was one of the chiefs of this
town, he did not desire to hear me on the subject of religion, for he
was resolved not to believe what might be said, nor pay any regard
to it. . . .

He said that they had lived a long time as they now do, and like

---

1. James Girty was the brother of the notorious frontiersman Simon Girty, who was
present when Col. William Crawford was burned at the stake in 1782. The Girty boys
were captured by Indians as children and raised by different tribes. They became reac-
quainted with each other later. Their loyalty to their Native American families and tribes
and to the British interest in Ohio made them hated by Americans.

it very well, and he and his people would live as they had done. This Indian seemed like some among us, who consider religion only as state policy. . . .

Jones left February 8, after buying a horse from Irwine. He traveled alone about twenty miles northeast, and lodged with Richard Butlar, who gave him some leggings to use as barter with the Indians.

My course to-day was about northeast. As I passed a certain place called the *Great Lick,* saw the last flock of parrots [Carolina parakeets]. These birds are in great abundance about Siota in winter, and in summer 'tis probable they may be seen much further towards the north.

My road was very small, and the night dark in this wide wilderness, made my travelling more disagreeable than can be easily expressed: but before nine o'clock, came safe to Mr. McCormick's at the Standing Stone [present-day Lancaster]. This town consists chiefly of Delaware Indians. It is situated on a creek called Hockhockin. The soil about this is equal to the highest wishes, but the creek appears muddy. Though it is not wide, yet it soon admits large canoes, and from hence peltry is transmitted to Fort Pitt. Overtook here Mr. David Duncan, a trader from Shippen's town, who was going to Fort Pitt.

Wednesday 10, intending to travel forty miles, set out early in the morning—our course more northerly than northeast—the land chiefly low and level—and where our horses broke thro' the frost, it might be called bad road and good land. There were no inhabitants by the way. Before night, came to the designed town, called Dan. Elleot's wife's; a man of that name was said to have here a squaa for his pretended wife. This is a small town consisting of Delawares and Shawannees. The chief is a Shawannee woman, who is esteemed very rich—she entertains travelers—there were four of us in company, and for our use, her negro quarter was evacuated this night, which had a fire in the middle without any chimney. This woman has a large stock, and supplied us with milk. Here also we got corn for our horses at a very expensive price: but Mr. Duncan paid for me here, and in our journey till we parted. . . .

Thursday, 11, set out for a small town called Conner's, a man of that name residing there. . . .

Mr. Conner, who is a white man, a native of Maryland, told me that he intended to sow wheat in the fall following, and was resolved to proceed to farming at all events. 'Tis probable that he will be as good as his word, for he is a man that seems not to fear GOD, and it is likely that he will not regard man. His connections will favour his attempts, for according to their way, he and the chief Indian of this town are married to two sisters. These women were captives, and it is likely from childhood, for they have the very actions of Indians, and speak broken English. It seemed strange to me to see the captives have the exact gestures of Indians. Might we not infer from hence, that if Indians were educated as we are, they would be like us? . . .

Jones arrived in present-day Newcomerstown, 130 miles, he noted, from Chillicothe. While he waited for permission from the chief to preach, he visited the Moravian towns. He arrived at Schoenbrunn, 10 miles up the Muskingum, on Sunday at the end of services conducted by the famous Moravian missionary, David Zeisberger. Jones was impressed by the conduct of the Indians and the tidiness of the town. The next day he preached to the Indians, which gave him great satisfaction after all his hardships.

But to proceed, I returned to New-Comer's Town in the afternoon, and went to see captain Killbuck [a Delaware chief, but not a Moravian], who is a sensible Indian, and uses us with part of the complaisance of a gentleman. He speaks good English, so that I conversed on the subject of preaching, and he was to meet me next morning to converse further. . . .
 Tuesday 16, met with captain Killbuck, spoke on many subjects. . . . [H]e related the distresses and dangers of the Moravian Indians last war, and how they were preserved at Philadelphia. Adding, that for all the assistance that the Moravians could give, their Indians might have been killed. Hence, argued, that it did not signify to be of that religion, that could not protect them in war time. . . .

Try as he might, Jones couldn't get permission to preach. Killbuck said the Indians were hostile because a soldier had come the previous year, taken an Indian wife, and later sold her as a slave. Jones and Killbuck argued over whether or not this could be true, but Killbuck had the last word: "He further said, 'What is become of the woman, she never came back to us again?'"
 Jones wanted to leave, but Killbuck advised him that "the weather was so cold, that it would kill even an Indian." Finally, on Thursday, February 25, Jones set out with an Indian guide. He left his horse at the Ohio River and was ferried across in a canoe by a white settler named McMechen from the Virginia (now West Virginia) side.

Moravian Indians Migrate to Ohio:
John Heckewelder's Diary of the Trip
to Gnadenhutten, 1773

The Moravian towns the Reverend David Jones visited had been established by German-speaking missionaries. The Moravian Brethren was an old Protestant sect whose members came to America in the early eighteenth century and set about aggressively evangelizing among the Indians. Under the missionary David Zeisberger, the sect was especially successful in converting Delwares in Pennsylvania. As relations between Indians and whites deteriorated, the situation of the peaceable Moravians in Pennsylvania became precarious. In 1773 a group of them, led by the missionary John Heckewaelder (or Heckewelder), traveled from their settlement, called Friedensstadt or Langundoutenunk, above present-day Beaver Falls, Pennsylvania, to Welhik Thuppeek, or Schoenbrunn, on the Tuscarawas River in Ohio, a distance down the Ohio and up the Muskingum and Tuscarawas Rivers of more than three hundred miles. They went to join the group that had traveled out the year before under the Reverend David Zeisberger. (This is the same group that had been there when the Reverend David Jones passed through.)

The Moravian Delawares kept an uneasy peace in the area for years. But they continually found themselves in the middle, not entirely trusted by either whites or warring Indians.

The *13th* of April, we departed together in twenty-two canoes from Langundoutenunk and reached the [Beaver] falls at night. Brother Schebosch, Johannes, and a few more Brethren reached us there too, to take our heaviest things with their horses by land as far as below the falls.

The *14th*, the latter turned back because the water was rising and they might have been cut off from journeying overland to Welhik Thuppeek.

The *16th*. The Indians found the head of a man close to our camp. The man had apparently been killed in the last war, since his skull had been split by an ax.

Our Indians pitied him, because he had died an innocent victim. It was still raining; hence, the strongest and most courageous Brethren resolved to ride the empty canoes over the falls. They endangered their lives by doing so, and two of our people were nearly drowned, but there were always a few Brethren with a canoe ready to help in case of emergency; yet they traveled safely down, although sometimes the canoes were half filled with water.

The *18th*. Now that we were on the Ohio, we made an agree-

The Reverend John Heckewelder,
Moravian missionary to the
Indians and father of Johanna,
"the first white child in Ohio."
From Emilius O. Randall, *History
of Ohio*, vol. 2 (1912).

ment with each other on how we would conduct our trip, namely,
that we would travel until evening, if the wind were quiet, because
the river is high. Today, now and then, we saw plantations of the
white people on the other side of the river; and in the evening we
made camp close to the Mingo Town [Mingo Junction].

The *19th*. . . . A few miles farther down, a white man called us
and invited us to come ashore and to rest a little, but we did not
want to delay ourselves. We told him the reason, to which he replied: "In that case, I wish you a happy journey, you good people."
Again we saw houses and plantations of white people on the east
side of the river in different places. No sooner had we gone ashore in
the evening than six white people appeared across the river from us
and started talking to me; but the river was so wide that we were
not able to understand each other very well, hence I paddled across
with the Brethren Anton and Boas. They questioned us about many
things for about half an hour, but they were quite modest, most of
their questions being about our religion and doctrine. . . .

The *20th*. Just when we were about to start on our journey again,
the same people came across the river and looked at all our people
and our whole outfit. They pitied the old people, because of the hardships of traveling; they fondled the children, and wished to all of us
a happy journey. Now I learned that they were Baptists; one of them
was a gentleman from Philadelphia. They sat down on the river bank
and were astonished at the general quietude of our people. In the

afternoon some of our men wanted to stop and hunt, because they had no more meat; but since the weather was so beautiful, and there was no wind, we did not want to lose any time. But after we had traveled a bit farther and encountered a little island [Captina], they had a notion that deer would be on the island. We encircled it with our canoes and put some people with a few hounds ashore, whereupon at once four deer jumped into the water, three of which we obtained.

The *22d*. We traveled through the most lovely countryside of our entire trip; crooked as the Ohio runs in other places, here it went straight ahead, and its course was W. S. W. nor did we see mountains any more, but level bottoms on both sides; the trees were for the most part in their full foliage, and many trees bloomed, as did all kinds of flowers, and the grass was about one foot high. Everyone was surprised to have such a beautiful vision of summer in this month. . . . At noon we left the Ohio and entered the Muskingum. . . . Today again a bear was shot.

The *25th*. We traveled on till noon, and since many complained of fatigue, we resolved to make camp near a huge rock [no longer in existence]. Some of the Brethren at once built a sweating oven to sweat out their fatigue; others went out hunting a little and encountered buffaloes, at which they shot, but without success. This night we did not find much rest because of the enormous number of toads, which greatly annoyed us. The Indians, therefore, call this place Tsquallutene, that means, town of the toads. About midnight we had a terrible thunderstorm accompanied by a heavy rain. A part of our people sought shelter beneath a rock which was standing beside the huge one. This big rock is 70 feet long, 25 high, and 22 wide, and is solid rock.

The *26th* and *27th*. . . . Together with some of our Brethren I went about ten miles up this creek to see the famous salt spring, which is imbedded in a sandbank, wells heavily, and has no visible outlet; evidently, it has an outlet underground, because after having been emptied it soon fills up again. We saw quite a few contraptions there for boiling salt. At the mouth of this creek there is a very fine mount of anthracite coal; it lies there like a wall of bricks, and not mixed with soil or other stones, as I have seen it in other places on the Ohio. This wall was 500 ells [1050 feet] long. . . .

The *29th*. We had to pass three bad rapids [Duncan Falls], which gave us much trouble because we had to tow up our canoes.

The *30th*. At noon we arrived at the Shawnee Town [Woaketammeki, or Wakatomica, now the site of Dresden] which had been visited by Brother David [Zeisberger] last fall. Some of our Brethren went into the town, but they found only a few people at home, who received them with kindness; most of them had already moved away. . . .

The *1st* of May, at noon, we rested again close to a Shawnee town. . . . I visited a white man who is living there and who has a white wife; she had been a prisoner and cannot talk anything but Shawnee. After that we journeyed on and were received very kindly in a town where Delaware and Monsey [a tribe of Delaware] are living; they showed us great hospitality and were not satisfied until we all had eaten enough. They would have liked us to stay with them for the night, but as we did not want to lose any time, we traveled on for a few more miles.

The *3d.* We again passed different towns, stopped at some and talked with the inhabitants, who showed themselves friendly toward us, and in the afternoon we passed Gekelemukpechunk and made camp at the upper end of the town. Passing by, I counted 106 spectators. They greeted us with their usual shout of joy. . . . I went with a few Brethren to visit Chief Netawatwes.[2] He, as well as others who were with him, was very friendly toward us. . . . Then I and another Brother went to see Killbuck,[3] who, among other things, asked the Brother who was with me: "Does this man really like the Indians?" — "Yes," he answered, "not only does *he* like them, but all the other Brethren who are with us like them, too. It would not be necessary for them to live as poorly as they do; I have seen with my own eyes how well they live at Bethlehem; but because they like the Indians, and want to acquaint them with the Savior, they are content with their poor mode of life and are happy when the Indians become believers in the Savior. There is nothing else they ask or demand of us." — He replied: "Well, well, now I know it."

The *4th.* . . . In the afternoon we arrived at Gnadenhutten, where everybody had been looking forward to our arrival. . . . Three families at once stayed there to live, and the rest of us, on the *5th,* arrived happily and safely at Welhik Thuppeek, where we were received

---

2. The chief of the Turtle tribe of the Delawares. The whites also called him King Newcomer, and his town was called Newcomer Town, or, in Delaware, Gekelemukpechunk. He was in his eighties at this time. He died in 1776.
3. There were two Delawares, father and son, called Killbuck. Both were alive in 1770. The son, whose Indian name was Gelelemund, was Netawatwees's successor as chief. He became a Christian in 1789 and died at the Moravian mission of Goshen in 1811.

by our Brethren and Sisters in the most affectionate and loving fashion.

The Massacre of Chief Logan's Family: Henry Jolley's Account, 1774

Logan, whose Indian name was Tachnechdorus, was born about 1725, the son of Shikellamy, a Cayuga who had been a friend of the Moravian missionary David Zeisberger. It is said Zeisberger nursed Shikellamy on his deathbed. Logan married a Shawnee woman and came to live in Ohio. Like his father, he was a friend of the white people until the massacre recounted below. After that, he declared a personal war against whites, and it is estimated he fulfilled his pledge to kill ten whites for each family member who had been murdered at Yellow Creek. He allied himself with the Shawnee chief Cornstalk in what came to be known as Lord Dunmore's War in 1774. The battle at Point Pleasant on the Ohio River was part of that war. When Dunmore and his men invaded Shawnee territory as far north as present Circleville, Cornstalk made peace. But Logan bitterly refused to participate in burying the tomahawk. He continued raiding white settlements throughout the Revolutionary War. The rest of his life is obscure. Some say he drank heavily and was murdered, possibly by his own nephew.

This account of the massacre of Logan's family was written by Henry Jolley, an early white settler who became a judge in Washington County.

I was about sixteen years of age, but I very well recollect what I then saw, and the information that I have since obtained, was derived from (I believe) good authority. In the spring of the year 1774, a party of Indians encamped on the northwest of the Ohio, near the mouth of the Yellow creek. A party of whites, called "Greathouse's party," lay on the opposite side of the river. The Indians came over to the white party, consisting, I think, of five men and one woman, with an infant. The whites gave them rum, which three of them drank, and in a short time they became very drunk. The other two men and the woman refused to drink. The sober Indians were challenged to shoot at a mark, to which they agreed; and as soon as they emptied their guns, the whites shot them down. The woman attempted to escape by flight, but was also shot down; she lived long enough, however, to beg mercy for her babe, telling them that it was a kin to themselves.

The whites had a man in the cabin, prepared with a tomahawk for the purpose of killing the three drunken Indians, which was immediately done. The party of men then moved off for the interior settlements, and came to "Catfish camp" on the evening of the next day where they tarried until the day following. I very well recollect my mother feeding and dressing the babe; chirruping to the little innocent, and its smiling.

However, they took it away, and talked of sending it to its supposed father, Col. George Gibson, of Carlisle, Pa., "who was then, and had been for many years, a trader among the Indians." The remainder of the party at the mouth of Yellow creek finding that their friends on the opposite side of the river were massacred, attempted to escape by descending the Ohio; and in order to prevent being discovered by the whites, passed on the west side of Wheeling Island and landed at Pipe creek, a small stream that empties into the Ohio a few miles below Grave creek, where they were overtaken by [Michael] Cresap with a party of men from Wheeling. They took one Indian scalp, and had one white man (Big Tarrener) badly wounded. They, I believe, carried him in a litter from Wheeling to Redstone. I saw the party on their return from their victorious campaign. The Indians had for some time before these events thought themselves intruded upon by the "Long Knife," as they at that time called the Virginians, and many of them were for war.

However, they called a council in which Logan acted a conspicuous part. He admitted their ground of complaint, but at the same time reminded them of some aggressions on the part of the Indians, and that by a war they could but harrass and distress the frontier settlements for a short time; that the "Long Knife" would come like the trees in the woods, and that ultimately they should be driven from the good lands which they now possessed. He therefore strongly recommended peace. To him they all agreed; grounded the hatchet, and everything wore a tranquil appearance, when behold the fugitives arrived from Yellow creek, and reported that Logan's father, brother and sister were murdered! Three of the nearest and dearest relations of Logan had been massacred by white men. The consequence was, that this same Logan, who a few days before was so pacific, raised the hatchet with a declaration that he would not ground it until he had taken *ten for one*, which I believe he completely fulfilled, by taking *thirty* scalps and prisoners in the summer of 1774. The above has often been related to me by several persons who were at the Indian towns at the time of the council alluded to, and also when the remains of the party came in from Yellow creek. . . .

Could any rational person believe for a moment that the Indians came to Yellow creek with hostile intentions, or that they had any suspicion of similar intentions on the part of the whites, against them? Would five men have crossed the river, three of them become in a short time dead drunk, while the other two discharged their guns, and thus put themselves entirely at the mercy of the whites; or would they have brought over a squaw with an infant pappoose, if they had not reposed the utmost confidence in the friendship of the whites? Every person who is at all acquainted with Indians knows better, and it was the belief of the inhabitants who were capable of reasoning on the subject that all the depredations committed on the frontiers, by Logan and his party, in 1774, were as a retaliation for the murder of Logan's friends at Yellow creek.

Who Is There to Mourn for Logan?
Chief Logan's Speech, 1774

Lord Dunmore's War, so called, ended with a peace treaty signed November, 1774, on Scippo Creek in Pickaway County. Logan refused to attend the treaty, but sent the following speech. This version is the one recorded by Thomas Jefferson in his Memorandum Book of 1774. As Judge Jolley said, Michael Cresap almost certainly had nothing to do with the death of Logan's relatives, although many Indians blamed it on him.

I appeal to any white man to say if ever he entered Logan's cabbin hungry and he gave him not meat; if ever he came cold and naked and he cloathed him not. During the course of the last long and bloody war, Logan remained idle in his cabbin, an advocate for peace. Nay, such was my affection for the Whites, that my country men hooted as they passed by and said "Logan is the friend of White men." I had even thought to have lived with you, but for the injuries of one man. Colo[nel] Cresap, the last spring, in cold blood and unprovoked, cut off all the Relations of Logan; not sparing even my women or children. There runs not a drop of my blood in the veins of any human creature. This called on me for revenge. I have sought it; I have killed many; I have fully glutted my vengeance. for my country, I rejoice at the beams of peace. but do not harbor a thought that mine is the joy of fear. Logan never felt fear. he will not turn on his heel to save his life. Who is there to mourn for Logan? Not one.

Trade and War: A Letter from
Governor John Penn to the Shawnees, 1774

Lieutenant Governor John Penn of Pennsylvania sent the following letter to the Shawnee Indians on August 6, 1774. Penn was right when he predicted that the whites would overwhelm the Indians. Although whites rarely won a battle in their long war against the Indians, they prevailed in the end by sheer numbers. Their armies were replaceable. The Indians' were not.

When I heard that you had taken Care of our Traders, and had sent some of your young Men to conduct them Home in Safety, it made my Heart glad, because I was satisfied that you kept fast hold of the Chain of Friendship. . . . But, Brethren, it gives me great concern, and my Heart is grieved to hear of the difference between you and our Brothers, the People of Virginia. . . . It is a very wicked Thing to kill innocent People, because some of their countrymen have been wicked, and killed some of you.
Brethren:
If you continue to act in this Manner the People of Virginia must do the same Thing by you, and then there will be nothing but War between you. Consider, Brethren, that the People of Virginia are like the Leaves upon the Trees, very numerous, and you are but few, and although you should kill ten of their People for one that they kill of yours, they will at last wear you out, and destroy you. . . .

An Early Tourist: The Journal of
Nicholas Cresswell, 1775

At the age of 24, Nicholas Cresswell traveled to America from his family's estate in England. After spending some time in the East, Cresswell ventured to the frontier in 1775, going by way of Fort Pitt and the Ohio River on his way to the Mississippi. He never reached his destination, turning back because his traveling companions were increasingly afraid of being attacked by Indians. After a short time back at Fort Pitt, Cresswell crossed the Ohio River into Ohio territory on a trading mission. He went to Schoenbrunn, Newcomerstown, and Coshocton, picking up a young Indian woman on the way who was his guide and lover until they returned to Fort Pitt.

    Cresswell visited many of the places others, such as the Reverend David Jones, had visited before him, but what brought him to Ohio was curiosity more than business or religion. Cresswell didn't stay in America. A loyal Tory, he went home and settled down to the life of a country squire.

Running through Cresswell's journal is the spirit of adventure he shared with many others on the frontier. He is one of the few writers who does not hesitate to speak of his sexual encounters. By his account, sex was free and easy in the forest. Cresswell also displayed the ignorance that got many settlers and explorers killed. Ohio was a dangerous place for a white tourist. The Indians regularly attacked rafts and canoes on the Ohio River, often plundering them and murdering the travelers. Luckily, Cresswell experienced only passing discomfort and occasional terror on his trip.

Thursday, May 4th, 1775. In the morning found ourselves opposite Yellow Creek on the W. Very heavy rain for several hours. Very few inhabitants, not a house to be seen in 40 miles, tho' the land is exceedingly rich, in general. The River is exceedingly crooked, full of small Islands and rapid. If there is high land on one side there is always a rich level bottom on the opposite shore. . . .

Sunday, May 7th, 1775. . . . Went ashore on the Big tree Island and measured a large Sycamore tree. It was 51 feet 4 inches in circumference one foot from the ground, and 46 foot circumference five feet from the ground. . . . Past the Muskingum River on the W. Fine land between that and the little Muskingum. . . .

Monday, May 8th, 1775. . . . Camped about 4 Miles below the Horseshoe, where we met with some people who gave us very bad encouragement, say that the Indians are broke out again and killed four men on the Kentucky River. My courageous companions' spirits begin to droop.

Friday, May 12th, 1775. This day held a Council whether we should proceed or turn back. After much altercation our company determined to persevere, tho' I believe they are a set of Dammd cowards. . . .

Tuesday, May 16th, 1775. Passed the mouth of the Sioto River in the night. This river is on the N.W. side. Stopped to cook our breakfast on a small gravelly Island where we found plenty of Turtle eggs, with which we made pancakes equal in goodness to those made with hen's eggs. . . .

The adventurers proceeded down the river, becoming increasingly fearful of attack. Also, the going got tougher as they encountered rapids. One man was almost killed as he slept in a canoe; a herd of buffalos crossed the river where he had tied up for the night. The store of flour was damaged and the travelers went on rations. All this frayed their nerves, and quarreling broke out. Finally, they arrived at Harwood's Landing, a settlement of about thirty cabins, where Cresswell, realizing he couldn't get anyone to proceed further down river, joined some men going back up. By June 18, they had paddled back to the mouth of the Great Miami.

Saturday, June 24th, 1775. [M]y shoesoles came off and I was obliged to walk bare foot for six miles. Find myself very unwell. Shot a Pole Cat. One of our Company missing. All the rest (except Tilling and myself) are going this evening, as they expect he is killed by the Indians. But I think he has lost himself in the Woods. Very arduous task to persuade them to stay, as they all expect to be killed before morning.

Sunday, June 25th, 1775. Slept little last night, over-fatigued. This morning our company are for setting out immediately, confident that the man is killed. With much importunity prevailed on them to stay till evening, but could not persuade any of them to go to seek the man. About sundown they all prepared for going, notwithstanding that Mr. Tilling and I could say against it, but just as we were going aboard saw the man come along the shore to our great joy. It had happened as I supposed—he lost himself in the Woods and had rambled all night. If we had left him he must have perished. Very unwell.

Wednesday, June 28th, 1775. This morning started early in a very thick fog. About three miles from our camp, the River was very broad and shallow a long way from the shore on that side we were on, which obliged us to keep out of sight of the shore for deeper water. Opening a point of a Bar, saw 4 Canoes full of Indians about two hundred yards ahead of us, upon which we pushed for the shore, but to our great surprise saw six other Canoes full of Indians betwixt us and the shore so that we were entirely surrounded.

Everything was prepared for an engagement, all our lumber and a great part of our provisions were hoved overboard. Out of twelve Guns five were rendered unfit for present use by the wet, mine happened to be in good order and I loaded her with an ounce bullet and seven swan shot. The command of our Canoes was given to me. We had only two Guns on board fit for use, Mr. Tilling's and mine. Tom O'Brien in the scuffle let his fall in the River and got her filled with water. He laid down in the bottom of the Canoe, begun to tell his beads and prayed and howled in Irish. Boassier's Gun was wet and unfit for use. He followed O'Brien's example. Weeping, praying, said Ave Mary's in abundance, at the same time hugging a little wooden crucifix he pulled from his bosom most heartily.

Jacob Nalen (a Swede) commanded a canoe had three rifle guns on board. Williams, the Welshman, commanded the other with two muskets. We held a short and confused council, wherein it was determined that Nalen should lead the Van, I in the centre, and Williams bring up the rear. The Indians had observed our confusion and lay on their paddleboxes 30 yards from shore. There were 23 Indians in the six Canoes betwixt us and the shore. All of them had poles or paddles, but our fears had converted them into Guns. These six we determined to attack as the River was shallow, if we by accident overset our Canoes we might wade ashore.

The Canoes above us with 21 Indians bore down upon us, we made for the shore. I ordered Tom O'Brien to steer the Canoes within ten yards of Nalen's vessel and Boassier and Clifton to take their paddles. Clifton, tho' a young boy, behaved with the greatest resolution. Tilling's countenance was not in the least changed, his behaviour animated me very much. Boassiers and O'Brien lay crying in the bottom of the Canoes and refused to stir. I set the muzzle of my Gun to O'Brien's head, threatening to blow his brains out if he did not immediately take his paddle. It had the desired effect, he begged for his life, invoked St. Patrick, took his paddle and howled most horribly. Dangerous and desperate as we imagined our situation to be, I could not forbear laughing to see the condition of this poor fellow. Boassiers pretended to be in a convulsion fit. Mr. Tilling threw several canfuls of water in his face, but he refused to stir. I put a pistol bullet upon the load I already had in my Gun. I was determined to give some of them their quietus. I confess I felt very uneasy. When we got within thirty yards of them some of Nalen's crew hailed them and to our great satisfaction they told us they were friends. They had seen our confusion and laughed at us for our fears. It proved to be one Catfish, a Delaware Indian, and a party with him going to hunt. They had several Squaws or Indian women with them, some of them very handsome We gave them some salt and Tobacco with which they seemed well pleased. Proceeded up the River very merry at the expense of our cowardly companions. . . .

At the mouth of the Kanawha, Cresswell heard of a battle at Boston between the colonists and the British. He wrote: "I hope it will prove that the English have killed several thousand of the Yankees." By the first of July, the group's little remaining food was infested with maggots, their fish hooks and lines were broken, and everyone was quarreling. At last arriving at Redstone Fort (present-day Brownsville, Pennsylvania), he was told of two "very severe engagements" at Boston. The Revolutionary War had begun.

With only two dollars left in his pocket, Cresswell found a man at Fort Pitt named John Anderson who advanced him cash and offered to accompany him on a trading trip into Ohio. Cresswell and Anderson set out, crossing the Allegheny River into "Indian country." On the first morning, they got drunk on rum and left their provisions behind. Nevertheless, they pressed on.

Wednesday, August 23rd, 1775. Proceeded on our journey, but not one morsel of provision. Crossed Great Beaver Creek at Captn. White-Eye's house. This is an Indian Warrior of the Dellawars Nation. Camped at Little Beaver Creek with three Indian Squaws and a man. Nothing to eat but berries such as we found in the woods. Find Mr. Anderson a good hearty companion. One of the Indian Squaws invited me to sleep with her, but I pretended to be sick. She was very kind and brought me some plums she got in the woods.

Friday, August 25th, 1775. Very heavy rain all day. Lost our horses, but an Indian brought them to us in the evening for which we gave him a pair of leggings. Breakfasted, dined and supped on Plums and Wild Cherries. . . .

Saturday, August 26th, 1775. . . . Just as the Sun went down we stopped to get our Supper on some Dewberries (a small berry something like a Gooseberry). Mr. Anderson had gone before me and said he would ride on about two miles to a small run where he intended to camp, as soon as I had got sufficient. I mounted my Horse and followed him till I came to a place where the road forked. I took the path that I supposed he had gone and rode till it began to be dark, when I imagined myself to be wrong, and there was not a possibility of me finding my way back in the night. Determined to stay where I was till morning, I had no sooner alighted from my horse, but I discovered the glimmering of a fire about four hundred yards from me. This rejoiced me exceedingly, supposing it was Mr. Anderson. When I got there, to my great disappointment and surprise found three Indian women and a little boy. I believe they were as much surprised as I was. None of them could speak English and I could not speak Indian. I alighted and marked the path I had come and that I had left, on the ground with the end of my stick, made a small channel in the earth which I poured full of water, laid some fire by the side of it, and then laid myself down by the side of the fire, repeating the name of Anderson which I soon understood they knew.

The youngest Girl immediately unsaddled my Horse, unstrapped the Belt, Hoppled him, and turned him out, then spread my Blankets at the fire and made signs for me to sit down. The Oldest made me a little hash of dried Venison and Bear's Oil, which eat very well, but neither Bread or Salt. After supper they made signs I must go to sleep. Then they held a consultation for some time which made me very uneasy, the two eldest women and the boy laid down on the opposite side of the fire and some distance away. The youngest (she had taken so much pains with my horse) came and placed herself very near me. I began to think she had some amorous design upon me. In about half an hour she began to creep nearer me and pulled my Blanket. I found what she wanted and lifted it up. She immediately came to me and made me as happy as it was in her power to do. She was young, handsome, and healthy. Fine regular features and fine eyes, had she not painted them with Red before she came to bed—and I suppose answers as well as My Lady in the dark.

Sunday, August 27th, 1775. This morning my Bedfellow went into the woods and caught her horse and mine, saddled them, put my Blanket on the saddle, and prepared everything ready, seemingly with a great deal of good nature. . . . In about an hour she brought me to Mr. Anderson's camp. . . . Proceeded on our journey and about noon got to an Indian Town called Wale-hack-tap-poke [Schoenbrunn], or the Town with a good Spring, on the Banks of the Muskingham and inhabited by Dellawar Indians. Christianized under the Moravian Sect, it is a pretty town consisting of about sixty houses, and is built of logs and covered with Clapboards. . . .

In the evening went to the meeting. But never was I more astonished in my life. I expected to have seen nothing but anarchy and confusion, as I have been taught to look upon these beings with contempt. Instead of that, here is the greatest regularity, order, and decorum, I ever saw in any place of Worship, in my life. With that solemnity of behaviour and modest, religious deportment would do honour to the first religious society on earth, and put a bigot or enthusiast out of countenance. The parson was a Dutchman [German], but preached in English. He had an Indian interpreter, who explained it to the Indians by sentences. . . .

Monday, August 28th, 1775. Left Wale-hack-tap-poke. . . . Lodged at White-Eye's Town only three houses in it. Kindly treated at a Dutch Blacksmith's, who lives with an Indian Squaw. Got a very hearty supper of a sort of Dumplings made of Indian Meal and dried Huckleberries which serves instead of currants. Dirty people, find it impossible to keep myself free from lice. Very disagreeable companions.

Tuesday, August 29th, 1775. Left White-Eye's town. Saw the bones of one Mr. Cammel, a White man, that had been killed by the Indians. Got to Co-a-shoking [Coshocton] about noon. It is at the forks of the Muskingham. The Indians have removed from Newcomer Town to this place. King Newcomer [Netawatwees] lives here. Sold part of my goods here to good advantage. Crossed a branch of Muskingham and went to Old Hundy, this is a scattering Indian settlement. Lodged at a Mohawk Indian's house, who offered me his Sister and Mr. Anderson his Daughter to sleep with us, which we were obliged to accept.

Wednesday, August 30th, 1775. My bedfellow very fond of me this morning and wants to go with me. . . . Agreed to take her. . . .

Thursday, August 31st, 1775. At Coashoskis [Coshocton]. . . . Sold all my goods for Furs. In the afternoon rambled about the Town, smoking Tobacco with the Indians and did everything in my power to make myself agreeable to them.

Friday, September 1st, 1775. . . . Saw an Indian Dance in which I bore a part. Painted by my Squaw in the most elegant manner. Divested of all my clothes, except my Calico short breech-clout, leggings, and Mockesons. A fire was made which we danced round with little order, whooping and hallooing in a most frightful manner. I was but a novice at the diversion and by endeavouring to act as they did made them a great deal of sport and ingratiated me much in their esteem. This is the most violent exercise to the adepts in the art I ever saw. No regular figure, but violent distortion of features, writhing and twisting the body in the most uncouth and antic postures imaginable. Their music is an old Keg with one head knocked out and covered with a skin and beat with sticks which regulates their times. The men have strings of Deer's hoofs tied round their ankles and knees, and gourds with shot or pebblestones in them in their hands which they continually rattle. The women have Morris bells or Thimbles with holes in the bottom and strung upon a leather thong tied round their ankles, knees and waists. . . .

Saturday, September 2nd, 1775. . . . Crossed the River and got to Newcomers Town. Very sick. Nancy [his Indian lover] is gone to fetch an old Indian woman to cure me as she says, therefore I must lay by my pen.

Sunday, September 3rd, 1775. Last night, Nancy brought an Indian Squaw which called me her Nilum. i.e. Nephew, as Mr. Anderson told me, and behaved very kindly to me. She put her hand on my head for some time, then took a small brown root out of her pocket and with her knife chopped part of it small, then mixed it with water which she gave me to drink, or rather swallow, being about a spoonful, but this I evaded by keeping it in my mouth till I found an opportunity to spit it out. She then took some in her mouth and chewed it and spit on the top of my head, rubbing my head well at the same time. Then she unbuttoned my shirt collar and spat another mouthful down my back. This was uncomfortable but I bore it with patience.

Cresswell recovered, and he and Anderson returned to Fort Pitt. Thus ended Nicholas Cresswell's adventures in Ohio.

Negotiating with the Indians: The Journal of Colonel Richard Butler, 1775

The atmosphere remained very tense on the Ohio frontier. The Ohio Indians were upset at the settlements beginning to spring up on their Kentucky hunting ground. The British, whose quarrel with the American colonists had just become a war, fanned the flames of Indian suspicions against the colonists. The Indians were constantly being pressured to choose sides, just as they had been when the British and French fought each other. The following journal entries relate to a trip Butler made to Ohio in 1775 to negotiate with the Indians. They convey the rumor, confusion, suspicion, and violence that pervaded the frontier. Some of the spelling and punctuation in these excerpts have been modernized.

Richard Butler was an Indian trader and government agent. As an Indian commissioner after the Revolutionary War, he helped negotiate the treaties of Fort McIntosh in 1785 and Fort Finney in 1786, in which some Indians signed over tribal claims to Ohio lands. However, other Indians who were not present at these treaties resented them bitterly, refused to accept them, and continued to fight for what they regarded as their own land. Butler was considered a villain by those who rejected the treaties.

In 1791 Butler (now a major general) was second in command to General Arthur St. Clair when their ragtag army of militia and regulars walked into an Indian ambush led by Little Turtle and Blue Jacket. About 650 Americans were killed. It was the largest defeat ever of white troops by Indians. A wounded Butler was left on the battlefield propped against a tree. When the Indians identified him, they killed him, scalped him, and then ate his heart in revenge.

Aug. 30. . . . Yesterday morning Kayasuta[4] told old Wingemund[5] that he thought the Shawnee people had something bad in their hearts as they always cast up the selling of the land to him. And the Corn-

4. A Seneca chief, acquainted with George Washington, who worked for years trying to maintain peace with the whites.
5. A Delaware chief, later present at the burning of Col. William Crawford at the stake.

stalk[6] had spoke very ill of him and of the Delawares who Wingemund said he looked on or called dogs or servants of the white people. . . .

Sept. 1st. Started at 6 o'clock for Pluggy's [present-day Delaware], it being the nighest way to the Wyandots from Cushockking [Coshocton] & no other road so good, which induced me to go that way. Arrived at the Big Lick [Mount Vernon] at sunset; the head men of the Mingoes had been 5 days gone to the Wyandot Town [Upper Sandusky] to hear a speech from Mr. Johnston[7] desiring them to give ear to no speech from the Big Knife [the colonists] as they only meant to deceive the Indians, and not to believe them or any message but his. And there had 2 Mingoes arrived that had been at Kaintuckky where they said they had seen a number of whitemen who told them after some discourse that they had built three strong forts [Harrodsburg, Boonesboro and McClelland's Station], that one was very near them, . . . that it was not quite finished but it soon would, and that as soon as done there would be a large garrison of men put in it, that they were on their way already, and the two beyond was then garrisoned. And as soon as the other was compleated that they would then go off to the Indian Country over the Ohio and see them, and see how they liked their country—which report put the Indians in a great panic till I saw them. . . .

The Cornstalk on his way down the Ohio called at the Big Kanawha [River] where he says he saw a man that had been prisoner with the Shawnees, . . . that he was in great fear for the Shawnees, that he expected very soon a great body of the Big Knife people there, and their intention was to go to their country over the Ohio to look at them and much more. This was reported to the Mingoes, Ottawas and Wyandots, and they were each to send two men to watch the big river to see these people. This report gave rise to an opinion that the white people intended to call them to a treaty, and the army to go in their absence and cut off their towns, women and children, and cut up the corn. These considerations, with the advice of a Frenchman at Detroit not to hear any of the messages from the Big Knife or any other but Johnston or him, had determined the Shawnees, Mingoes, Ottawas and Wyandots not to go to the treaty as they looked on all had been said to them a deception, and that it would be running too great a risk.

---

6. A Shawnee chief who had led the Indians against a force of white frontiersmen at the Battle of Point Pleasant in 1774; he was murdered by whites at Fort Randolph in 1777.
7. Colonel Guy Johnston was the British superintendent of Indian affairs.

Butler set about getting all the Indians to attend a conference in Pittsburgh and not to listen to Johnston about how the colonists and British were quarreling with each other.

[Sept.] 3rd, Sun. Started at 6 o'clock, arrived at the Wyandot Town at 11 o'clock where I found the Wyandots and Ottawas in the council house. They seemed very much pleased at our arrival. They welcomed us and told us they would be glad to hear our errand. . . . I then delivered the message. . . . They then told us that it was a message of consequence and would require us to be properly considered. You must stay tomorrow and we will give our answer.

Just at this juncture came in a woman called Spitfire with a piece of very bad news that had like to ruined all.

A hand of Mr. Heron's called John Edwards was coming to the Wyandots from the Shawnees' Towns with some goods belonging to Messers Heron, Beveard & Dodge . . . and a Wyandot called the Doctor. They were under a necessity of stopping to camp at the Scioto. Said Edwards had lay down to rest himself he being sick. The Indian was making a fire when an Indian called Snip, a Wyandot, came up and asked the Indian what ailed his friend. The Indian told him he was sick and lay down to rest. Said Snip went to the young man and pulled the blanket off his face and struck a tomahawk in his head and scalped him. The Indian called the Doctor ran off, and the murderer took and opened the goods and took what he pleased.

The Half King [Pomoacan, a Wyandot from Upper Sandusky] was told of the affair privately and he called out some of the other head men and acquainted them of it. He then came in & with tears in his eyes told us he was very sorry that they, the Wyandots, had done us much wrong, that they had struck the tomahawk in our heads for which they also were now very sorry, and it had struck the message we brought them. But as an act done could not be undone, begged of us not to be surprised or angry or more sorry than we could help, as it would be of no use or could not bring back our lost friend. He then told the above related affair, which really surprised us all.

But after our surprise was over a bit, the Half King spoke again and begged of us to stay & hear what they would conclude upon. We waited about two hours, when we were again called, and he spoke as follows:

"Brothers, we are very sorry for this bad act of a bad man. It is not the sense of this tribe to hurt you or do they by any means approve of this action, but on the contrary do condemn and disclaim it, therefore hope you will consider what has been said as our true meaning.

Therefore with this string [of wampum] wipe the tears from your eyes and open your ears to hear us. And with this we wash away all ill from your minds and all sorrow from your hearts and hope you will be sorry no more. We will send and bury your dear friend and bring your effects to you again."

They sat awhile, and addressed us again as follows:

"Brothers, having told you our true meaning, we now with this belt [of wampum] draw the tomahawk out of your heads and heal the wound and bury the tomahawk so deep that it shall no more be seen by us or you and we wash away the blood never to be thought of more."

The white people present considered that to show any resentment was of no use as they had declared themselves in the above manner. We therefore got a few strings of white wampum and addressed them as follows:

"We believe that you are sorry for this sad affair as well as us and that you knew nothing of the matter. Therefore, we desire you to hearken to us. We tell you to be strong and advise your people to take care for the future, not to be guilty of the like any more; that we do not come here to do mischief to you or to fight you, that we come here as brothers and friends to buy your skins and sell you our goods, that we think it very hard that ourselves and our people is in so much danger of our and their lives in doing this business. Therefore tell you, you ought to protect us and not hurt us. We do expect you will bury our dear friend out of our sight and that you will bring back our property and restore it to us. . . . We don't blame you, but we blame the bad man that did it and leave it to the great men to settle the past affair with you. . . ."

5th Tuesday. . . . Kayasuta told me a great deal of the talk he had with the Half King. It was chiefly to clear off his doubts concerning the ill intentions of the white people on getting them up to the treaty, as the reports had made so deep an impression on their minds they with reluctance believed anything else. Some of them brought two small kegs of rum, and the Ottawas and some Wyandots got drunk together and in a dispute a Wyandot man bit off an Ottawa man's nose. We left the Wyandot town about 11 o'clock and rode through the village to take our leave of them and the Ottawas, who were still a little drunk.

An Official Description of the Ohio Country: Selections from Thomas Pownall, 1776

Thomas Pownall was the author of a topographical description of the Ohio country in 1776. Pownall got his information second hand, it seems, from sources such as the journals of Captain Harry Gordon (1766) and Christopher Gist (1750). His description of the rivers suggests how from earliest times white people who came to Ohio looked upon the country as a place to be developed by and for white people.

Muskingum is a fine gentle River, confined within high Banks that prevent its Floods from damaging the surrounding Land. It is 250 Yards wide at its Confluence with the Ohio. It is passable with large Batteaux to the Three Logs, and with small Ones to a little Lake at its Head, without any Obstruction from Falls or Rifts. From hence to Cayahoga is a Portage a Mile long. *Cayahoga,* the Creek that leads from this Portage to lake Erie, is muddy and middling swift, but no where obstructed with Falls or Rifts. As this has fine Land, wide extended Meadows, lofty Timber, Oak and Mulberry fitted for Shipbuilding, Walnut, Chesnut, and Poplar for domestic Services, and furnishes the shortest and best Portage between Ohio and Lake Erie; and its Mouth is sufficient to receive good Sloops from the Lake: it will in Time become a Place of consequence. *Muskingum,* though so wide extended in its Branches, spreads all in most excellent Land, abounding in good Springs and Conveniencies, particularly adapted for Settlements remote from marine Navigation, as Coal, Clay, and Freestone. In 1748 a Coal Mine, opposite Lamenshikola [possibly Sandy Creek in Stark County] Mouth, took Fire, and kept burning above a Twelve-month, where great Quantities are still left. Near the same Place is excellent Whetstone; and about Eight Miles higher up the River is Plenty of white and blue Clay for Glass Works and Pottery. Though the Quantity of good Land on Ohio, and its Branches, is vastly great, and the Conveniencies attending it so likewise; we may esteem that [land] on Muskingum the Flower of it all.

HOCKHOCKING is passable with Batteaux Seventy or Eighty Miles up; it has fine rich Land, and vast grassy Meadows, high Banks, and seldom overflows. It has Coals about Fifteen Miles up, and some Knowls of Freestone. . . .

Sioto [Scioto] is a large gentle River, bordered with rich Flats, which it overflows in the Spring. . . . Opposite the Mouth of this River is the Lower Shawane Town, removed from the other Side, which was One of the most noted Places of English Trade with the

Indians. This River, besides vast Extents of good Land, is furnished
with Salt on an Eastern Branch [Salt Creek], and Red Bole on Necunsia
Skeintat [probably Paint Creek]. The Stream is very gentle, and passable with large Batteaux a great Way up, and with Canoes near 200
Miles to a Portage near the Head, where you carry over good Ground
Four Miles to Sanduski. *Sanduski* is a considerable River, abounding in rich level Land, its Stream gentle all the Way to the Mouth,
where it will receive considerable Sloops. This River is an important Pass, and the French have secured it as such; the Northern Indians cross the Lake here from Island to Island, land at Sanduski, and
go by a direct Path to the Lower Shawane Town, and thence to the
Gap of Ouasioto [Cumberland Gap], in their Way to the Cuttawas
[Catawbas'] Country. This will, no Doubt, be the Way that the French
will take from *Detroit* to *Moville* [Mobile], unless the English will
be advised to secure it, now that it is in their Power.

The Rescue of Jane Stoops from the Indians: Three Accounts of Samuel Brady's Rescue of Jane Stoops, 1780

The Stoopses were settlers on Chartiers Creek in Pennsylvania when, in 1780,
Indians attacked their cabin and captured Jane Stoops and her son, William. As
they and their captors entered Ohio, near what is now Lowellville, in Mahoning
County, they encountered a small party of white men led by Captain Samuel
Brady, who later became famous for reputedly leaping the Cuyahoga River to
escape Indians. Brady rescued Jane Stoops, but her son remained a captive. She
died in Pittsburgh in 1793. Eventually, William Stoops bought land and built a
cabin on the spot where his mother had been rescued.

The three versions of the story below show how the details of events on the
frontier often changed subtly as they were told and retold. Even such questions
as how long William remained a prisoner and whether his mother lived to see
him again remain unresolved. The first excerpt is the story as Samuel Brady
supposedly told it to his brother, General Hugh Brady.

. . . The captain at the solicitation of his colonel visited the upper
Sandusky town with only eight men. On his near approach to the
village he discovered men, women, and children amusing themselves
in horse racing. . . . As no chance of taking a warrior prisoner presented, he caught two squaws and started for home. That night it
commenced raining very hard and continued throughout all the next

day, which destroyed their provisions and all the powder but a few
charges which the captain had in a priming horn. The weather continued cloudy for several days after. . . . Having then been two days
without provisions, he informed his men he would go in advance
and try to kill something to eat. He had proceeded but a little way
when he met on the path a party of Indians. The man in advance
was riding, and accosted the Captain as a friend, who being disguised
in Indian costume he mistook as such. And turning his head to an-
nounce him to his friends the Captain shot him. As he fell out of his
saddle, the captain gave the war whoop, which being answered by
his friends in the rear (they supposing he had killed something for
supper) induced the Indians to retreat. When the captain got to the
dead Indian, he found a white boy fastened to his back. Before he
could extricate him he discovered the Indians returning, and seizing
the mother of the child, dragged her off much against her will, and
escaped the Indians.

His own men, on seeing the Indians, supposing the captain was
killed and having no powder, let the squaws run and made their way
to Fort McIntosh below the mouth of the Big Beaver. About 12 miles
from the fort the captain was met by a detachment sent out to bury
him, his men having arrived and reported him killed. (Here I think it
not out of place to say that the boy remained with the Indians until
after Wayne's Treaty in 1795, when agreeably to its stipulations he
was surrendered and brought to Pittsburgh. . . .)

The following account was told to the historian and archivist, Dr. Lyman Draper,
by John Sprott, son of Samuel Sprott, who had been a scout under Brady. Samuel
Sprott claimed to have heard the story of the rescue of Jane Stoops from Brady
himself.

Brady with a party—four or five altogether—went to Sandusky to
catch a prisoner & learn information about the Indian towns and
designs in that quarter. They were returning, had run out of provisions, & had only one load [of powder] left, & that was in Brady's
gun—they came on the Mahoning, & Brady bleated up a doe, he
snapped, but his gun missed fire. He picked out a few dry grains of
powder from his horn & re-primed his gun, & started after the re-
treating deer to try to bleat her up again; and as he came round a
large log, he discovered a party of Indians approaching—one Indian
on horseback with a small boy fastened behind him—Mrs. Stoops, a
prisoner, also mounted—the rest all on foot. Brady said he happened
to discover a little hand around the Indian's breast—it instantly

flashed upon his mind that it was a prisoner child, & he aimed a little higher & shot—the gun fired clear, and the Indian fell from his horse, with the lad fastened to him—Brady ran up, & tried to jerk loose the Indian's powder horn, as he had no powder to re-load with; one of the Indians flashed his gun at Brady, the Indians having treed— & Brady's men, having no loads nor amunition, could only halloo & thus help to scare the enemy. Brady driven by the enemy's fire and position from securing the coveted powder horn, now less exposed jerked Mrs. Stoops from her horse, & ran taking her by the hand. Brady's party now scattered, & the Indians did not pursue.

Following is the account of Nancy Stoops, the widow of William Stoops, the captive child. She stated that she had married him in 1808 and that he died in 1835. This is the story as she heard it from him.

Three of the children were at Pittsburgh attending school. Mrs. Stoops thought all day she had seen the shadows of Indians on the hill in the woods near the house, but her husband hooted at it. In the night they were awakened by Indians trying to break into the front door. Mr. S. made several efforts to carry off the child, but every time he [William] would cry out lustily. Finally Mrs. S. seeing the futility of an attempted escape with the little affrighted boy, and not willing to abandon him herself, she urged her husband to escape, that he might be a father to the children in town. And perhaps he might be able to get help in time to rescue her and the child. He went off through the back door in his shirttail, taking the gun; he soon shot at the Indians, and made off, they following him some distance.

Mrs. Stoops got into the potato-hole under the floor, leaving little William (between 3 & 4 years old) in bed. The Indians first set the house on fire, then broke in, going to the bed where the child was. A mother's affection prevailed, and she called out in agony, begging them to spare her child. One of the Indians replied by asking in broken English, where she was? She told, and directed which board to lift up, and let her out of her hiding place. Both mother & child were saved.

After robbing the house, particularly of victuals, as also milk from the milk-house, they departed with their prisoners, leaving the house in flames. Mrs. Stoops would break twigs by the way, to enable her husband to pursue, and discovering this, the Indians beat her. They cut off her petticoats, squaw fashion, to enable her to travel better.

On the northern bank of Mahoning Creek, 33 miles from Beaver, & about a mile & a half below where the state line crosses the

Mahoning, and two miles below Lowell[ville] . . . was where Mrs. Jane Stoops was rescued, & the Indian killed.

Brady & 2 or 3 others were returning from Sandusky with one squaw prisoner. Brady was in advance, with (as Mrs. S. thinks) his last load of powder but one, in his rifle—met the seven Indians— only the head one on horseback, with little William tied behind him— Mrs. Stoops near her son, & the other Indians following behind on foot. Brady shot the Indian dead, to whom the little boy was tied. He fell off his horse. The other Indians quickly treed. Don't recollect about Brady trying to get the powder-horn, nor of an Indian snapping his gun at him. Mrs. Stoops, seeing Brady in Indian dress, & painted, & not doubting but he was a real Indian, enquired, "What did you kill your brother for?"

"Brother, be d—d," replied Brady, "come with me!"

Neither Brady nor Mrs. Stoops, though well acquainted, at first recognized each other, though soon discovered. They made off. Near by, Brady & his party crossed the Mahoning, and the squaw waded (or swam) over, carrying Mrs. Stoops on her back, and once over, she exclaimed to Mrs. Stoops, "Puck-e-she! Puck-e-she!" which meant, "make your escape—clear yourself!" And then the squaw recrossed the stream and disappeared. Either Brady did not notice it, or if he did was indifferent about her under the new circumstances of the case.

When the squaw arrived where the Indians were, they were debating whether to kill the little white boy, since his mother had escaped and their leader had been killed, & one of the Indians had already struck him a tomahawk blow on the head, inflicting a wound an inch & a half long. The squaw now coming up, begged the boy's life, which was granted her, she becoming nurse. At Detroit he was sold to the British, & sent to school.

That night Brady & his party lay under a shelving rock, & the Indians in pursuit came so close by, that the whites held their breath to avoid the least noise. Brady went to Fort McIntosh. Mrs. Stoops was badly scratched & lacerated with thorns & bushes, & was lame a considerable time. After she reached home, she became so much affected with reflections upon her captivity, & the uncertain fate of her little boy, that her friends thought she would go crazy.

William Stoops was detained in captivity 3 years. Recollects something about an Indian giving information about the boy, & being offered a reward to return him to his parents. He probably failed in his efforts to do so. He was sent with other prisoners to the East & Samuel Stoops, his oldest brother, went & got him, aided by General Hand,

& brought him home to Pittsburgh on a salt pack-horse. His mother at the time of his arrival, was 3 miles distant attending a sick woman, and returned in haste, not putting on her clothes. She knew her boy by a mark on his body.

An Expedition against the Indians: Henry Wilson's Account of George Rogers Clark's Campaign against the Shawnees, 1780

George Rogers Clark, a Virginian, was trained as a surveyor, but spent much of his colorful life as a soldier. As it turned out, he was a very good one, achieving the rank of general in 1781. Nevertheless, he died poor and forgotten in Kentucky in 1818.

His military career began with Lord Dunmore's War, the expedition of 1774 against the Shawnees. As a major in the militia in 1776, he led the settlers in defense of their Kentucky settlements. In 1778 he captured the fort at Kaskaskia and the nearby French villages without firing a shot. Then he took the British fort, Vincennes, in another surprise attack in early 1779. In August, 1780, he led an expedition of settlers against the Ohio Shawnees. Enraged at the settlements and blockhouses that had been springing up in their Kentucky hunting grounds, the Indians continued to cross the river to raid and try to drive out the whites. Once again, the settlers raided the Shawnee villages to punish them.

Henry Wilson was in Colonel James Harrod's regiment during the raid. Writing in the third person, Wilson tells of an expedition typical for its bumbling and confusion. Militiamen outfitted themselves, so they were only as well equipped as they could afford. The only unusual thing about this raid was that the soldiers didn't just run away from the fight.

For the Shawnees this was a serious affair. Their homes, crops, and families were threatened. Afterward, they would never again feel as safe, even deep inside their Ohio home.

There were 200 men in Col. James Harrod's reg[imen]t, mostly dressed in hunting shirts & breech clouts, some linen & others buckskin. The mouth of Licking was the place of rendevouz. . . .

Every man was to furnish his own provisions. In Harrod's reg[imen]t every six men formed a mess, & had a pack horse, to carry blankets, kettle, the axe, parched corn meal and salt. The boats proceeded up from the Falls along the Kentucky shore, made such a noise that all the game was scared away.

Some of the men tried to hunt on the north shore of the river, but they ran into an Indian encampment and were attacked. Nine of them were killed or wounded.

This little check put a stop to hunting on shore. The men were now on half allowance of parched meal, & almost despaired of continuing the campaign. Near the mouth of Licking, a flat bottomed boat was met, loaded with corn, & destined for the Falls of Ohio for market. This was impressed & divided among the men. . . .
    . . . Logan's was the largest reg[imen]t, Boone was with him. There were some 1200 men altogether. . . . Marched on up the valley of the Lit. Miami, nothing occurred, until within five miles of Old Chillicothe [near present Xenia], when the spies returned, gave information that the Indians appeared to be moving off from the town. The army now commenced a run, kept a good smart trot, but when they reached the town about mid-day, they found the Indians had all gone & burnt their own town. Some pots were found over the fires, boiling green corn & snaps. The troops found a great relief in green roasting ears & string (snap) beans. That afternoon was spent in feasting & recruiting themselves. The next day the corn was all cut up, except five or six acres reserved for roasting ears on their return. Marched on to the Piqua town on the Big Miami, reached there about 8 o'clock in the morning, crossed half a mile below the town, water but knee deep. . . . Soon after had crossed, passing through a prairie, there met a large body of Indians chiefly behind a fence and in a piece of woods. Came second to the woods, the Indians fired, the whites returned it, & then the former broke & run 200 yards and again rallied & formed on a hill covered with timber. To the right along the stream & just before reaching the woods, was a large cornfield, along the margin of this field & parallel with the river ran a pole fence, behind which were the main body of the Indians—they fired upon the troops but fifty yards as they ran along through the prairie, a little before the party fired in the woods, then fled through the corn, and took a circuitous rout & gained their position with the others on the elevation. . . .
    The Indians finally retreated a hundred yards off, to a couple of large oak trees wh[ich] lay prostrate in a parallel line, on the top of these were placed chunks and poles stretched along lengthwise on their top forming a very good breast work with something like port holes between the pole & main body of the tree. Here some fifty Indians posted themselves undiscovered to fire upon the advancing whites. Capt Joseph McMultry, when within thirty steps of the Indian breast work, without knowing that Indians were there, seeing

some Indians quite a distance ahead, rested his rifle against a sapling & tumbled over his Indian, who however imediately arose & ran on. McMultry had his horn up filling his charger, when the Indians behind the oak trees all fired nearly at the same time, & though the large body of the men were not more than 200 feet off, but a single man was hurt, & that was Capt McMultry. A ball completely cut off his right hand fore finger, passing on through the top of his powder horn, shivering it to pieces, & entered his left breast.

Four men—Henry Wilson among the number—remained with him. McMultry expecting he was mortally wounded began giving some directions about his affairs & some word for his wife. Wilson wished to mount him on a horse they had with them, fearing the Indians might gain their rear. The wounded Captain desired not to be moved, as he shd not live long, "about as long as a deer shot through the lights."

Wilson thought they had better examine the wound & not take it for granted, without knowing, that the wound was mortal—felt the bullet lodged against the breast-bone. McMultry inserted his thumb & finger in the wound & flirted out the ball, which has been flattened in passing throught the horn, & before entering the breast, making a large wound, it had nearly spent its force. His finger was done up with a handkerchief & then all dashed on & overtook the troops a quarter of a mile off. Wilson, being thirsty, & seeing a spot where he thought might be water, & near the troops ran there, but found none, he then saw three Indians dodging through the bushes—one with a cocked hat on, at whom he aimed & shot through the belly & fell, skulked through the bushes to a tree top nearby, leaving his military hat where he fell.

As Wilson was picking up his booty, Capt Wm McAfee came running to his aid, & both ran up to the tree top, & looking for the Indian, who drew up & shot McAfee through the body less than ten feet off. A soldier now ran up, When the Indian was pouring powder into his rifle without measuring it—& shot him under the arm. The other two Indians were also shot, & all scalped. McAfee lived to be carried to the mouth of the Licking on a litter, & thence by water to a friends on Bear grass near the Falls of Ohio, his wife was sent for & reached him two days before his death.

The Indians were driven from tree to tree, and stand to stand, first in one direction two miles from town, & then in another till finally, about 3 o'clock P. M., they retreated gradually to their fort in the lower part of their town. It was a triangular stockade, covering perhaps half an acre—a new one, just made for the expected inva-sion of Clarke. Their women & children had all been sent off some twenty in all, & all the warriors collected in from far & near.

Clark's men set to work pounding the little stockade with a small cannon.

This hot work, & Clarke's being beyond the reach of their rifles, induced the Indians to divide their men—altogether about 1500—one half secretly left the fort, entered the cornfield which came up close, undiscovered, & thus gained the woods in Clarke's rear. The other half opened the only gate of the fort which fronted Clark & marched out & took position on the flat below, & formed into a single line. It was a novel movement & Clarke ordered the cannon to cease firing, thinking they had got tired of fighting & were about to propose to treat.

A few minutes dissipated this delusion—a heavy fire upon the rear now opened from the woods along the whole Indian line, this was briskly returned. The Indians on the flat came running in line, & fired when within gun shot. Clark gave strict orders for the men to reserve theirs until the Indians should come close—some of the soldiers along the line, hollered "let them come near enough before we fire that we can singe their eye-brows."

When within forty steps Clark's front some few treed, when near a tree—showered a volly upon the Indians, which mowed them down terribly, & which checked their advancing, & the second fire caused them to retreat.

In this action a cousin of Clark's on his mother's side, named Rogers, was mortally wounded, & crept behind a stump. Some of Clark's men were shooting at some of the wounded Indians crawling off, when Rogers hollered out to them not to shoot him for he was a white man. Some 3 or 4 ran down to him, said he was own cousin to Gen. Clark, & wanted to see the General. Clark soon rode up, & remarked he was sorry to see him in that situation, & expressed an opinion that as he knew that army was coming in time to have escaped & joined his countrymen, he shd have done it. He said he had no opportunity, & couldnt. He was taken into the rear & died an hour or two after. He had been taken prisoner two years before at the mouth of Big Miami. . . .

The fighting ended when the Indians made their escape.

The previous day had been one continued fight from 8 o'clock till night—had lost 20 killed, double that number wounded—had taken

73 scalps from the enemy—some of their dead & many wounded, were doubtless carried off. The greatest loss on both sides was in the action in the town above the fort.

Two days were now spent in destroying corn & village—it was estimated that 1000 acres were destroyed. Some thirty or 40 horses were taken, sold at auction at the mouth of Licking where Covington now is; there, too, the army disbanded, & the men scattered to hunt—the roasting ears got on their return at Chillicothe had given out. Camped no supper that night—left next morning. Some of them well nigh starved before reaching the settlements. No commissaries, no baggage waggons to convey regular rations, &, but too often, day after day without a particle of food, or if any but a sorry pittance of jerk, parched meal, or green corn, snaps or pumpkins—never all these luxuries at once—these were the conquerors of the West, these the protectors & saviors of the country. . . .

The First White Child in Ohio: John Heckewelder's Memoir of the Birth of His Daughter, 1781

It is debatable whether Johanna Maria Heckewelder, called "Aunt Polly" in her later years, actually was the first full-blooded white child born in Ohio. But she long held the honor. People traveled to her house in Bethlehem, Pennsylvania, to visit her as a tourist attraction. The following account of her birth was written for her by her father, the Moravian missionary John Heckewelder. It was translated from German by the (unnamed) editor of the Moravian newspaper in Bethlehem. Aunt Polly died in 1868 at the age of 87. She and her father are both buried in the Moravian cemetery in Bethlehem.

The Moravian Indians, who were mostly Delawares, lived under almost constant threat from both whites and other Indians during the Revolutionary War. They were mistrusted by both sides and often considered spies or at least sympathizers for one side or the other. In this account they were first rounded up by Indians on the British side then later, ninety-six of them were massacred at Gnadenhutten by Americans. That infamous event, in which peaceable men, women, and children were slaughtered, incited the cruel treatment of Colonel William Crawford by the Indians who captured him after the so-called Battle of the Olentangy in 1782.

Johanna Maria Heckewelder was born on Easter monday, April 16th, 1781, at Salem, a village of Christian Indians on the Muskingum river. She was baptized on the day following by Rev. William Edwards, minister at Gnadenhutten. A few days after her birth the Indians in that region were thrown into a state of great alarm by the sudden attack of an American army upon a town of the savages, named "Goschachking" [Coshocton], and a number of the latter were killed. About eighty warriors came to our settlements, determined to break up the Indian congregation at Shoenbrun, Gnadenhutten and Salem, or at least remove them about one hundred miles further westward; but during their stay amongst us they changed their minds and the majority of them, especially the chief, said they considered us a happy people, to injure whom would be a great sin, and that they wished that they themselves were partakers of the same happiness. . . .

After this event the three Indian congregations continued for some time to live in peace, and increased in spiritual knowledge and grace, so that we were filled with great joy. But in the beginning of the month of August we heard that there was a new movement amongst the Indians to drive us away, some even being in favor of destroying our settlements, but as they failed to find amongst their own number any who were ready to undertake this, certain wicked white persons joined them, and on the 12th of August they arrived at Salem with the advance-guard. The others arrived during the following days numbering in all 300 warriors, who camped in the square at Gnadenhutten. They endeavored by all sorts of promises to entice our Indian brethren and sisters to leave our stations and to come and live with them. After spending three weeks in these efforts, which were entirely unsuccessful, and being in the end disposed to leave the matter drop, they found that they had compromised themselves to such an extent that they were compelled to use force.

They accordingly set apart the 2d of September for a general council, and all the brethren at the three stations were summoned to be in attendance. Brother David Zeisberger repaired to Shoenbrun, eight miles above, I to Salem, about six miles below Gnadenhutten, and the Brethren Edwards and Senseman to the latter place. Brother Jungmann and wife remained at Shoenbrun with Sisters Zeisberger and Senseman, the latter of whom had an infant at the breast, and Brother Michael Jung remained at Salem with you and your mother. We passed the night in much sorrow, but without fear. Finally on the 3d of September, as we were walking up and down on a level spot behind the gardens, several warriors of the Wyandotte nation came up and took us prisoners to their camp. Here we were stripped of our best clothes, and one of them, who probably did not know what he was about, seized us by the head and shook us, saying in a scornful tone, "Welcome, my friends."

After a while we were placed in charge of a guard. When we were taken prisoners the appearance of the Indians was indeed terrible, as they all grasped their arms and we thought we should be dispatched on the spot, but our grief at the thought of your mother and yourself and the others, was more terrible than everything else, for just as we were led into the camp about twenty warriors, brandishing their arms and with terrible cries, galloped off on their horses towards Salem and Shoenbrun. When he saw them coming at a distance, Brother Jung locked the door of the house. You were lying in your cradle asleep. Finding the outer door locked, they burst it open by force and would have killed Brother Jung on the spot, but a white man who was with them prevented them. Your mother snatched you from the cradle and was told that she was a prisoner and must accompany them to Gnadenhutten. The house was then plundered from top to bottom. In the meanwhile it had commenced to rain, and some of the Indian sisters begged very urgently that you and your mother might remain with them over night, promising to bring you to Gnadenhutten the next day. Brother Jung they took with them, arriving at the camp about midnight. We had heard the scalp-cries all the while as we sat on the banks of the river, and the night was thereby made all the more horrible to us.

Heckewelder and his family and the other prisoners were marched to Upper Sandusky. At the beginning of October, they began to build themselves shelters nearby, but before they finished, the British commandant at Detroit ordered the missionaries be brought there.

This was a new and severe trial. Winter was at hand, and we were to leave our wives and children behind without any provision. In addition, the savages daily threatened to kill us. The day of our departure was fixed, and the Brethren Zeisberger, Edwards, Senseman and myself set out on the long journey. Brother Schebosch promised to provide our families with provisions brought from our deserted village.

The little group had a cold, hard journey. The soldiers became drunk and threatening, and the Moravian missionaries were met at Fort Detroit by an angry commandant, who believed the Moravians had been collaborating with the Americans during the war.

For a week we remained in a state of great uncertainty as to what was to become of us. We were not permitted to appear before the Commandant to make any statements, nor were we permitted to

address any written communications to him. At last, our accusers
being all assembled, we were summoned to attend, and after a thor-
ough examination into the accusations brought against us, the result was that two of our accusers were completely silenced, and the
third became our defender. . . . Thus even here the glory of God's
name was protected.

With the commandant's blessing, they returned to Upper Sandusky in November.

On the very day of our return the winter set in, a great deal of snow
fell and the cold became intense. The distress of our Indians became
terrible. In a short time they lost 150 head of cattle, which were their
main dependence for food. The wild Indians again threatened to stop
the preaching of the Gospel, and the power of the prince of darkness
seemed almost supreme. The scarcity of food became so great that
we began to fear that some, especially the little children, would perish from hunger.

A number of Indian brethren and sisters accordingly resolved to
return with their families to their deserted villages and gather in the
harvest, which was yet standing in the fields, and little by little to
forward the proceeds to this place. They had almost finished this
work and were preparing to return to us, when they were attacked
by a party of American militia, taken prisoners, and butchered in
cold blood. These dear martyrs, ninety-six in number, resigned themselves cheerfully to God's will. They united together in prayer to the
Savior, begged each other's forgiveness for past offenses, sang hymns
of faith and trust, and testified that they died as Christians. The many
little children in this company shared the same fate as their parents.
Thus a whole Indian congregation was in one night 7th-8th of March,
1782, translated from earth to heaven.

In the meanwhile, we who remained at Upper Sandusky, were
suddenly summoned to appear at Detroit, whilst our Christian Indians were to unite themselves to some of the wild tribes in the vicinity. Our poor Indian brethren could not understand nor reconcile
themselves to these orders. . . . Those were days of bitter suffering
and most distressing doubts, but the Savior comforted and strength-
ened us. . . .

April 14th, 1782, we set out in the boats, descending Sandusky
river for thirty miles and then crossing Lake Erie to Detroit. On the
16th, your first birthday anniversary, we were compelled at four different times to draw our boat to the shore during a storm, once at

great risk to us all. As I was afflicted with rheumatism and could not help myself, brother Edwards built a shelter against the wind for your mother and you out of cedar boughs. April 29th, we crossed Miami Bay, not without considerable danger, and next day we arrived at Detroit.

Here our whole company remained until August. Our Indians, who had been scattered in many different places, received permission to assemble here, and after several families had come, we commenced a settlement on the Huron river, which empties into Lake St. Clair. Many of our Indians joined us here, and the Commandant, now Colonel De Peyster, provided us with provisions. As the Brethren Jungmann and Senseman were in the year 1785 to return to Bethlehem your parents concluded to send you with them to the school at Bethlehem. After a farewell love-feast, these Brethren set out, May 16th, your father accompanying you as far as Detroit. The journey was made by boat across Lake Erie, and after being detained at Niagara for two weeks, in the same way across Lake Ontario to Wood's Creek, and thence by way of Schenectady and Albany to Bethlehem, at which place you arrived July 8th.

Colonel Crawford's Death at the Stake: William Croghan's Report on the Tragic Aftermath of the Battle of the Olentangy, 1782

In 1782, as the Revolutionary War, was coming to a close, there was constant friction between whites and natives on the frontier. After a group of white militia massacred peaceable Moravian Delawares at Gnadenhutten in March, the Ohio country exploded in war. One horror led to another. Colonel William Crawford, George Washington's associate in the land speculation business, was sent out with the militia from Pittsburgh to subdue the Indians. They marched toward the Indian towns at Upper Sandusky. After a brief battle, the militia, who were not disciplined soldiers and were tired of the whole business, retreated. During their disorderly retreat, Crawford and some others were captured.

The following letter is from William Croghan at Fort Pitt to Colonel William Davies of the Virginia Board of War. It was written soon after the ill-fated expedition that became known as the Battle of the Olentangy. Croghan was the nephew of George Croghan, a famous Indian agent, and the brother-in-law of George Rogers Clark.

Gen. Irvine commands at this post, where he has so few Continental troops (about 200 for duty) that 'tis not in his power to go from the garrison against the Indians, who are daily comitting murders through this country. The Pennsylvania militia formed an expedition against the Indians about three months ago; but instead of going against the enemies of the country, they turned their thoughts on a robbing, plundering, murdering scheme, on our well-known friends, the Moravian Indians, all of whom they met they . . . in the most cool and deliberate manner (after living with them apparently in a friendly manner for three days) men, women & children, in all ninety three, tomahawked, scalped & burned, except one boy, who after being scalped made his escape to the Delaware Indians (relations of the Moravians) who have ever since been exceeding cruel to all prisoner they have taken.

About six weeks ago, 500 volunteers of this country, commanded by (our old) Colonel William Crawford, went on an expedition against the Indian towns—the men behaved amiss (were cowardly) no more than about 100 having fought the Indians, who came out from their towns to meet them—the firing continued at long shot with rifles for near two days—the second evening our party broke off & retreated in the most disorderly manner—Colonel Crawford and a few others, finding the men would pay no attention to orders, were going on coolly in the rear, leaving the road in case the Indians should pursue, until the second day when they thought they might venture on the road, but before they had marched two miles, a body of Indians fell in between them and the rear of the party, & took them prisoners. We had no certainty of this unhappy affair until yesterday, when Doctor [John] Knight [surgeon's mate], who was taken with Crawford, came into the garrison in the most deplorable condition man could be in and be alive. He says that the second day after they were taken, they were carried to an Indian town, stripped and then blacked, and made to march through the Indians, when men, women, & children beat them with clubs, sticks, fists, &c., in the most cruel manner. Colo Crawford and the Doctor were confined together all night; the next day they were taken out, blacked again, and their hands tied behind their backs, when Col. Crawford was led by a long rope to a high stake, to the top of which the rope about the colonel was tied; all around the stake a great quantity of red hot coals were laid, on which the poor colonel was obliged to walk barefoot, and at the same time the Indians firing squibs of powder at him, while others poked burning sticks on every part of his body; thus they continued torturing him for about two hours, when he begged of Simon Girty, a white renegade who was standing by, to shoot him, when the fellow said "Don't you see I have no gun." — Some little time after they scalped him, & struck him on the bare scull several times with sticks. Being now nearly exhausted, he lay down on the burning embers, when the squaws put shovels full of coals on his body, which, dying as he was, made him move and creep a little. The Doctor was obliged to stand by and see the cruelty performed. When the colonel was scalped, they slapped the scalp over the Doctor's face, saying "This is your great Captain's scalp; to-morrow we will serve you so." The Doctor was to be served in the same manner in another town some distance off; and on his way to his place of torment he passed by where Col. Crawford's dead body had been dragged to & burned, & saw his bones. The Doctor was guarded by but one Indian, who seemed pretty kind to him; on the way the Indian wanted a fire made, and untied the Doctor, ordering him to make it. The Doctor appeared willing to obey, and was collecting wood till he got a good chunk in his hand, with which he gave the Indian so severe blow as levelled him; the Indian sprang up, but seeing the Doctor seize his gun, he ran away; the Doctor could not get the gun off, otherwise would have shot the Indian. He steered through the woods, and arrived here the twenty first day after he left the Indian, having no clothes, the gun being wood bound,[8] he left it after carrying it a few days.

For the twenty one days, and two or three more while he had been under sentence of death, he never ate anything but such vegetables as the woods afforded. None of the prisoners were put to death but those that fell into the hands of the Delawares, who say they will shew no mercy to any white man, as they would shew none to their friends and relations, the religious Moravians. I believe I have not told you, that the whole of the five hundred who went out with Crawford returned, except about fifty. Colonel Harrison & Mr. William Crawford, relatives of Col. Crawford, were likewise taken prisoners, but fortunately fell into the hands of the Shawanees, who did not kill their prisoners.

---

8. Wood bound: exposed to moisture to the point that the wooden stock has swelled up and interferes with the movements of the metal parts of the gun, making it inoperable.

PART TWO

The Tomahawk, the Sword,
and the Plough
1783-1815

This day the axe is laid to the root of the trees.
—Colonel John May

The Revolutionary War ended in 1783. Soon afterward the floodgates on the frontier opened. What had been a stream of colonists who made their way over the mountains or down the river to Kentucky became a torrent. And they didn't just stay in Kentucky.

Squatters often were the first on the scene in Ohio. They settled down where they pleased and stayed until they were driven off by the Indians or the American government or until someone bought them off by paying them for the improvements they had made. Try as it might, the fledgling American government never was very successful at keeping squatters off Indian territory in Ohio.

Worse from the perspective of the Indians were the government-sanctioned permanent settlements that the Ohio and Scioto land companies were developing along the Ohio side of the Ohio River. To regulate the development of lands gained from the British in the War of Independence, the fledgling Congress of the Confederation passed ordinances in 1785 and 1787. The second of the two, known as the Northwest Ordinance, is regarded as one of the most significant accomplishments of the Confederation Congress.

The 1785 ordinance provided for the survey of the newly-gained lands. The basic unit of the survey was a six-mile-square township made up of thirty-six sections of 640 acres each. Within each township four sections were reserved for the national government and one for the support of education within the township. Other provisions governed the sale of the land once it had been surveyed. This survey was later extended to all the western lands acquired by the United States.

The Northwest Ordinance of 1787 set up the framework for the governance of the territory. It provided for the appointment of a governor, magistrates and courts, and for the election of a legislative body. Specific articles ensured religious and civil liberties, encouraged schools and, ironically, urged the

Ohio about 1815, drawn by John Melish, showing the major tracts
of land, including land company purchases, the Connecticut
Reserve granted to that state by King Charles II, and the Virginia
Military District, set aside by Congress to pay Revolutionary War
soldiers. By permission of the Ohio Historical Society.

protection of the Indians. It also permitted the formation of new states when an
area had achieved a population of sixty thousand free inhabitants. Finally, it
prohibited slavery within the territory.

Together these ordinances established the principles and, largely, the practices that shaped the development not only of the Old Northwest but also of
the entire extent of the modern-day United States. They oversaw the expansion
of a young seaboard nation into a continental power.

In 1785, Fort Harmar was built near present-day Marietta. In 1788, Marietta
became the first recognized town of the Northwest Territory. White settlers
such as Colonel John May actually arrived with land deeds in hand and proceeded cutting down the ancient forests, building houses, and planting crops.

It was a recipe for trouble. The Native Americans were shocked that the

Treaty of Paris ending the Revolutionary War had failed to consider their land claims. And while some Indians had signed the subsequent treaties forfeiting large portions of Ohio, others had steadfastly refused to do so and were more than ready to draw their line at the Ohio River. Having moved repeatedly away from the encroaching whites, they decided to take a stand. The Shawnees, already having lost their hunting grounds in Kentucky, were especially hostile to white settlements in Ohio.

Native American methods of confrontation usually were hit-and-run. They hijacked the big, slow, settlers' barges as they floated down the river, or they attacked isolated cabins or individual colonists who strayed from the safety of the town or fort. They even went so far as to kill most of the game in the area of Marietta and pile it up to rot. John May, Joseph Barker, and Luke Foster all give some idea of how the settlers felt living on the edge of this chaos.

Jonathan Alder, who was kidnapped as a child by Indians and raised among them, gives an insider's view of tribal life in those days, describing how threatened the natives felt by the coming of the settlements. Once the whites had a foothold in Ohio, they were freer to return the hit-and-run raids, and in turn they took an awful toll on the natives. Alder writes: "Driven from place to place, our favorite hunting grounds taken from us, our crops destroyed, towns burned, and our women and children sent off in the midst of winter, perhaps to starve, while the warriors stood between them and their enemies, like a mob to be shot down!"

The earliest white settlers, for their part, risked everything to live in Ohio. Their tales of life in those days are harrowing. Some couldn't take the strain of pioneer life and went back east. Some died in Ohio of accident, war, or disease. Those who stayed often worked extraordinarily hard under challenging conditions to establish in Ohio the kind of life they had left back home. Of course, not all white settlers were striving, hardworking, clean-living people. Some were adventurers, even criminals. Some were colorful backwoods folk. A variety of frontier characters are introduced in these pages.

The conjunction of gullible emigrants looking for a better life and sharp real estate developers working on the edge of the law caused grave misfortune at Gallipolis in 1792. Some descriptions of Ohio were written with a rose-colored pen for the benefit of naive newspaper readers in Europe. As a result, a group of French people decided to buy land along the Ohio River from the Scioto Company. The French immigrants arrived in America, however, to find that the Scioto Company had no title to the land. They had been defrauded. Being ill-suited to frontier life, the French spent a miserable winter in Ohio, during which many of their group died. In the spring, as Joseph Barker recalls, they drifted away to Canada or back to France. A very few stayed and founded Gallipolis.

The biggest threat during the period 1783-1815 was that shaky relations with the Indians would deteriorate into war. And most of the time the frontier was in a state of undeclared war. The white settlements—Marietta, Gallipolis,

Columbia, and Cincinnati—established themselves against a background of unrest. Under the circumstances, growth was slow.

Then, in 1790, war broke out in earnest. Ironically, the Indians usually won the battles. In 1790 the Indians routed miltia and regulars under General Josiah Harmar. In 1791, allied tribes under the leadership of the Miami chief, Little Turtle, crushed the army of General (and governor) Arthur St. Clair in the worst defeat American troops ever suffered at the hands of Native Americans.

But the Indians were in a position similar to that of the South in the Civil War. The war was conducted on their land. Their villages and crops no longer were secure. Every victory depleted their small forces. While the warriors fought, their families suffered from hunger. In the long run, they couldn't win. In 1794, they were defeated at the Battle of Fallen Timbers, and in 1795 they signed the Treaty of Greenville, giving up two-thirds of Ohio to the whites.

After that, white settlements sprang up rapidly. The Western Reserve encompassed all or part of fourteen counties in northeastern Ohio. The area had been claimed by Connecticut under a king's charter of 1622. In 1795, the Connecticut Land Company acquired it, subdivided it into townships, and sold it off, mainly to pioneers from New England. The east central counties attracted Quakers and Germans from the overpopulated counties of Pennsylvania. Travelers penetrated Ohio up the rivers and established such towns as Chillicothe and Franklinton on the Scioto River, Youngstown on the Mahoning, and Waynesburg on the Little Miami. Sadly, many of these towns were created on the sites of Indian villages. Indians sometimes wandered through their old homelands, but no longer as overlords of a vast domain. They appear as wretched, displaced figures in the background of the burgeoning white communities. When John Melish passed through Schoenbrunn in 1811 he noted, "The Indians look wretchedly poor." Jonathan Alder had already decided it was a good time to be white again, and he bought land and settled among his own kind. His Indian wife left him in disgust.

By 1800 Ohio had some forty-five thousand inhabitants. In 1803, it became the first state of the Old Northwest. Two years later, Indians relinquished about a third of their remaining land, including the section south of Lake Erie called the Firelands. Two more cessions of land followed. By the time the Englishman Fortescue Cuming visited the state in 1807 and wrote about his trip, he could travel in safety up Zane's Trace from the Ohio River across from Maysville, Kentucky, all the way to Wheeling, West Virginia, never far from farmhouses and inns the whole way.

While the new Ohioans subdued the land, some native Ohioans felt themselves not yet subdued. When the War of 1812 broke out with the British, a few tribal leaders who had not attended the Treaty of Greenville—especially the charismatic Tecumseh and his brother, The Prophet, who preached a return to traditional Indian ways and the rejection of white values and lifestyle—saw an opportunity to take back what had been theirs. They attempted to form a tribal federation to make one last push against their adversaries. The three years of the war brought with them once again the threat of attack by the Indians and British. At times, things looked grim indeed. Several writers in this section describe the perils of wartime Ohio. In 1813, Cynthia Barker wrote to her friend Julia Buttles that the news from Worthington, in Franklin County, was "WORSE & WORSE."

But shortly thereafter, in October, 1813, Tecumseh was killed in battle in Canada, and the last Ohio Indian resistance collapsed. In the future, Ohio would belong to the conquerors. Within months, Benjamin Stickney, the Indian agent, was writing about white intrusions into the remaining Indian land: "As the fear of Indian hostility has now ceased in this quarter, something decisive appears to be necessary at this time, to convince those disposed to intrude themselves, that it will not be winked at. . . ."

The collapse of Indian opposition was now so complete that huge sections of the Northwest Territory opened for settlement. Indiana became a state in 1816, Illinois in 1818. (Michigan and Wisconsin followed more slowly, in 1837 and 1848 respectively.) Settlers from Ohio helped populate these states, as will be seen in the next section.

Perhaps nothing characterizes this period in Ohio history more than fear— on both sides, white and native. While life continued to be challenging on the frontier after this, as may be seen in Part Three, henceforth fear of the enemy was dispelled. It was replaced in the white community by pity and some contempt for former opponents. In the native community, it was replaced with a growing despair.

Rousting the Squatters: Ensign Armstrong's Report on Destroying Squatters' Cabins, 1785

While the Revolutionary War continued, there was little the government could do about white settlers squatting on Indian lands west of the Ohio River. It was a constant worry, however, for the Indians had no patience with invasions of the territory that was theirs by treaty. They often murdered white interlopers to make their point, thereby setting off continual frontier wars.

In 1779, Colonel Daniel Brodhead sent sixty men to burn some cabins between the Muskingum River and Fort McIntosh (near present Beaver Falls, Pennsylvania) and to inform the Indians at Coshocton of what he had done. Later he wrote to Major Richard Taylor: "I sincerely wish [Captain Vance] had taken under guard some of those fellows who, by their unlicensed encroachments on the Indian's Hunting grounds, seem determined to provoke new calamities to the already much distressed inhabitants of the frontier."

After the war, the "unlicensed encroachments" increased. In spring, 1785, soldiers destroyed cabins that had been built around the salt springs in

Weathersfield Township, Trumbull County, and then sought to evict settlers who had built along Yellow Creek and the west bank of the Ohio. The following report was made by Ensign John Armstrong, commander of the operation.

Agreeable to your orders, I proceeded with my party early on the 31st of March down the river Ohio. On the 1st instant we crossed little Beaver and dispossessed one family. Four miles from there we found three families living in sheds, but they having no raft to transport their effects, I thought proper to give till the 12th inst., at which time they promised to demolish their sheds and move to the east side of the river.

At Yellow Creek [near Wellsville, Columbiana County] I disposessed two families and destroyed their buildings. The 2d being stormy, no business could be done. The 3d we dispossessed eight families. The 4th we arrived at Mingo Bottom, or Old Town [below present-day Steubenville]. I read my instructions to the prisoner Ross, who declared they never came from Congress, for he had late accounts from that Honorable body, who he was well convinced gave no such instructions to the Comissioners. Neither did he care from whom they came, for he was determined to hold his possession, and if I should destroy his house he would build six more in the course of a week. He also cast many reflections on the Honorable, the Congress, the Commissioners and the commanding officer. I conceived him to be a dangerous man, and sent him under guard to Wheeling. Finding most of the settlers in this place were tenants under the prisoner, I gave them a few days at which time they promised to move to the eastern side of the Ohio, and that they would demolish their buildings. On the evening of the 4th, Charles Norris, with a party of armed men, came to my quarters in a hostile manner and demanded my instructions. After conversing with them for some time and showing my instructions, the warmth with which they first expressed themselves appeared to abate, and from some motive lodged their arms with me till morning.

I learnt from the conversation of the party that at Norrises Town (by them so called) eleven miles further down the river [about fourteen miles below Steubenville] a party of seventy or eighty men were assembled with a determination to oppose me.

Finding Norris to be a man of influence in that country I conceived it to my interest to make use of him as an instrument which I effected by informing him it was my intention to treat any armed party I saw as enemies to my country, and would fire on them if they did not disperse.

On the 5th when I arrived within two miles of the town or place

where I expected to meet with opposition, I ordered my men to load
their arms in presence of Norris and then desired him to go to the
party and inform them of my instructions. . . .

When I arrived at the town there were about forty men assembled
who had deposited their arms. After I had read to them my instructions they agreed to move off by the 19th inst. This indulgence I
thought proper to grant, the weather being too severe to turn them
out of doors. . . .

Marietta in Its Infancy: The Journal of Colonel John May, 1788-1789

Colonel John May was a rich Massachusetts patriot and merchant who participated in the Boston Tea Party. After the war, when some colonists wanted to
move west to escape high land prices in the east or because the family farm was
too small to accommodate second and third sons, May saw Ohio as a good
place to make an investment. He went there on behalf of the Ohio Company in
1788 to draw lots of land at the mouth of the Muskingum River. He traveled
on horseback from Boston to Pittsburgh, where he had to wait some time for a
boat. The trip down the Ohio River was beautiful, he wrote later, but overshad-
owed by stories he heard of recent Indian attacks, robberies, and murders. He
arrived in time to record some of the earliest days of Marietta.

Tuesday, [May] 27th. Slept on board last night, and rose early this
morning. Have spent the day in reconnoitering the spot where the
city is to be laid out, and find it to answer the best descriptions I
have ever heard of it. The situation delightfully agreeable, and well
calculated for an elegant city. . . .

As to our surveying, buildings, etc., they are in a very backward
way. Little appears to be done, and a great deal of time and money
misspent. There are now here about thirty Indians, who appear to be
friendly enough; but they are a set of creatures not to be trusted. . . .

Thursday, 29th. This day the axe is laid to the root of the trees. . . .
Find the soil very good, but was tormented beyond measure by myriads of gnats. They not only bite surprisingly, but get down one's
throat.

This evening, arrived two long boats from the Rapids [Louisville,
Kentucky], with officers and soldiers, the number about one hundred. On their passage up the river they were fired upon by a strong
party of Indians, headed by a white man. They returned the fire, and
had two men killed. They were obliged to drop down the river a piece,

Campus Martius, a fortification built to protect early Marietta settlers from Indian attacks. From *American Pioneer, vol. 1 (1884)*

and come by the place in the night. There are various reports about the hostilities of the savages, but nothing to be depended on. The Indians are frequently in here, and seem to be on friendly terms. I have shaken hands with many of them. . . .

Monday, [June] 9th. I have been clearing land for eight days, and now begin to feel the effects of poison—from ivy, doubtless. I hope it will not prove very bad. . . . Colonel Battelle and myself went out this morning and killed a fine raccoon. The settlers are zealously at work, and the land is opening fast, and looks finely; but we are in great want of [ox] teams.

Sunday, 15th. . . . A number of poor devils—five in all—took their departure homeward this morning. They came from home moneyless and brainless, and have returned as they came. . . .

Sunday 22d. . . . Had a fine dinner to-day on gammon, parsley, and so on; excellent bread, mustard, vinegar. Our luck has been heretofore to have good provisions—the best of bread, fine venison, and turkeys—when we pleased; also, gray and black squirrels at any time when we want them, and as great a variety of fish as can be named in any market. The gardens of the garrison, also, much at our service. I have received innumerable civilities from the officers of the fort. In a word, we live superbly. However, lying so long on board ship (which is four weeks yesterday) I think unwholesome. Some of us are beginning to complain of aches and pains. I, amongst the rest, am full of rambling pains, and my limbs drag after me. I am afraid the worst is not come yet. But I don't intend to grumble, or get into the dumps. . . .

Thursday, 26th. Some gone to raising, some to drawing timber, and some to sawing in the pit,—myself grunting, but often seizing the axe in order to stir my blood as well as to stimulate others. I have assisted in cutting two black-walnut trees, either of which would make four hundred feet boards. These I shall have sawed into stuff for furniture for the new house. . . .

Tuesday, July 1st. . . . We were alarmed to-day by a letter from Major Doughty, at Pittsburg, stating that they had just received intelligence from Detroit, that two parties of Indian warriors, about forty in each party, were started on a hostile expedition against our settlement and Kentucky. Our people were called in from labor at 11 o'clock, and a guard consisting of a subaltern and thirty men sent to reconnoiter and scour the woods. They took a day's provisions with them. . . .

Thursday, 3d. . . . At the first of our coming here there were no robins; but for a fortnight back there have been several about here, and it seems as if they would exhaust themselves in praising our works and Him who sent us here and protects us here. . . . I returned from labor at sunset, and found hanging up in my cellar a pike that weighed twenty-one pounds, and a perch twenty-four and one-half pounds. . . . In short, fish are so various, and of such magnitude, that one can hardly exaggerate in speaking about them.

Friday, 4th. . . . All labor comes to a pause today in memory of the Declaration of Independence. Our long bowery is built on the east bank of the Muskingum; a table laid sixty feet long, in plain sight of the garrison, at one-quarter of a mile distance. . . . On the whole . . . we had a handsome dinner; all kinds of wild meat, turkey, and other fowls of the woods; gammon, a variety of fish, and plenty of vegetables; a bowl of punch, also grog, wine, etc. Our toasts were as follows:

1. The United States.
2. Congress.
3. His Most Christian Majesty the King of France.
4. The United Netherlands.
5. The Friendly Powers throughout the World.
6. The New Federal Constitution.
7. General Washington and the Society of Cincinnati.
8. His Excellency Governor St. Clair and the Western Territory.
9. The Memory of Heroes.

10. Patriots.

11. Captain Pipes, and a Successful Treaty.

12. The Amiable Partners of our Lives.

13. All Mankind. . . .

Saturday, 5th. . . . I am of opinion that deer are plentier in this country than horned cattle are in New England. However, this state of things will not last long; for whenever a country begins to be settled, the native inhabitants must either flee or perish outright. . . .

Thursday, 10th. Wind at southwest, and rainy. Streets—mud, mud, mud. . . .

Friday, 11th. A delightful day. All hands at work on the house. This an arduous undertaking, and will cost more than I intended. Am building from several motives. First, for the benefit of the settlement; second, from a prospect or hope of gain hereafter; third, for an asylum for myself and family, should we ever want it; fourth, as a place where I can leave my stores and baggage in safety; and lastly, to gratify a foolish ambition, I suppose it is. The house is thirty-six feet long, eighteen wide, and fifteen high; a good cellar under it, and drain; and is the first (of the kind) built in Marietta.

Thursday, 24th. Fine weather, and work enough for willing hands to do. For several days we have had plenty of vegetables from our own industry; and I dare say that there is not a market in the world which will have a greater variety of good things than we shall have this fall. And what makes it extraordinary is, that they were grown on land where, six weeks ago, stood the lofty trees of the forest, from eight to ten rods long.

Friday and Saturday, 1st and 2d August. . . . We begin now to knock the boat to pieces, in order to obtain board suitable for flooring the house. . . . In the evening, went over the Ohio river, and visited Mrs. Williams, and made a visit also to General Harmer.[1] Here I was introduced to old Pipes, chief of the Delaware nation,[2] and his suite, dressed and acting like the offspring of Satan. They did not stay long before they went to their camp in the woods, and I crossed the river back again to my lodgings. Went to bed at 12, but got little rest. The Indians made one of their hellish pow-wows, which lasted till the hour of rising. . . .

Sunday, 3d. Got up at 3 o'clock, and put myself in order for em-

---

1. General Josiah Harmar was a Revolutionary War veteran and Indian fighter for whom Fort Harmar, near Marietta, had been named. In 1790 his troops were badly defeated by Indians led by the Miami chief Little Turtle.

2. A well-known chief from the Delaware towns in northeastern Ohio.

barkation. the company with whom I am to ascend the Ohio is composed of all officers and all men: consequently every little matter
proposed has to be stated and discussed an hour or so before it can be
determined how it shall be. . . . We did not quit the quay at Marietta,
until half after 8. . . .

Monday, 4th. . . . Nothing material happened. Could not help remarking again the beauties of the river. On each side mountains,
with valleys between, rising progressively to view, and filling the
mind with admiration and wonder. . . .

These Beautiful Shores: Descriptions of Ohio by Manasseh Cutler and St. John de Crevecoeur, circa 1789

The following description of the Ohio country was written by Manasseh Cutler, a founding member and agent of the Ohio Company (though this was a
different Ohio Company from the one that sent Christopher Gist to Ohio) and
one of the founders of Marietta. It was published in English and then, in 1789,
in French, to encourage emigration and settlement along the Ohio River. The
version printed here was translated back into English from the French in 1888.
It describes the rivers, identifies the navigable ones, and talks about transportation of goods and the fertility of the soil. It is pure ad copy. Its rhapsodic account of the Ohio country lured the French settlers who bought land from the
Scioto Company only to discover when they arrived in Ohio in 1792 that their
land titles were invalid. What people on the scene, such as Joseph Barker and
Luke Foster, had to tell about the real conditions in the wilderness, demon-
strates just how false is this developer's-eye view of Ohio.

The great level plains which one meets with here and which form
natural prairies, have a circumference of from twenty to fifty miles,
they are found interspersed almost everywhere along the rivers. These
plains have a soil as rich as can be imagined and which with very
little labor can be devoted to any species of cultivation which one
wishes to give it. They say that in many of these prairies one can
cultivate an acre of land per day and prepare it for the plough. There
is no undergrowth on them and the trees which grow very high and
become very large only need to be deprived of their bark in order to
become fit for use.

. . . One finds both on the hills and on the plains a great quantity of grapes growing wild, and of which the inhabitants make a red wine, which suffices for their own consumption. They have tried the experiment of pressing these grapes at the settlement of Saint Vincent [Vincennes], and the result is a wine which, by keeping a little while, becomes preferable to the many wines of Europe. Cotton of an excellent quality is also a product of the country. . . .

There is a very little bad land in this territory, and no marsh. There are plenty of hills; their position is agreeable, and they are not high enough to interfere with their cultivation. Their soil is deep, rich, covered with trees of good growth, and adapted to the cultivation of wheat, rye, indigo, tobacco, etc.

Cutler goes on to quote St. John de Crevecoeur, French consul to America, who himself quotes from the "letters of an American farmer" on his travels down the Ohio River.

Never before had I felt so disposed to meditation and revery; involuntarily my imagination darted into the future, the remoteness of which gave me no trouble, because it appeared to be near. I saw in fancy these beautiful shores ornamented with handsome houses, covered with crops, the fields well cultivated; on the declivities of the hills exposed to the north I saw orchards planted, on the others vineyards, plantations of mulberries, acacias, etc. . . . What an immense chain of plantations! What a great career of activity, of industry, of culture and commerce is offered to the Americans. I consider therefore the settlement of the country watered by this great river as one of the greatest enterprises ever presented to man. It will be the more glorious because it will be legally acquired with the consent of the ancient proprietors and without the shedding of a drop of blood. It is destined to become the foundation of the power, wealth and future glory of the United States. . . .

If a poor man, who had nothing but his hands, should ask me, "Where shall I go to establish myself in order to live with the most ease, without the help of horses or oxen?" I would say to him, "Go to the banks of one of the creeks in the Scioto bottoms; all that you will have to do will be first to obtain permission from the Indians from the neighboring village (this permission is no longer necessary since the treaty with them); second, scratch the surface of the earth and deposit there your wheat, your corn, your potatoes, your beans, your cabbage, your tobacco, etc., and leave the rest to nature. In the meantime amuse yourself with fishing and the chase."

Recollections of an Early Cincinnati Settler:
A Letter from Luke Foster, 1789

Luke Foster arrived in Columbia, just below the mouth of the Little Miami River, in April, 1789. He joined the small settlement there whose proprietor was Benjamin Stites. Columbia would soon be outstripped in size by nearby Cincinnati.

The first year Foster spent in Columbia was a cruel one, threatened by Indian attacks and near starvation. He wrote a letter in 1819 that described some of the settlers' experiences there. Foster was barely literate, but he conveyed the scene with chilling detail. Some of his spelling has been corrected for easier reading.

On the 27ᵗʰ. of the (same) month, August, 1789; I met the first party of hostile indians, that ever came with hostile designs, against these settlements. . . . The party I met was four indians, on the road or rather path, to our cornfield, about 1 1/4 mile from our fort. . . . The next day, my self, with eight others, pursued them, when coming on their trail, found they had taken our horses, which made their trail more plain, we followed them on horseback, up the east fork of Little Miami; about 30 miles, (as near as we could guess) when to our surprise, we heard a yell, it was their Sentry a mile back on their trail: we put too our best mettle, & soon past their fire, where they had stopt to refresh; at which we made no stop, but pursued in full speed, about 1 1/2 mile, when from the extraordinary speed of their horses, & from a consideration, that 2 of our men whose horses were tired & not able to keep up, we feared for their safety, returned back to the fire; where were our two men, who had by this time exchanged their tired horses for two of the indian horses, they had left six; four of their own; & two they had taken; which we took back & restored. . . . About 6 weeks after this; Obediah & John Seward, was taken, the latter attempting to escape, was killed, by a pipe tomahawk, twice drove through his skull; so that his brains ran out; the whole scalp was taken off his head, yet he lived 39 days, & was rational.— Obediah, was taken nearly to the town, there shot by one of his captors; who alleged it to have been an accident; but they cut off his head, & skinned his body, below the breast, & set it up on a stake. Two weeks after Edʳᵈ Larkins, was taken the same route, who recognized the head of Seward. . . .

At this time living in garrison became disagreeable, to my self & some others, we returned to our huts, made them as strong as possible, & chose rather to defend ourselves, than live confined in garrison. After this, surprises were frequent, deaths & captures often, though I cannot recollect the dates: but many were the victims. That winter, was a winter of warfare, & we all minute men. . . .

In the spring, a still more serious evil was found to exist, than even a savage war, with all its horrors. A famine! being harassed, & pent up by the indians, that we could take no wild meat, and our corn so frosted, that it would not sprout, neither would a hungry horse eat it; for I tryed mine, with the best I had, & he would not taste it: but what was still worse there was not enough of it for every one to have a little. There were, perhaps, in Columbia, near 200 persons, of all sex & ages; & I believe not one pound of pork, or any other kind of salted or any other meat; & but little milk, & no flour. In fact, our subsistance, was an insufficiency of such poor corn ground by hand, or boiled whole; & the roots of beargrass, which was found on the rich bottoms, boiled mashed up, & baked, some times with, & some times without a mixture of our hand mill meal: but then it was good, I dont know how it would eat now.

Growing Up Indian: The Memoir
of Jonathan Alder, 1786-1805

Like James Smith twenty-five years before, Jonathan Alder was captured by Indians and learned to love and respect them. At age 7, in 1781, Alder lived with his widowed mother and brother in Wythe County, Virginia. One day his mother sent the boys out to look for a mare and colt that had wandered away. They were captured in the woods by Indians, who immediately killed and scalped Jonathan's brother and took Jonathan captive. The child was marched north across the Ohio, then up the Scioto to a Shawnee town at Chillicothe. After running the gauntlet, he was adopted into a Shawnee family and treated as a family member. So attached did he become to them that in 1783, when a Kentucky trader offered to exchange Jonathan as a prisoner, Alder stayed with the Shawnees.

Eventually, he married an Indian woman. They settled near present Plain City in Madison County, along the Big Darby Creek, among white settlers. But Alder's wife didn't like their white neighbors or the white way of life, and finally the two agreed to part. She went back to her people in northern Ohio. Alder later married Mary Blont of Virginia and fathered twelve children. He died in 1849.

This is Alder's history as he told it to his son late in life. Like many other captives who stayed among the Indians for some time, Alder became warmly attached to them. He saw their troubles as his own. In many ways he became

Jonathan Alder's cabin, once along the Big Darby Creek near Plain City, now at the Madison County Historical Society, London.

one of them. By the time he told his story, however, he had re-identified himself as white. This should be remembered when reading his accounts of Indian raids. He may not be completely frank about his role in them.

One incident that I remember and should have spoken of before, and which occurred before I had commenced to hunt, I will now relate. Sometimes one Indian, and sometimes another, would take me out hunting for a single day. One cold winter day, Big Turtle asked me to go with him hunting. We then lived near the Sandusky Plains. I got ready and started. We wandered about for some time, and finally he said we would cross the Plains. After we had crossed over a short distance, he killed a fine deer, skinned it and hung the meat up.

We were then a good distance from camp, and it was too late to bring it in that day. The weather had been changing all day, so by that time it was very cold. When he finished, we started for our hut, but had not gone far before he killed a large wild turkey; he gave it to me and told me to run and that would keep me warm, but presently we struck the prairie, and the difference in the temperature was so great that had I been half naked in the timber I would not have felt the cold so severely as I did, with all my clothes on, when we started across the plains. We had not gone more than a mile before I began to get very numb. I threw the turkey down, and had gone some distance before Big Turtle discovered it, and ran back past me to get it but before he got back, I had fallen down three or four times in the snow.

When he came up to me, he discovered I was freezing. He took me by the hand and told me to run. He ran, holding me by the hand, carrying his gun and the turkey in the other. He encouraged me to hold out and help myself all I could. We had about two miles to go before we would reach timber; as soon as we got under the shelter of the timber, there seemed to be about as much difference in the temperature as if a warm blanket had been wrapped around me. Big Turtle never stopped, or let go of my hand, until we got into camp, and then was very careful not to let me get warm too rapidly.

As soon as I had recovered sufficiently, they gave me something to eat, some warm drink, and then prepared my bed and put me in it. I soon fell asleep and did not awake until the next morning. . . .

I was about twelve years old when an Indian came to me one day and said he had killed a buffalo and wanted help to carry in the meat. I had frequently gone out with them when they had killed large game, and they gave me the head to carry, which, by-the-way, is a very convenient thing to carry, when it has horns on; so I told them I wanted to go along, and carry the head, and laughed. They told me to come along. I had never been near a buffalo as yet, and did not think about its large size. When we got to the game, I found the Indian had killed the largest bull buffalo I ever saw, and after the head was cut off, I was hardly able to raise it from the ground; they all laughed and said, "Carry it! Why don't you carry it?" I felt very much ashamed and really did all I could to carry it, but that was impossible; so after some merriment at my expense, they carried it. But my inability to carry the huge monster's head, was quite an amusing scene for the Indians and boys, and for a long time, they plagued me about the affair. My [Indian] mother always took my part, by saying: "Poor fellow, he did all he could, and if he could not carry such a big load, you should not tease him about it."

In 1790, Alder went on a raid into Kentucky with eight Indians to steal horses from the white settlers.

I had never owned a horse but was very desirous of doing so and did not reflect upon the mode proposed to obtain them. To me nothing seemed wrong so far as the whites were concerned. We had suffered so much at their hands that all seemed to be fair. . . .

We were then in the neighborhood of the Mack-a-chack towns and from thence we passed down through what are now called Logan, Union, Madison, Pickaway and Ross counties. We stopped a few days on the Pickaway plains, hunted, and passed on slowly, for Indians on such trips are never in a hurry. . . .

They crossed the river at present-day Portsmouth and traveled for two days into Kentucky, camping at night without a fire. On the third day, they came to a white settlement and hid nearby.

About sundown we began to hear bells all around us. The settlers all belled their horses in those days. We could hear men at every cabin, chopping wood. The head Indian remarked that the whites had a day which they kept and on which they did not work. He said tomorrow will be that day; and their horses will all be turned out until day after tomorrow, and the men will be in and about their cabins; so, we may just as well commence now and gather up the horses, as it is the best time we will have to do so; and we went to work as soon as possible.

Before it was quite dark we had a number of horses caught and taken back and tied in a secret place. We had the advantage of the moon, as it was then full. . . . We had in all, thirty-two horses, young and old. I had a mare, a two-year old and a yearling colt. The head Indian said if any of us were not satisfied, he would give more time to get other horses but we told him we did not want anymore. . . .

After some time we got home and, as usual, . . . our story, with all the particulars, was told. My old Indian father and mother were greatly pleased at my success. . . .

During my stay with the Indians, and until after the great victory of Gen. Wayne [at the Battle of Fallen Timbers in 1795], we were frequently attacked or disturbed by the whites. In fact not a year passed without suffering some loss on our part by attacks of the white armies. The fall of the year was generally chosen as the time best suited to march against the Indians for the reason, perhaps, that at that time our crops were raised and preparations made for winter; and if our subsistance should be destroyed we would be reduced to greater distress at that season, than at other periods of the year. Many bitter and sorrowful hours have we passed in consequence of such

difficulties and privations. When peace prevailed we enjoyed ourselves freely, but when these terrible troubles and scourges came,
attended as they were, with the loss of everything an Indian holds
dear on earth, we became very much disheartened. Driven from place
to place, our favorite hunting grounds taken from us, our crops destroyed, towns burned, and our women and children sent off in the
midst of winter, perhaps to starve, while the warriors stood between
them and their enemies, like a mob to be shot down! All these things
engendered animosities and caused cruel retaliation. The whites were
strong and powerful; the Indians few and feeble and hence were driven
back and their lands occupied by the whites. This state of things
will account for many, if not all of the cruelties charged to the Indian. I was rapidly becoming an Indian in the true sense of the word,
and felt sorely for the wrongs on these occasions and acted as they
do—revengeful and hateful toward the white race. I felt keenly the
wrong of robbing them of their lands while the whole race was being
pressed further and further back into the wild forests; and that too,
from lands for which the whites never could have had any claim
whatever. Even the theory of purchase was but another pretext to
rob. We had no choice but to sell and take what they chose to give or
be driven off and get nothing! The price offered was always governed
by what it would cost to drive us off, and if the latter cost the least,
it would always be the first resort. This is but a true statement of
the case. . . .

I was now drawing toward manhood and had become accustomed
to the ways, habits, diet and general mode of living, among the Indians, and so far reconciled that I had lost all desire to return to my
home and kindred. . . .

A couple of years after their first horse stealing expedition, Alder and some
other young braves went to Kentucky on another one. This time they were almost caught by white settlers. As they retreated toward Ohio, the Indians passed
a lone cabin in the woods.

We halted and held a council and it was finally concluded that as we
had been discovered, and having missed the object of our expedition,
we would wait until after dark and kill the family in the cabin! . . .

About dark some of the Indians reconnoitered the cabin and pre-
mises. We fell back about a half mile and waited until near midnight, and then got ready for the slaughter of this unsuspecting and
innocent family. I would have done anything consistent with my own

safety to have saved them; but there was no way of escape. It must be done and I dared not oppose it as I would have been unfaithful and my life would have paid the forfeit at once, or at least I thought so.

It had been cloudy before night and continued getting more so until we were ready to start, by which time it was so dark we could not see a foot before us. The head Indian gave the word to move on, he taking the lead. We crept along very cautiously until we thought we had got far enough to be at the house. We then wandered around for some time hunting the house but could not find it! Finally we halted and all gathered close to each other to consult. I being but a boy, did not engage in such consultations, but retired a few steps.

As soon as all got together the head Indian made a remark: "If you recollect it was a clear day until just before sundown and then it commenced clouding until it has got so dark we cannot see one another standing here close together, although it is full moon. Now the Great Spirit does not want us to kill these people, and when the Great Spirit does not want us to do something He will not let us do it, so we had just as well leave for we will not find them!"

At that time I was standing about a rod from them as was usual for me when a council was held. I heard the door creak on its wooden hinges as it opened and in about one minute I heard it creak again as it shut. It could have been but a very short distance from me and the people evidently were on the lookout for the Indians! I trembled from head to foot when I heard the door; for I fully expected the Indians would hear it and then I would have to witness the horrible deed of murder and butchery of innocent persons, old and young; for under our circumstances none would have been saved had we been able to have surprised them. But the Indians still kept talking so that I was soon convinced that neither of them heard the door open. After a little more parley the word was given and we moved on. . . .

They picked up a few stray horses the next day and headed home.

We had returned without any loss or serious trouble. One thing gave me great consolation, that we had made the trip and neither killed nor hurt anyone; yet I was very careful never to tell about my hearing the door of the cabin open, for fear of their suspecting me of being not a true and trusty partner.

Eventually Alder's Indian father died, and Alder hunted and trapped alone on the Darby Plains and along Paint Creek. He also courted Barshaw, a sister of

Big Turtle. After the Battle of Fallen Timbers and the subsequent treaty, he and Barshaw married and settled in the Darby Plains near present Plain City. But as he mingled with the white settlers who came there, learned English, and took to the white people's ways, Barshaw grew unhappy.

I soon had a fine stock of hogs and cattle and also of horses. I could almost beat any of my white neighbors for I had greatly the advantage if any of my stock strayed off it was no trouble for me to find them. I began to sell horses and hogs to the white settlers as they came in and we sold milk and butter to the Indians and furs and skins to the traders. I was now in a manner happy. I could lie down at night without fear, a condition that had been rare with us and I could rise up in the morning and shake hands with the white man and the Indians all in perfect peace and safety. Here I had my own white race for neighbors and the redman that I loved all mingling together. . . .

But Barshaw didn't like living among white people. She left Alder and returned to her family. Eventually Alder heard from his white family. In November, 1805, he set out with neighbors John and Nicholas Moore to visit them in Virginia.

We arrived at my brother Paul Alder's the first Sunday after New Year 1805 at about 11 o'clock, dismounted, hitched our horses and walked up to the house. We passed ourselves off as strangers and travelers and called for our dinner and to have our horses fed, which was readily granted, and inquired who lived there. The man of the house said, "Paul Alder." I had concluded not to make myself known for sometime and thought when I would see my mother I would know her by a mole on the side of her face. I wanted to make all the close observations I could before I made myself known to see if I could recognize any of them. There was an old lady sitting there whom I eyed very close to see if I could recognize her as my mother. When I was taken prisoner my mother's hair was as black as a crow and this old lady's hair was almost as white as wool. I supposed she was my mother but could not tell. I then eyed my brother as close as I could but could not see any features that I could recognize at all. There were two young women in the house at the time. One of them was my half sister that I knew nothing of. My mother had been married in my absence and had had one child which was one of the young women present. I noticed that the young women were scrutinizing me very close and they commenced whispering together. I heard one of them say: "He looks very much like Mark." That was my brother.

I saw they were about to discover me so I turned my chair around to my brother and remarked to him, "You say your name is Alder?" "Yes," said he, "my name is Paul Alder." "Well," said I, "my name is Jonathan Alder."

Now it is hardly necessary to undertake to describe our feelings at that time but mine was very different from those I had when I saw the Indian coming with the scalp of my brother David in his hand shaking off the blood. When I told my brother that my name was Alder he rose to shake hands but he was so overjoyed that he could scarcely utter one word after giving me a hearty shake by both hands he left the room to give vent to his feelings. My mother rose from her seat and threw her arms around my neck and kissed me. She too was not able to speak for a short time but the first word she spoke was, "Jonathan, how you have grown!"

Alder convinced his brother Paul to leave his poor farm in Virginia and return with him to Ohio, where they settled near what is now Plain City.

Early Marietta Settlers: Joseph Barker's Journal, 1795 and After

Joseph Barker, born 1765, and his wife, Eliza, went west from Massachusetts with her family. Her father had lost his fortune during the Revolutionary War, and was seeking a new life in the Ohio country. They arrived in Marietta in 1789. Barker served with the militia during the Indian war. In 1795 they moved to one hundred acres on the Muskingum that Barker had been given for his war service.

Over the years Barker expanded his holdings at Wiseman's Bottom to some six hundred acres. A man of many talents, Barker ran a shipbuilding yard at his farm on the Muskingum, and also built houses. One of these was a mansion for a rich Irishman, Harmon Blennerhassett, and his beautiful wife on an island in the Ohio River. Blennerhassett unfortunately became involved with Aaron Burr in a scheme to invade Texas and possibly Mexico in order to establish a new country. Barker built fifteen boats for Burr. All but one were captured when the government foiled the plot. Barker died in 1843.

He wrote his memoirs of Marietta for Dr. Samuel Prescott Hildreth, a physician and pioneer historian. Barker was present for the city's first Fourth of July celebration, the arrival of the French settlers who had been cheated by the Scioto Company, the first smallpox inoculations, and the infamous Big Bottom massacre.

In January, 1790, a Boat on the Way to Kentuckey put on shore a very sick Man & his family, by the Name of Welch. . . . Mr Welches disorder proved to be the small pox. As the small pox had not been in Marietta a Town meeting was called, a small house was built not far from where the college now stands, to which he was removed with necessary attendants, but he lived but a few days. . . . A Town Meeting was called & held in the Northwest Blockhouse at Campus marcus [Martius], at which it was decided that all persons who had not [suffered] the small pox should accomodate themselves with houses back on the plain & there be inoculated. Doc^t Farley procured matter & inoculated & tended the Whole. One house at the upper end of the Big cornfield had twenty three; they were strung along down the plain. Col^o Wm Stacy had a house near the Creek below Mr Prentices, his two sons & son in Law & families, near twenty. Old Mrs. Stacy, aged about 70, died & an elderly Lady, Mrs. Winsor, from Campus Marcus, the only two lost by inoculation. A number of Families had not left Marietta who soon after moved out to Belprie & Waterford.

The Intermittant, or the Fever & Ague, was the fashionable disorder among all classes along the streams the first, second or third year after their arrival. It commenced about the first of August—& continued with Variations until the sap run in the spring. . . .

THE SEASONS. It is the Opinion of Most people with whome I have conversed on the subject that our Winters Generally were more moist & mild before the Land was cleared than they have been since, & our summers more humid & sultry. I never knew the Ground freeze in the Bottoms in Winters, where it was covered with leaves & had not been disturbed by Hoggs (at the same time, having ocasion to set posts on cleared land on the Bank, I found the ground froze 15 Inches). All the Alluvial lands were covered with a dense Forest which kept off the wind & sun; the moisture was retained much longer than in cleared Land. An exhalation was generally seen rising from those Forests in Winter, when not prevented by hard frosts or snow. These vapours, when it was not too cold, seemed to ameliorate the air & render it more mild; the Banks of the Streams being lined with a heavy growth of Trees confined the Wind from sweeping over the Bottoms & carrying off the warm vapour. . . .

The Black Cat & the Pike were the leargest Fish, the yellow Cat next, the salmon, the Buffalo, the perch & sturgeon next, the suckers & pouts, least. I saw a Black Cat, caught by Mr James Patterson in 1790, which weighed 96 lbs. . . .

But the Pike is the King of Fish in our Waters. Judge Gilbert Devol took a Pike from the Muskingum which weighed ninety six pounds, on the second day of July, 1788. He was a tall man, & when he had the Pike on his gigg Pole & the Pole on his shoulder, the Pike drew on the ground. . . .

Previous to the landing of the Ohio Comp[an]y, Wild Game had been very plenty in the neighbourhood of Marietta—Deer & Turkies, & ocasionally Elk & Buffalo. In the Winter of 1792, H[amilton] Kerr & [Peter] Niswonger killed six or seven Buffalos on Duck [Creek] about Ceder Narrows; they were fat & the first Quality of Beef, Judge Gilman said, better than any Beef he ever eat. . . .

The Indians who were in at the Treaty [of Fort Harmar] concluded on the 9th of Jan^y, 1789 had destroyed, wasted & drove back the Deer so that they were very scarce for a year or two; but in the fall of 1790 the Beech & other Moss was plenty on the bottoms, which brot in Turkies in abundance—so many that people were obliged to secure their Corn before it was ripe, & if there was any stacks of Oats or Wheat they were obliged to cover them thick with brush to prevent their being distroyed. They were kill^d in all ways—one Man killed forty with a Rifle one day. They were trap'd, kill^d with clubs & dogs, until a Turkey would not sell for a pip because people were cloyed, & they could not be used. . . .

That the Turkies should beat in, in persuit of Beech Moss, is not surprising: But that the squerrels, by millions, should simultainously become Itinerant, taking their course, swiming learge Waters without apparently seeking for food, but like the Locusts in Africa, stop long Just enough to distroy every thing they could eat which fel in their way, & perhaps before cold weather would turn & come back— is not so easy for me to account for.

They would get in &, before people were aware, the side of the Cornfield next the Woods would be distroyed, & the field must be imediately gathered. I was at Belprie [where] Capt Dana had got about two bushels of uncleaned Hempseed on a sheat a few rods from the House; when we came back from dinner it was so compleatly covered with sqerrels that nothing could be seen of the hempseed. No one who had not seen them could have any correct Idea of their Numbers. . . .

In september, 1790, What has been called the French emigrants arrived & were permitted by Col^o Sproat (who then had Charge of the Garrison) to take possession of all the vacant rooms in Fort Harmer. They arrived in the Night, in six Kentuckey Boats, & [were] said to be four hundred & fifty Men, Women, & children—there was but few children. This company came from Paris to settle on lands which were purchased from Joel Barlow [of the Scioto Company], & which they expected to find immediately below the Ohio Compys purchase.

. . . Towards spring they began to scatter. The Marquis Debutts, & some other Gentlemen went over the Mountains & back to France. A goodly Number Went to Gallipolis, some to Canada, some staid about Marietta & got Donation Land. I suppose they had been defrauded in their purpose of Land—they were disappointed, put out, & illnatured. . . .

Barker writes that he was not present when the Indians hung about Marietta during the winter of 1788-89 waiting for a treaty. Barker arrived in 1789, and heard of what had happened when the Indians became frustrated and angry at the delay.

As the Indians Came in to the Treaty they imployed themselves in Hunting & distrying the Game for which they had no use (as they drew rations from the public), except for the skins of the Deer. So greate was their Industry & perseverence that, in the fall & Winter, they brot in Deer & Turkeys & piled them up on the Bank of the Muskingum, west of Doc^t Cottons, like a rick of Hay, until the Inhabitents were obliged to Assemble & throw them into the River to Abate the Neusance. They left the Carcous about the Woods, which brot in the Wolves & Panthers but distroyed all the Deer—(A man by the Name of Bagley, fidler, coming from Wolf Creek, towards spring one cold, Snowey, frozen Afternoon, was attacked by learge gang of Wolves who drove him up a Tree, where he had to sit & play the Fiddle for them until they saw fit to leave him next day.) When interigated why they distroyed & wasted the Game? the Indians Answered, they meant to destroy & Starve out every white face North of the Ohio. They frequently alluded to the prospect of repossesing their Lands & recovering their good hunting Ground. One Old Indian, when he drew his Blanket, threw it Over his shoulders saying he had got his cornfield on his back, but he would have it to walk on next Year.

It was said There were better than four hundred Indians—men, Woman, & children—& so thoroughly did they distroy the game within ten Miles of Marietta that rarely a deer Could be seen, where before a good hunter could kill from 10 to 15 of a day. . . .

To the circumstance of the Indians distroying nearly all the game in the Neighbourhood, combined with that of a severe frost in the early part of september, 1789, may be attributed the very great Scarcity of Bread & Meat in the spring & Summer of 1790. Many families were destitute of Cows; there were a few Yoak of Oxon which could not be spared from the Clearing & the Plow, & No Young stock, a few breeding Sows. A learge Majority of the Emigrants had literally strewed all their Money on the Mountains, &, in the injoyment that they had got to the Land of promase, they forgot to provide for the future. . . . But those who had not means Could not buy, & by the Middle of May a Majority of the People were out of Bread, Meat, & Milck, & especially those families the leargest & most necessitious. Where Poverty, Improvidence & Scarcity meet, Charity & benevolance only Could give relief. It was no time for "Catch penny & Chuck farthing." Genuine hospitality prevailed; those who had, dealt out freely but sparingly, without Money or price, to those who had not, which soon brot on a general scarcity. Those the most forehanded adopted the strictest economy & management that they might assist the Needy. Nettles were the first herbs up in the spring & were freely used, next pigweed & Poke sprouts.

The latter part of May, Gen[l] Putnam Wrote on to Col[o] R. J. Meigs[3] to Open a hole of Po[ta]toes he had at Campus Martius & distribute them among the people for planting. . . . Coffee, Tea, & Sugar were out of the Question—spice Bush & Sassafras were the Common drinks. Some Maple sugar was made, but most people were not prepared for want of Metal to Boil in. In this way the People got along until the Season brot relief. . . .

Lots had been surveyed & drawn for by a number of Persons who had associated to make a settlement at Big Bottom, Who, about the beginning of Winter, determined to go on & Cultivate their Lands. Those best acquanted with the Indians & those best Capable of Judging from appearences had but little doubt that the Indians were preparing to Commence hostilities, strongly opposed the settlement going out that fall, & advised their remaining until spring, by which time probably the Question of War or peace would be setled. Even Gen[l] Putnam & the Directors of the Ohio Co, Who gave away the Land to have it setled, thought it riskey & imprudent, & strongly remonstrated against venturing out at that time.

---

3. Rufus Putnam and Return Jonathan Meigs were officers of the Ohio Company, which developed Marietta. Putnam had made the original request to Congress for the land. Before government had been set up in Ohio, Meigs administered justice in Marietta. He later was a U.S. senator and governor of the state.

But the Young men were impatient—Confident in their own prudance & ability to protect themselves, & sanguine in a hope of sucsess. They went.

They put up a learge Blockhouse which might accomodate the Whole on an immergancy, Covered it, & laid punchen floors & stairs, &c. the House was laid up of learge Beech Logs & rather Open, & it was not Chinked—this Job was left for a rainy day or some more convenient season. Here was their first greate Error, here their building of Babel stop'd and the generel interest was lost in that of the convenience of each individual, & with this, all was lost.

The second greate Error was: they kept No Century [sentry]. . . . The Indians proceeded down the Westerly side of the Muskingum, opposite the Blockhouse, where there was a high hill near the River, from which they could view as much of the Bottom as was not obstructed by trees, see how every Man was imployed & what was transacting about the Blockhouse.

As was observed, the general business of Fortification & security had been suspended; stopping the Cracks between the Logs of the House & picketing & a sentry had been neglected. No system of defence & disipline was introduced—their Guns were laying in different places without order about the house. About twenty Men incampd in the Block house & each Individual & Mess Cooked for themselves. One end of the Blockhouse was appropriated for a fire place, & when the day Closed in all Came in, built a learge fire & Commenced Cooking & eating their supper.

The Indians from the opposite hill had watched their Motions—the Ground was froze, the River was froze Over strong & covered with snow. When it began to grow dusk, the Indian[s] slipped across the River, surrounded the Blockhouse, & each had a deliberate ame [aim] at the inmates through the Door & cracks between the Logs. Part of the Indians rushed in at the Door, other kept up the fire from without & secured those who attempted to escape. Those who were not crippled [by] the first fire endeavored to escape be getting into the Chamber, & severel got through the roof & jumped down, but were all Killed or taken. Two Mr Bullards had a small Camp back in the Bottom which probably had escaped the Notice of the Indians, Who, on hearing the Guns at the Blockhouse, made their escape & got in to Waterford & gave the alarm. The Indians took up the Puncheon floor & built a fire & attempted to burn the slain & the house; but, as the wood had been recently cut & was all green, the fire subsided, burning some so as to disfigure them, others partially. The arm of a Mr William James was found clinching a piece of Indian Bread in his right hand, which probably he was eating at the time he was Shot. . . .

Campus Martius in Marietta was subsequently fortified, and pickets were set out in preparation for a possible Indian attack. But one never came. However, an Indian was seen lurking about the post one night, and signs of other Indians were found in the morning. In 1791, Captain Joseph Rogers of the settlement was killed and scalped nearby, and the rumor flew that the Indians were at the very gates of the fort.

All was consternation, but every One made immediately for his alaram Post. Some little circumstances served to mark the propensity of different Individuals:

The first person for Admittance at the Central Blockhouse Was Col° E. Sproat with a Box of papers, then came some Young Men with their Arms, then a Woman with her Bed & Children, then came old Mr. William Moulton, from Nubury Port [Massachusetts], aged 70, with his leather Apron full of Old Goldsmiths tools and tobacco. His daughter, Anna, brot the China Teapot, Cups & sausers. Lydia brot the Greate Bible, but when all were in Mother was missing. Where was mother. She must be killd. No, says Lydia, Mother said she would not leave a house looking so, she would put things a little to rights, & then she would come. Directly mother Came, bringing the Looking Glass, knives, forks & spoons, &c.

Soon messingers were exchanged with Campus Martius & no appearence of hostilities were discovered. All returned to their homes in the Morning & a party from the Point & Campus Martius Went out, about 10 O Clock, & brot in Capt Rogers & buried him in second street, on the East side, a little North of the learge Brick House built by Mr Waldo Putnam the last Year [1790].

A Winter Journey Down the Ohio:
Francis Baily's Journal of a Tour to Unsettled Parts, 1796-1797

Francis Baily was just twenty-two when he came to Ohio in December, 1796. He had arrived in America the preceding year probably to establish business connections in the New World, but also to have a great adventure. He returned to England in January, 1798, and never traveled back to America again. Instead he became a wealthy and well-known stock broker, insurance expert, and amateur astronomer there. He died in 1844.

In this excerpt from his *Journal of a Tour in Unsettled Parts of North America in 1796 and 1797*, Baily was traveling down the Ohio River by boat with a party of men and women. They stopped for the night below Grave Creek in present West Virginia, and awoke December 21 to hear the terrifying sound of the ice breaking and the river rising.

Only conceive a river near 1,500 miles long, frozen to a prodigious depth (capable of bearing loaded waggons) from its source to its mouth, and this river by a sudden torrent of water breaking those bands by which it had been so long fettered! Conceive this vast body of ice put in motion at the same instant, and carried along with an astonishing rapidity, grating with a most tremendous noise against the sides of the river, and bearing down everything which opposed its progress!—the tallest and the stoutest trees obliged to submit to its destructive fury, and hurried along with the general wreck! In this scene of confusion and desolation, what was to be done?

The party quickly began to unload the eleven tons of goods on the boat, including food, "articles of barter," and "other necessaries." They hauled their stores up a steep bank and made a crude camp, where they remained until the thaw in February. Then they set out again.

We anchored (or rather fastened our boat to the shore) about the middle of Long Reach this evening. Long Reach is the most beautiful place I ever saw in my life; the river at this spot preserves one straight course for fifteen miles, and is agreeably interspersed with a number of islands through its whole length. It runs nearly in a westerly direction, and the setting sun at the extreme end, reflecting itself in the smooth water, and beautifully tingeing the distant trees, rendered it at once one of the most sublime views I ever was witness to. The river looked like a little sea of fire before us; and, by the rapidity and smoothness of its current, seemed to be silently hurrying us on towards it. . . .

Tuesday, February 21st—about five o'clock, we started and came to Muskingham [Marietta] about one. Muskingham, so called from the river of that name, at the mouth of which it is built, consists of about one hundred houses agreeably situated on the eastern point where the Muskingham joins the Ohio. . . .

Monday, February 27th—We started again, at six o'clock, and about half-past three we came to Columbia, our long-wished-for port, having, through unforeseen difficulties and unavoidable delays, been six months on our journey.

We put our boat into the mouth of the Little Miami river; and my friend H[eighway][4] having some business to do with a gentleman in the town, whose house was about a mile off, he took the canoe and went down to him this afternoon, and did not return till quite late. H. had purchased, in company with two other gentlemen of this place, about thirty or forty thousand acres of land on the banks of the Little Miami, and about forty miles up that river; and he was now going to form a plantation on that land, and to encourage settlers to do the same. He was down here about a twelvemonth ago, and then made the contract. He gave Judge Symms[5] 1 1/4 dollars per acre for it, payable by instalments. . . . He informed me that nearly half of his land was sold, and great part of it settled; the price he asked for it was two dollars per acre; but it will increase in value as the settlements increase. The lots in the town which he had laid out were six dollars. They consist of half an acre of ground, and you are obliged to build a house within a certain time.

Tuesday, February 28th, 1797—This morning we dropped down the river about half a mile to a convenient landing, and here we had a much better view of the town than we had where we lay last night. The houses lie very scattered along the bottom of a hill which is about one-eighth of a mile from the river. The town is laid out on a regular plan, but it was never in a very flourishing state; the neighbouring and well-settled country round and at Cincinnati, prevents it from being a place of any great importance; besides it lies very low, and is often overflowed from the river. . . .

After breakfast we went ashore to view the town, and H introduced me to Mr. Smith and Dr. Bean. The former gentleman is a man of very good property, which he has acquired in several different ways in this place: he is a farmer, a merchant, and a parson; all these occupations, though seemingly so different, he carries on with the greatest regularity and without confusion. The latter is a man of good education, and practises physic here. . . .

As Dr. Bean would insist upon our sleeping at his house, and in fact stopping with him altogether during our residence here, we ac-

---

4. Samuel Heighway, who founded the town of Waynesville in Warren County.
5. John Cleves Symmes, another early land speculator, gambled on the Miami River valley. He ended up in a dispute with Congress about how much land between the two Miami rivers he actually owned and died in 1814 financially ruined.

companied him home. His house was built of logs, as all the houses
in these new settlements are, and consisted of a ground floor containing two rooms, one of which was appropriated to lumber: the
other served all the purposes of parlour, bedroom, shop, and everything else; (though there was a little outhouse, where they occasionally cooked their victuals, and also washed); and it did not appear as
if it had been cleaned out this half-year. There were two windows to
throw light into the room; but there had been so many of the panes
of glass broken whose places were supplied by old hats and pieces of
paper, that it was very little benefited by the kind intention of the
architect. I saw a few phials and gallipots on a shelf in one corner of
the room, and near them a few books of different descriptions; and
this I believe comprised all the medicine and knowledge he was possessed of. . . .

At dinner time I observed a table prepared in the middle of the
room, with some knives and forks and pewter plates placed on it,
but without any tablecloth; and when the dinner was ready, two of
his servants who were working out in the fields were called in, and
sat down at the same table and partook of the same provisions as
ourselves; and I observed that they did not seem to treat their master or any of his company with any degree of reserve, but behaved as
if they were with his equals, though without behaving at all improp-
erly, or stepping beyond the bounds which this state of society has
prescribed. . . .

Baily decided to accompany Heighway to his new settlement. So Heighway
and two wagons with provisions set off on March 4, and Baily and Dr. Bean
and some others followed on March 6. They caught up with Heighway about
noon the following day, and he told them a tale of woe, that his wagons had
overturned and the strain of trying to pull them through the swampy terrain
had almost worn out the horses.

The next morning, *Wednesday, March 8th,* by daylight, our cavalcade was in motion; and some of the party rode on first to discover
the spot, for we were travelling without any other guide than what
little knowledge of the country the men had acquired by hunting
over it. I could not but with pleasure behold with what expedition
the pioneers in front cleared the way for the waggon: there were but
three or four of them, and they got the road clear as fast as the waggon
could proceed. Whilst we were continuing on at this rate, we observed at some distance before us, a human being dart into the woods,
and endeavour to flee from us. Ignorant what this might mean, we

delayed the waggons, and some of us went into the woods and tracked the footsteps of a man for some little distance, when suddenly a negro made his appearance from behind some bushes, and hastily inquired whether there were any Indians in our party, or whether we had met with any. The hideousness of the man's countenance, (which was painted with large red spots upon a black ground,) and his sudden appearance, startled us at first; but soon guessing his situation, we put him beyond all apprehension, and informed him he was perfectly safe.

He then began to inform us that he had been a prisoner amongst the Indians ever since the close of the last American war; and that he had meditated his escape ever since he had been in their hands, but that never, till now, had he been able to accompolish it. He asked us what course the nearest town lay from us; and after telling him, he said that the Indians no doubt were pursuing him ever since they had missed him, and that he intended to escape to the first town for protection. He said that they had used him remarkably well ever since he had been with them, treating him as one of their own children, and doing everything in their power to render his situation comfortable. They had given a wife, a *mother*, and plenty of land to cultivate if he chose it, and the liberty of doing everything but making his escape. With all these inducements, he said he could not give up the idea of never seeing again those friends and relations whom he left in his early days. This man, when he was taken prisoner, was a *slave* to a person in Kentucky; and though amongst the Indians he enjoyed liberty and all the comforts which can be expected in a state of nature, and which were more (I may safely pronounce) than when he tasted of the bitter cup of slavery, yet was this man, who so lately enjoyed all these blessings of Heaven, going to render himself up a voluntary slave to his former master. For what? That he might there once more embrace those friends and relations from whom he had been so long separated. . . .

Baily, Heighway, and the others arrived that afternoon, March 8, at the Little Miami River.

The next morning nothing was to be heard but the noise of the axe resounding through the woods. . . .

I have seen oak-trees, and those not uncommon, which measured near four feet diameter at the bottom, and which had a straight trunk *without a single branch* for seventy feet; and from that part to the termination of the upper branch it has measured seventy more; and these immense trees I have seen cut down for the sole purpose of making a few shingles from them to cover a house with; and even for the sake of killing a poor bear who had taken refuge therein against the inclemency of the weather; and even for less than that: I have often seen them set on fire merely to dislodge a paltry raccoon!

A Picnic in Old Chillicothe: From the Diary of the Reverend James Smith, 1797

The Reverend James Smith, a native of Virginia, came to Ohio as a member of the Republican Methodist Church. He traveled and preached in Kentucky and Ohio. Eventually, he bought land on the Little Miami and moved there with his family of nine children in 1800. But he died soon afterward at the age of 43. He kept diaries of his earlier travels to the state. This journey was one he made in 1797.

Already, there can be seen a little of the romantic tourist in Smith, waxing nostalgic about the savages who had sat on the very spot where he was having a picnic. The further white settlers got from the horrors of the Indian wars, the more sentimental they were about them.

Thurs. [October] 12th. Mr [Samuel] Heighway after compelling us to take breakfast with him [in Waynesville], accompanied us some distance and put us into the right way to Old Chillecothe.[6] About 1 o'clock we were saluted with a view of one of those beautiful plains, which are known in this country by the name of pararas [prairies]. Here we could see many miles in a straight direction, and not a tree or bush to obstruct the sight. The grass in the parara, we found higher than our heads on horseback as we rode thro it. After riding about 2 miles thro this enchanting parara we arrived on the spot, where the old town of Chillecothe stood, of which scarcely a vestige now remains. We saw a few slabs and something like an old breastwork but so decayed and covered with grass that it was scarcely discernable. The stumps of some gate posts were still to be seen, but the houses were all destroyed, having been burned a few years ago, by the order of the commander of an expedition against the Indians. We sat us down on the green grass and ate our dinner of bread and cheese on the very spot where a few years ago, the bloody savages held their grand councils. While we rested here there came a man to us, and

---

6. Not the present city of Chillicothe, but a Shawnee village of the same name located at present Oldtown in Greene County, north of Xenia.

informed us that himself and his two brothers (who lived about a mile from the place) had found 60 beehives within a mile and a half of their house; 3 of which they had taken the week before and had gotten 14 or 15 gallons of honey. The land about this town, I think is equal for wheat and grass to any that I ever saw. . . .

Fri. 12th. We took in our way the town of Deerfield. It has 30 or 40 families residing in it. It is a new town, having only been settled since spring 12 mo. It is something surprizing to see with what I suppose is owing to two causes: (1st) the fertility of the land, which induces new adventurers to settle there and (2nd) that excellent regulation which shuts out slavery; this induces the mechanic and the manufaturer, who choose to settle in towns to carry on their different employments. O, what a country will this be at a future day! What field of delights! What a garden of spices! What a paradise of pleasures! when these forests shall be cultivated and the gospel of Christ spread through this rising republic, unshackled by the power of kings and religious oppression on the one hand and slavery, that bane of true Godliness, on the other. . . .

The Pioneer Household: Thomas Ewing's Childhood Adventures, 1798-1800

Thomas Ewing's family came to Ohio from West Virginia (then still part of Virginia) in 1798, after the Treaty of Greenville made the country safer for settlers. Ewing left an autobiography for his children in which he described frontier life in Athens County. He also submitted some remembrances of the early days for Charles Walker's *History of Athens County, Ohio* (1869). Despite growing up in a land without schools, where the nearest neighbor was fourteen miles away, Ewing got himself educated and became a successful lawyer and later a member of the United States Senate. His memoirs demonstrate the resourcefulness of the early settlers and, more remarkable to the modern mind, the independence and self-sufficiency of the children.

At the time of my father's removal, I was with my aunt, Mrs. Morgan, near West Liberty, Virginia, going to school. I was a few months in my ninth year. Early in the year 1798, I think in May, my uncle brought me home. We descended the Ohio river in a flat boat to the mouth of the Little Hocking, and crossed a bottom and a pine hill along a dim footpath, some ten or fifteen miles, and took quarters for the night at Dailey's camp. I was tired and slept well on the bearskin bed which the rough old dame spread for me, and in the morning my uncle engaged a son of our host, a boy of eighteen, who had seen my father's cabin, to pilot us.

I was now at home, and fairly an inceptive citizen of the future Athens county. The young savage, our pilot, was much struck with some of the rude implements of civilization which he saw my brother using, especially the auger, and expressed the opinion that with an axe and an auger a man could make everything he wanted except a gun and bullet molds. My brother [George, age 16] was engaged in making some bedsteads. He had already finished a table, in the manufacture of which he had used also an adze to smooth the plank, which he split in good width from straight grained trees. Transportation was exceedingly difficult, and our furniture, of the rudest kind, composed of articles of the first necessity. Our kitchen utensils were "the big kettle," "the little kettle," the bake oven, frying pan, and pot; the latter had a small hole in the bottom which was mended with a button, keyed with a nail through the eye on the outside of the pot. We had no table furniture that would break—little of any kind. Our meat—bear meat, or raccoon, with venison or turkey, cooked together and seasoned to the taste (a most savory dish)—was cut up in morsels and placed in the centre of the table, and the younger members of the family, armed with sharpened sticks, helped themselves about as well as with four-tined forks; great care was taken in selecting wholesome sticks, as sassafras, spice-bush, hazel, or hickory. Sometimes the children were allowed, by way of pic-nic, to cut with the butcher-knife from the fresh bear meat and venison their slices and stick them, alternately, on a sharpened spit and roast before a fine hickory fire; this made a most royal dish. . . .

This year [1799], in April, I went with George to Wolf Creek Mills, about eighteen miles distant to bring home some meal. We had each a horse and he had his gun, and the little Spaniel was one of the party. On our return as we were about descending the Laurel Hill into Wolf Creek bottom George gave me a rope attached to his horse's bridle and told me to lead him & come on slowly, and he would go forward into the valley & try to kill some game to take home with us—it was a dim narrow path, but I was able to follow it. In a few minutes after he left me I heard the crack of his rifle & the bark of the dog. I hastened on and soon heard a sound of a third crack of the gun, and saw on the right of the path George running with his gun in his hand closely pursued by a very large bear and the dog following snapping & barking at the bear. George leaped behind a tree and loaded his gun and the bear turned, ran a little way pursued and worried by the dog, and climbed a tree, a small beach broken off about

30 feet high & held on near the top, his head between his forepaws looking down at man & dog below—by this time I had tied my horses and joined George who had his gun loaded and at a moderate distance fired at the bear's head, but missed it, and shot him through one of his fore-paws. The bear fell, and rolled down the hillside towards us, and ran slowly toward the creek which was near—before he got to the water George shot again, but the bear limped on without heeding him and got into the water and lay down—the dog followed and the bear seized him with his sound paw and drew him under water. George took aim at the bear's head and attempted to fire, but his flint flew out and was lost in the grass and sand—he then drew his knife and was about leaping in to save the dog, when I held by his hunting shirt & prevented him—just then the bear let go the dog and went to shore on the other side and lay down in the sand quite exhausted—the dog followed and sat down & barked and the bear replied with a growl. George had no second flint—his gun therefore was useless—he said he could kill the bear disabled as he was with his knife but to this I would not consent—he then said he could tie his knife to a pole, with leatherwood bark, and spear him at a safe distance. I agreed to this, but while he was preparing his lance I got on my hands and knees & searching closely found the flint—he then waded across and shot the bear in the head. All his other shots had taken effect, but none in a vital part. We were about ten miles from home. George climbed a tall slender sapling which stood nearby—bent it down & secured the hind legs of the bear to it—cut off the top above, and with a forked pole on each side raised the huge carcass high enough to be out of the reach of wolves, and we left it till next day when we went with the necessary aid and brought it home. It was very fat—had just left its winter den in the rocks and come down to the creek bottom to feed on young nettles, their earliest spring food.

Much of Ewing's account of his childhood is about his struggle to get an education in the wilderness. It was catch as catch can. His sister taught him to read, his mother told stories at the fireplace, and he read whatever heavy reading material was in his parents' possession. But he was starved for more.

We had yet no physician in the neighborhood, and some one of the family being sick, my father went to Waterford about twenty miles for Doctor Baker. He at once made my acquaintance, & told me he had a book which he would lend me if I would come for it—one he said I would like to read—not long after I got leave of my Father and went, on foot, with the little spaniel, Ring, for company and as a body guard—it was on the same path that was the scene with the bear fight the year before, and still a space of thirteen miles without a house. I made the journey without any adventure, was kindly received by the Doctor and brought home the book—it was a translation of Virgil's Aeneid, I do not know by whom as the title page was torn out. . . .

I read it with great interest. My Father at that time had several hired men, rough frontiersmen—I read at noon, in the evenings and on Sundays to them and never had a more attentive audience.

A Circuit-Riding Preacher in the Western Reserve: A Memoir of the Reverend Joseph Badger, 1801-1803 and After

The Reverend Joseph Badger, after whom the Trumbull County town of Badger is named, was a Revolutionary War veteran from Massachusetts who studied theology at Yale. In 1784 he married Lois Noble, and together they had six children. Upon leaving his first parish in 1800, he accepted an appointment to go to the Connecticut Western Reserve as a Presbyterian missionary. At first he went to Ohio alone, leaving his family behind. In 1802, he returned for them, and all eight emigrated to the frontier.

Badger became famous as a circuit-riding preacher of the hellfire and brimstone school. He describes many camp meetings at which people fell senseless to the ground while listening to his sermons. Meanwhile, his wife and six children often remained at their crude cabin in the Western Reserve in the direst distress. In his diary, Badger unconsciously paints himself as a neglectful husband and father while he did the work of the Lord. One can only wonder what his wife thought of her life. Nevertheless, Badger's efforts on behalf of religion were almost superhuman. He traveled incessantly from settlement to settlement over terrible roads or no roads at all, through snow and rain, crossing swollen rivers and fighting fevers. He preached, visited, and nursed the sick everywhere he stopped.

There was only one road leading from Beaver to the Reserve, and that almost impassable. I was directed to take a *blazed* path which led to the Mahoning river, a mile or two east of Poland. When I came to the river the water was high, the current strong, and how deep I could not tell. But there was no alternative; I must pass or sleep in

the woods. I ventured in; the water soon came over the tops of my
boots, and my horse beat down stream fast toward swimming water;
but happily reached the shore in time to escape the deep water; got
on the state line, and arrived at the cabin of Rev. Mr. Wick about
dark. I was received by this brother and sister as a familiar friend.
The Lord brought me through safely. . . .

On Monday I rode to Vienna, where was one family; thence to
Hartford, in which were three families. Here I rested a day or two,
and rode to Vernon. In this place were five families. Here I preached
on the Sabbath, the people all collecting, with the three families from
Hartford.

January, 1801. The frequent snows and rains rendered it difficult
passing from one settlement to another. This was the last opening
toward the lake. Here I tarried two weeks; in which time Mr. Palmer
of Vienna, was taken sick. I was requested to go and see him. There
was no doctor in the country. I found him very sick, and stayed and
nursed him about eight days, when he got better.

The next place I visited was Warren; was received courteously by
Mr. John Leavitt and family. I preached here on the Sabbath. In this
place were eleven families, and one in Howland. From this I went to
Canfield by the salt springs, where was one family employed in making salt, at three or four dollars a bushel. In Canfield there were eleven
families. Preached here on the Sabbath, and on Monday rode to
Deerfield, fifteen miles, and preached a lecture; five families, and all
attended. On my way I saw a large wolf that followed me several
miles. Crossed the Mahoning on the ice, and returned the next day.
One family west of this in Atwater; all beyond was an unbroken wilderness. From Canfield I visited Boardman and Poland; five or six
families in each place.

I now revisited all the settlements in this part of the Reserve,
and endeavored to encourage the people with hopes of a brighter day.
Their hard beginning would soon pass away. The soil was good, and
industry would soon produce plenty. Found here and there profess-
ing Christians mourning the loss of their former privileges, and won-
dering why they had come to this wilderness, where there was no
house of worship nor gospel ordinances. I observed to them that they
had been moved here by the hand of God, to plant the church in this
wilderness. . . .

In December, Badger returned to Massachusetts and, packing up his wife and
six children, he set out for Ohio on February 23 and arrived in July. By the end
of that month he was off on his missionary labors.

About this time it was necessary to extend my missionary labors to other parts of the Reserve. I had only made such arrangements as to shelter my family from the storm, and supply them with bread for about two months. Having committed them to the care of our Heavenly Father, on the last week in July I set out; reached Painesville on Saturday.

Sabbath preached to about twenty, consisting of two families and several workmen; not one seemed to have the least regard for the Sabbath; I was, however, treated decently.

Monday, rode on to a small settlement of five families, in a place called the "Marsh," in Mentor, and preached a lecture; . . .

From this I passed on to Mr. Burke's in Euclid. This family came out with the surveyors; had been in this lone situation over three years. The woman had been obliged to spin and weave cattle's hair to make covering for her children's bed. . . .

Except for a week's break in September, Badger didn't return to his family for three months.

It became necessary that something should be done to our cabin, to prepare for the increasing cold and winter's frost. Hitherto we had only half a floor of split logs, and no chimney; cracks between the logs open, without plastering or mudding. I preached in four settlements; Conneaut, twenty-five miles from my house; Morgan, two and a half; Harpersfield, ten miles, and Austinburg, and made arrangements to leave my family as comfortable as I could for a winter's tour. . . .

Wednesday, 17th [August, 1803]—Rode to Windsor; stopped at Judge Griswold's about two hours, during a heavy shower. Rode on through the woods, without path or marked trees. . . .

Had by this time become drenched with water, but continued my course, until nearly dark I came to the only ford on Grand River within ten miles: passed over, intending to encamp on the upland bank where some trees were broken down. Rode up to the place and started some animal on the opposite side. I rode a little around to see what company I had fallen into, and was met by a large bear. Supposing the brute would run, as several had done with which I had met before, I slapped my hands and halloed at him. But instead of running, he raised his hair on end, and snapped his teeth violently. As I had no weapon for defense, I thought best to leave the ground, turned to the left, and walked my horse partly by him, when the brute stepped directly on behind and within a few paces.

By this time it had become so dark I could see nothing around, not even my hand holding the bridle, and the bear was snapping and approaching nearer. I had in my hand a large heavy horse-shoe, took aim by his noise, and threw the shoe, but effected no alarm of the enemy. To ride away was impossible, in a pathless wood, thick with brush and old fallen timber. I concluded to resort to a tree, if I could find one. I reined my horse first to the right, and then to the left, at which instant some sloping limbs brushed my hat. On feeling them, I found them to be long, pliable, beech limbs. I reined my horse again, and he came with his shoulder close to the tree. I tied the bridle to the limbs, raised myself on the saddle, and by aid of the small limbs began to climb. I soon got hold of a limb large enough to bear me, and at this instant the evil beast came to the tree with a violent snuffling and snapping. . . .

I then ascended about forty feet, as near the top of the tree as I thought was safe; found a convenient place to sit on a limb, and tied myself with a large bandanna to the tree, so as not to fall if I fell into a drowse. . . . By the roaring of the thunder it appeared a heavy gust was approaching. It soon began to rain powerfully, with heavy peals of thunder with wind. At this time the horse shook himself, which started the bear to a quick rush a few rods, at which point he stopped and snapped his teeth violently, and there continued, until a few minutes before light he went off. My horse standing at the tree without moving a foot from the place I left him, and in no way frightened by the approach and management of the bear, seemed peculiarly Providential. This was the only time I was disturbed in camping out many times. . . .

Saturday [late September], rode to Hubbard, preached twice on the Sabbath to about three hundred attentive hearers. . . . A reviving spirit appears to be extending over this new population. . . .

Sabbath [October] preached twice and administered the Lord's Supper. The evening was spent in singing and prayer. My support being scanty, and almost all my time absent from them, my family are in pretty difficult circumstances in regard to clothes, shoes, and house. . . .

November 6th,— . . . Preached twice to a very solemn assembly. Several were in deep distress, and became unable to support themselves. . . . As three children, twelve or thirteen years old, were going from the barn to my house, about twenty rods, they all fell helpless. They were taken up and taken care of: one of them continued in a perfectly helpless situation for more than six hours. . . .

A certain man took opportunity, between him and me, to say that such exercises would not do; that I ought to frown upon them and stop them. I told him the work was evidently supernatural, and I should not dare to oppose it.

Incredibly, the Connecticut Missionary Society voted to reduce Badger's stipend from $7 a week to $6. Nevertheless, he stayed on in Ohio. His work extended beyond the white settlers. He had long preached to Delawares and Shawnees who lived in Ohio. He had to contend with the powerful influence of Tecumseh's brother, called The Prophet, who preached that the Indians should cleanse themselves of evil white influences and return to the ways of their ancestors. The Prophet was the religious arm of Tecumseh's political movement to overthrow white domination. The following entry is from 1806.

On our arrival, we found the Indians were gathered at the Lower Sandusky, attending to the prophet, who was pointing out several of their women to be killed as witches. I immediately sent to them, informing them of my arrival, and requested Crane [Tarhe]⁷, the head chief, to sit still until the interpreter should come; upon which the chiefs stopped the prophet from proceeding any farther. . . . At the Upper Sandusky there was a small settlement of black people, to whom I preached frequently. There were seven adults and several children, and one white man, a silver smith, whose name was Wright, married to one of the colored women. Wright afterwards left his wife. She was a sensible, industrious woman. . . . I spent much time in conversation and preaching: but there was a constant and powerful opposition, both from the Indian traders and several officers of Government. But the influence I obtained over the Indians, in persuading them not to use strong drink of any kind, broke up the traders, and they went off.

Work and Play in Trumbull County: Leonard Case's Memoir, 1800 and After

Leonard Case came to Ohio with his family when he was about fourteen years old. They traveled overland from Washington County, Pennsylvania, to present-day Warren, Ohio, arriving on April 18, 1800. He wrote the following memoir in later life.

---

7. Tarhe, also called The Crane, was a famous Wyandot chief. William Henry Harrison had great respect for him as a man and a leader. He was at the Treaty of Greenville and later, as an old man, he led his warriors under Harrison in the War of 1812.

Tecumseh's brother, called The
Prophet, who gave religious
legitimacy to Tecumseh's war
against the white invaders.
From Emilius O. Randall,
History of Ohio, vol. 2 (1912).

The usual incidents attended the journey until crossing the south
line, on 41° N.L. [North Latitude]. From there to Yellow Creek, in
Poland, was a very muddy road called "The Swamp." In Poland, a
settlement was begun, Judge Turhand Kirtland and family living on
the east side, and Jonathan Fowler and wife, a sister of the Judge,
keeping a tavern on the west side. From thence our way was through
woods to where was a family by the name of Stevens, who had been
there three years or more. The wife's name was Hannah. With her,
our family had been acquainted. She said she had been there three
years, without seeing the face of a white woman. There our party
and cattle stayed over night. Next morning, we passed up the west
side of the river, (for want of means to cross it,) to James Hillman's,
and then through woods, on the old road made by the Connecticut
Land Company, to the Salt Spring. . . .

     After our passage through woods and mud, the leeks on the In-
dian Field on Mahoning Bottom made a most beautiful appearance. . . .

In a footnote, Case wrote:

Wolves and bears committed depredations almost continually upon
the cattle and hogs, and other smaller vermin upon the domestic
fowls. The wolves would approach even within two rods of the cabin,
seize a pig, run off with it and eat it, and as soon as the flock became
still again, would return again and seize another in like manner pur-

suing their depredations to such an extent as to render it difficult to raise anything. The wolves would likewise seize and destroy the weaker cattle. In winter, when quite hungry, they were bold and would come among the settlers' cabins. The writer recollects one night in February, 1801, when the weather had been stormy—the wind then blowing a severe gale—when the wolves attacked the cattle on the Bottoms, on Lots 35 & 42 in Warren. The cattle gathered together in large numbers; the oxen and stronger ones endeavoring to defend the weaker ones. They ran, bellowing, from one place to another and the wolves, trying to seize their prey, howled fearfully. In the morning, it was evident, that the oxen had pitched at the wolves, burying their horns up to their sculls in the mud and earth. Several of the weaker cattle were found badly bitten. . . .

FOURTH OF JULY

In 1800 there was a 4th of July celebration at the place of Mr. Quinby. They were much at a loss for musical instruments.—Elam and Eli Blair, the twin young men who came with John Leavitt, Esq.—one a drummer and the other a fifer—surmounted the difficulty. One found a large, strong stem-elder and soon made a fife. The other cut down a hollow pepperidge tree and with only a hand-axe and jack plane made a drum-cylinder. With the skin of a fawn, killed for him by William Crooks, he made heads for the drum and for the cords used a pair of new plow-lines belonging to M. Case. They discoursed most patriotic music. Of course, all had guns. So, the usual amount of patriotism was demonstrated in proper style by music and the burning of gunpowder. John Leavitt, Esq. played the militia captain. A good dinner was had in a bowery. Toasts were duly given and honored with the needful amount of stimulus. All went off merrily. . . .

In February 1801, Benj'n. Davison, Esq., . . . his son Samuel, a lad about 16 or 17, and Ebenezer Earle . . . a bachelor about 30, agreed to take a sled load of wheat and corn to the mill on Mill creek in Boardman.

The sled had a new wood rack with two yoke of oxen. There was snow, but rather thin sledding. These three with the team started pretty early in the day for the mill, twelve miles distant. Soon after they started it grew warmer and began to thaw. It was after dark before they got their grain ground, but knowing that the road (the road which the Connecticut Land Co. caused to be opened from Poland, by the Salt Springs, Warren and to Painesville) would soon break, and likewise the ice over the Big Meander, they started for home in the night. They had not gone far before the ice over the mud-holes began to give way. Old Mr. Davison went forward to pilot the boys along the muddy places, particularly where the brush and logs were turned out and piled up like win[d]rows. He would frequently break through. Then he would call to the boys, "Turn out, boys, turn out!" "a bad place here." When they came to the Meander it had risen so as to be above their sled beams. In order to save their load from the wet, they placed chains crosswise at the top of their rack, laid poles, crosswise with the chains, on them and piled their bags upon the poles. At a little more than half way across, the weight crushed down the rack. They and their load together found the water. It was up to their knees. However, they drove on. It was about four o'clock in the morning when we heard them half a mile off. Soon after, they reached my father's—the first house after leaving the Salt Springs—not much the worse, after they got dry. The water did not penetrate into the meal bags much. . . .

A Waynesville Quaker: A Letter from Samuel Linton, 1804

Samuel Linton was persuaded by his son, Nathan, to emigrate to Waynesville, Ohio, from Bucks County, Pennsylvania, in 1802. He was then a Quaker widower with five children. He stayed in Ohio the rest of his life, dying in Clinton County in 1835. He wrote the following letter on May 5, 1804, to a Quaker friend back home.

Friends Saterthwaites—I am about to visit you with another letter, and inform you it is fine growing weather here at this date after a cold, snowy winter; the northeast wind, about the 10th of the first month [January], made its way around the North Bluff of the mountain, and found us and blowed us up a big snow, above eighteen inches deep, a thing unprecedented in this country—and, also that we are in good health. . . .

The emigration into this country is so prodigious that, notwithstanding the fertility of the soil, there is scarce enough raised to supply their immediate wants at this time (without our Exporting Company sending it away), which makes produce high at the present: wheat, two-thirds of a dollar; corn, half a dollar; bacon, 8 cents per pound, etc. . . .

We have four head of horses, old and young; and thirteen head of cattle, old and young. It begins to be time to enlarge our borders. . . .

A straight-coated Friend (a millwright), is about purchasing some hundreds of acres of land adjoining my plantation, and intends to have grist-mill running, in less than a year from now, on his land. He has a sweet, pretty daughter, just cleverly merchantable. There is a fine chance for young men in this country—good land and pretty girls plenty; there were six fair ones passing my door this morning in a troop. . . .

A Letter from Worthington: Ruhamah Mays Writes to Friends Back in Conecticut, 1805

The following letter was written on August 23, 1805 by Ruhumah Mays in Worthington, Ohio, to her friend, Elizabeth Case, back in Granby, Connecticut. The letter is in the collection of Julia Buttles Case, who married Job Case in 1815. Julia's father was one of the investors in the settlements at Worthington and Granville. He brought the family to the area in 1804. He died of a fever in June, 1805. The "Mr. Buttles" mentioned in the letter probably is Julia's brother, Joel, who had become the family breadwinner. Ruhamah Mays herself remains a mystery.

Most respected friend,
     Can I withhold my pen from writing to one on whom I so much depend as we have left most of our good neighbours those few that we hope to enjoy seem particularly near & not hearing from you we have had some anxiety on your account fearing you would not come this fall. I assure you Miss Buttles is & the rest of us would be greatly disappointed should you fail. I should be glad to inform you more respecting our journey & present situation than I can at present for want of time. We overtook our team at the north river & the crossing was the most pleasant part of our journey altho so much dreaded. . . . [A]ll things went on well with us until we had sad news of the DEATH of Lieut. Bullolph announced to us which we are sensible was very alarming to you as well as to us the particulars you have doubtless heard—when we arrived at Licking Mr. Mays was so well pleased we staid several days & I was something out of health & began to think it was high time to have a home. We then took a road that was newly cut that the [illegible] that went with Mrs. Sessions had made & their carriages were narrower than ours so that we had to cut & tug three days in the wilderness & see no human being nor scarce any water I thot it a poor time to be sick but the third day just at evening we came in sight of a small settlement It gave me much joy to see the face of a woman here we was treated with much kindness put up at Mr. Curtises from Southington & should not have reached

here the next day had had [*sic*] it not been for the timely exertions of our friends here who heard of our coming & came with teams to meet us. We made our home with Mr. Buttles until we have another which you may see when you come here. If you wish to know how I am suited with this living here I can tell you that the ladies in general apear to be well pleased but as for my self I do not make up my mind at once though I think you may wait the next post to find that intelligence. We have many good things of life here pork is easy made but no cellars to put it in the best of beer but no cider. . . . A barrel of whiskey stands in one corner of one of our front rooms we have the best of wheat flour & I think the indian meal preferable to that in new england but we have no other place to store it only in bags & we are overrun with mice but I believe there is not a rat in Ohio. Respecting preparing for the journey our loads were made a little too heavy or at least too bulky bringing our clock was a wrong calculation If I had brot the top part of my case of drawers it would have been better. . . . If I was to take the journey again I would not use one article of crockery on the road for we broke the most of ours. tin will doo for almost any use & you can borrow teacups at most places where you put up. If you calculate for smooth road free from hills you will be disappointed, if you expec to dress & keep your clothes clean you will miss your aim. . . .

Mahoning County Hero: Roswell Grant Remembers James Hillman, circa 1806

Among the early settlers of Mahoning County, Colonel James Hillman stood out as a leader. He served in the War of 1812 and later was a member of the legislature. Several stories have come down to us of how he mediated problems between the Indians in the area and the white pioneers. He left his name to a neighborhood of Youngstown.

The following story was told by Roswell M. Grant, uncle of President Ulysses S. Grant, in a letter to the Mahoning Valley Historical Society in 1875. Grant contributed his memories of pioneer life to the first annual reunion of the pioneers of Mahoning and Trumbull counties. According to Grant, the following incident took place about 1815. The historian Henry Howe dates it in 1806, others in 1807, which would mean Grant may not have been an eyewitness as he claims. Howe also gives a different version of the story. Finally, Grant misremembers the family name of the brothers in the story. It is Diver, not Diven.

Although blinded, Daniel Diver did not die from his terrible gunshot wound.

He lived for many years afterward, and he and his brother are buried in Deerfield cemetery, Portage County.

Last night I wrote a sketch of James Hillman. The first part is verbatim of what I have heard Hillman and wife speak of many times, but from 1807, and up to the time I left Youngstown, I was an eyewitness of what I have stated. All I have seen or heard I never forget. . . .

Some two years after the above there was a party of Indians lived near Ravenna, Deerfield, and Atwater, of about four hundred strong, and of all ages and sizes. John Diven lived in Deerfield; he had traded horses with an Indian. The Indian thought he was cheated. John Diven refused to trade back. On Christmas night there was a ball at the house of Judge Day. John Diven and his brother Daniel was there. John Diven married a Miss Ely, of Deerfield. Daniel Diven was to be married New-years' day; all the parties were at the ball. About dark the Indian came to the door and wanted to see John Diven; he refused to go out. Daniel Diven told John to swap coat and hat and he would go out. They done so. Just as Daniel Diven stepped out of the door the Indian shot Daniel Diven through both eyes, laying both eye-balls on his cheeks. The Indians all left that night. It was twenty-five miles to Youngstown, but two messengers came to James Hillman in the night and told their business. After feeding their horses and eating something themselves, they left for Deerfield before day.

Upon arriving there they found some fifty or sixty men ready to start in pursuit of the Indians. J. Hillman told them if they wanted to go they could do so, but if he went he went by himself. They had to consent, and James Hillman started by himself. There was no snow on the ground, but the ground was very rough. He could track them; as the rough ground had wore out their moccasins, their feet were cut and bleeding. After a hard day's ride he came upon their camp. He fell back out of sight and encamped for the night.

Early next morning he went up to their camp. The squaws were getting breakfast. The men were asleep. The Indians had a small fork stuck in the ground, with their guns leaning on it, and their shot-pouch and powder-horns hanging in the fork. The squaws did not see him until he came within fifty yards of them. They gave the alarm; in a moment every Indian was upon his feet. He drew his gun upon the chief; told him to order every man to stack his gun against a certain tree or he would pull the trigger. The chief knew the Colonel so well that he gave the order. So soon as their guns, tomahawks, and knives were stuck against the tree, Colonel Hillman took possession of the tree. He then told them his business; told him one of

The grave of Daniel Diver, Deerfield Cemetery, Deerfield, Portage
County

his men had shot Daniel Diven; that they had to return; that he knew
the man that shot Daniel Diven; if they would return peaceably and
give up the man that shot Daniel Diven none of the balance would
be hurt, and that they all knew him. If they refused he would kill at
least twenty before they could recover their arms; that the chief
would be the first man to fall. He told them to eat their breakfast,
and told them to send him his breakfast; after that he would hear
what they had to say. . . .

They came back with the emblem of peace. He then told them to
send out hunters for meat, and for them to mend their moccasins,
and to remain where they were until morning.

The fourth day after, he brought the whole party into Warren,
where the authority put the chief under guard. They remained there
for some time. How it was settled I have forgotten. I have seen Daniel

Diven in Youngstown frequently. I was in Deerfield in July, 1824. I called to see him. He appeared very cheerful, and was very pleasant; thanked me for calling upon him. He had not forgotten me.

A German Missionary in Ohio:
The Reverend Paul Henkel Preaches
at Brush Creek, 1806

The Lutheran Ministerium of Pennsylvania sent the Reverend Paul Henkel and his wife on a mission to Ohio in 1806 to seek out and preach to the German settlers. At that time many of them, emigrants from German settlements in Pennsylvania, could not speak English. In fact, as this selection from Henkel's diary shows, many of them were not encouraged to give up their language and traditions and become Anglicized, though most had lived in America for many years, some for more than a generation. Preachers such as Henkel addressed the settlers in English or German, whichever was necessary at the moment for successful evangelizing. This typical day of his missionary journey gives a good idea just how diligently he worked on his mission labors. Henkel's trip took him from New Market, Shenandoah County, Virginia, to Chillicothe; then he detoured to Brush Creek to see some old friends and, of course, preach. His diary was translated from German.

Sunday, the 17 [August].
    This morning we leave the household of Friend Roth. He himself goes with us to service. His wife very much lamented her fate that she could not go with us. Within the first three miles all who had promised to go along, besides others, joined us. Our company is composed of 7 persons who are going along to service. We must ride through a forest a distance of 13 miles. It is half past ten by the time we arrive at the place. . . . Upon our arrival, we find all the Germans assembled, who are living in the whole neighborhood, as well as many English. Here we again meet our friend Rausch. As this place has just newly been settled, and as it has as yet mostly small houses, there is none large enough. The wind blows very strongly, or we would use the forest for this purpose. Nevertheless we secured a frame inn, into which as many gathered as could. Yesterday I was the first German preacher who had been at the Brush Creek, and so here today, in this place. The first sermon was for the Germans, during which all were quiet and very attentive. Certainly several must have been touched by it. I baptized eight children here. After this followed an English sermon. But what shall I say to this assembly? Several of

them are even drunk, and the others look very dissolute. What more could I wish than that the sermon would fall as heavily upon them; as it was for me to preach. But I do my duty. They are not all drunk. The Germans understand some of it. yes, in fact, it goes better than was expected, but what the fruits thereof may be, the Lord alone knows. . . . After the conclusion of the service, I rode home with a German, one and one-half miles away, and baptized his child. I reproved him that he held his and his wife's mother tongue in such little esteem, and did not teach it to their children. . . . I rode home with Friend Wilkin, a distance of three miles. Upon our arrival, which was at twilight, we found the house full, and to these I had to speak, at their request. Here I again recorded all the German households, to the number of thirty-five, but most of them just lately settled here. A number of households were from my former congregation; some from Pastor Schmucker's, who were delighted to hear that we were also acquainted with him. At 10 o'clock we broke up; the work for today is ended, and I am glad that I can go to rest. Tomorrow, God willing, we intend to go to the Little Miami.

A Trip along Zane's Trace: Selections from Fortescue Cuming's Travel Book, 1807

Although we know almost nothing about Fortescue Cuming, the author of these travel journals, he left a literate and interesting account of his adventures in America. He started his western travels in Philadelphia in January, 1807, and walked to Pittsburg in twenty-seven days. There he stayed until July, when he took a boat down the Ohio River to Maysville, Kentucky. After a brief tour of Kentucky, he crossed the Ohio and traveled by foot, horse, and stagecoach along Zane's Trace to Wheeling, then back to Pittsburgh, where he arrived again on August 1. He traveled mainly for pleasure and curiosity, but he also paused near West Union, Ohio, to inspect a piece of land he had bought, sight unseen, in Europe.

The Ohio Cuming describes was a far cry from the one Nicholas Cresswell had visited in 1775 or Colonel John May in 1788-89. Settlements and farms now dotted the forest. Towns were pushing up on the river banks and state roads. However crude, European civilization was taking hold. But there were still plenty of hard-bitten frontiersmen to provide local color and frighten travelers.

After a leisurely trip down the Ohio River, stopping at farms along the way, Cuming arrived in Marietta on July 23.

This town is finely situated on both banks of the Muskingum, at the confluence of that river with the Ohio. It is principally built on the left bank, where there are ninety-seven houses, including a court-house, a market-house, an academy, and a post-office. There are about thirty houses on the opposite bank, the former site of Fort Harmar, which was a United States' garrison during the Indian wars, but of which no vestige now remains. . . .

The land on which Marietta is built was purchased during the Indian war, from the United States, by some New England land specu-lators, who named themselves the Ohio Company. They chose the land facing the Ohio, with a depth from the river of only from twenty to thirty miles to the northward, thinking the proximity of the river would add to its value, but since the state of Ohio has began to be generally settled, the rich levels in the interior have been preferred, but not before the company had made large sales. . . .

On July 24, Cuming landed on Blennerhassett Island. Owner Harman Blennerhassett had begun construction of a showplace mansion there in 1798. Blennerhassett got involved with Aaron Burr, possibly to plan a military inva-sion of Texas and Mexico. (No one is sure even now what they intended.) In 1806 Blennerhassett fled just ahead of the militia, who came to arrest him for treason. His house burned down in 1811.

On ascending the bank from the landing, we entered at a handsome double gate, with hewn stone square pilasters, a gravel walk, which led us about a hundred and fifty paces, to Mr. Blennerhasset's house, with a meadow on the left, and a shrubbery on the right, separated from the avenue by a low hedge of privy-sally, through which innu-merable columbines, and various other hardy flowers were display-ing themselves to the sun, at present almost their only observer.

We were received with politeness by Mrs. Cushing, whose hus-band, Col. Cushing, has a lease of this extensive and well cultivated farm, where he and his family now reside in preference to his own farm at Belle-pre [Belpre].

The house occupies a square of about fifty-four feet each side, is two stories high, and in just proportion. On the ground floor is a din-ing room of twenty-seven feet by twenty, with a door at each end communicating with two small parlours, in the rear of each of which is another room, one of which was appropriate by Mr. B. for holding a chymical apparatus, and as a dispensary for drugs and medicines. . . .

The body of the house is connected with two wings, by a semi-

circular portico or corridor running from each front corner. In one
wing is the kitchen and scullery, and in the other was the library,
now used as a lumber room.

It is to be regretted that so tasty and so handsome a house had not
been constructed of more lasting materials than wood. . . .

The house was finished in a suitable style, but all the furniture
and moveables were attached by the creditors to whom Mr. B. had
made himself liable by endorsing Col. Burr's bills, and they were
lately sold at publick auction at Wood county court house, for perhaps less than one twentieth of their first cost.

At Buffington's Island, they tied up at Peter Neisanger's (or Niswonger's) farm.

Fastening our skiff to a tree, we ascended the steep sloping bank to
the house where we were received with cautious taciturnity by Mrs.
Neisanger, whose ungracious reception would have induced us to
have proceeded further, had not the evening been too far advanced
for us to arrive at better quarters before dark; and besides the state of
our stomachs rendered us insensible to an uncourteous reception:
We determined therefore to make our quarters good, though a few
minutes after, friend A—, repented of our resolution, on seeing a figure scarcely meriting the name of human approaching him, where
he had gone alone in quest of some of the males of the family. It had
the appearance of a man above the middle age, strong and robust,
fantastically covered with ragged cloathing, but so dirty that it was
impossible to distinguish whether he was naturally a white or an
Indian—in either case he equally merited the appellation of *savage.*
A—, acosted him as lord of the soil, but he did not deign any reply,
on which he returned to me, where I was in the boat adjusting our
baggage, to consult with me whether we had not better proceed farther; but first resolving to make one more attempt, we again mounted
the bank and found two men with rifles in their hands sitting at the
door, neither of whose aspects, nor the circumstance of their being
armed, were very inviting: As however we did not see the strange
appartition which A—, had described to me, we ventured to accost
them.

The elder of the two was Neisanger.—Though he did not say us
"nay," to our request of supper, his *"yea"* was in the very extreme of
bluntness, and without either the manner or expression which sometimes merits its having joined to it the adjective *honest.*

They laid aside their rifles, and supper being announced by the
mistress of the cabin, we made a hearty meal on her brown bread
and milk, while she attended her self-important lord with all due

humility, as Sarah did Abraham; which patriarchal record in the scrip-
tures, is perhaps the original cause of a custom which I have observed
to be very common in the remote parts of the United States, of the
wife not sitting down to table until the husband and the strangers
have finished their meal.

During supper, Mr. Neisanger gradually relaxed from his blunt
and cautious brevity of speech, and we gathered from him that he
had been a great hunter and woodsman, in which occupation, he said
that one man may in one season kill two hundred deer and eighty
bears.

He had changed his pursuit of the wild inhabitants of the forest
about nine years ago, for an agricultural life. Since that time he had
cleared a large tract of land, had planted three thousand fruit trees
on his farm, and had carried on a distillery of whiskey and peach
brandy, for the first of which he gets seventy-five cents per gallon,
and for the last a dollar. . . .

The next morning, "three miles below Neisanger's," Cuming was hailed from
shore by two men. One was the son of the man for whom Buffington's Island
was named.

Buffington was a very stout young man, and was going to the falls to
attend a gathering (as they phrase it in this country) at a justice's
court, which squire Sears, who resides at the falls [Letart Falls, in
Letart Township, Meigs County] holds on the last Saturday of every
month: He supposed there would be sixty or seventy men there—
some plaintiffs, and some defendants in causes of small debts, actions of defamation, assaults, &c. and some to wrestle, fight, shoot
at a mark with the rifle for wagers, gamble at other games, or drink
whiskey. He had his rifle with him and was prepared for any kind of
frolick which might be going forward. . . .

Next stop, Gallipolis.

We got an excellent breakfast at Mr. Menager's, a French emigrant
who keeps a tavern and a store of very well assorted goods, which he
goes yearly to Baltimore to purchase. He is a native of Franche
Comté,[8] and his wife is from Burgundy. They are very civil and oblig-
ing, and have a fine family. It is fifteen years since they arrived in
this country, together with nearly 800 emigrants from France, of

---

8. The mountainous region around Besançon on the Swiss border.

whom only about twenty families now remain at Galliopolis; the rest having either returned to France, descended the Ohio to French Grant, proceeded to the banks of the Mississippi, or fallen victims to the insalubrity of the climate, which however no longer, or only partially exists, as it has gradually ameliorated in proportion to the progress of settlement. . . .

In August, Cuming crossed the Ohio from Maysville, Kentucky, and walked to the land he had bought in Europe the year before. Then he set out along Zane's Trace on his journey across the state.

I had expected to have found a mere wilderness, as soon as I should quit the high road, but to my agreeable surprise, I found my land surrounded on every side by fine farms, some of them ten years settled, and the land itself, both in quality and situation, not exceeded by any in this fine country. . . .

On Saturday [August 8] I returned to Ellis's ferry opposite Maysville, to give directions for my baggage being sent after me by the stage to Chillicothe.

Having registered his property deed at the clerk's office in West Union, Cuming continued on his way Monday, August 10. He walked about seven and a half miles to Jacob Platter's tavern on Brush Creek.

Having rested and taken some refreshment, the growling of distant thunder warned me to hasten my journey, as I had five miles through the woods to the next habitation. The road was fine and level,—the gust approached with terrifick warning—one flash of lightning succeeding another in most rapid succession, so that the woods frequently appeared as in a flame, and several trees were struck in every direction around me, one being shattered within fifty paces on my right, while the thunder without intermission of an instant was heard in every variety of sound, from the deafening burst, shaking the whole surrounding atmosphere to the long solemn cadence always interrupted by a new and more heavy peal before it had reached its pause. This elemental war would have been sublimely awful to me, had I been in an open country, but the frequent crash of the falling bolts on the surrounding trees, gave me such incessant warnings of danger, that the sublimity was lost in the awe. I had been accustomed to thunder storms in every climate, and I had heard the roar of sixty ships of the line in battle, but I never before was witness to so tremendous an elemental uproar. I suppose the heaviest part of the electrick cloud was impelled upon the very spot I was passing.

I walked the five miles within an hour, but my speed did not avail me to escape a torrent of rain which fell during the last mile, so that long before I arrived at the hospitable dwelling of the Pennsylvania hunter who occupied the next cabin, I was drenched and soaked most completely. . . .

The next day, he walked on past Sinking Spring to a house owned by the Bradleys.

Bradley and his wife are about sixteen years from Stewartstown, county Tyrone in Ireland, and have a daughter lately married to a young shoemaker named Irons at the next cabin, where I stopped to get my shoes mended. I here found a dozen of stout young fellows who had been at work repairing the road, and were now sheltering themselves from the increasing storm, and listening to some indifferent musick made by their host on a tolerably good violin. I proposed taking the violin while he repaired my shoes. He consented and sat down to work, and in a few minutes I had all the lads jigging it on the floor merrily; Irons himself, as soon as he had repaired the shoes, jumping up and joining them.

The next day, he walked through Bainbridge and followed Paint Creek thirteen miles to the Rogers house, where he spent the night. The next morning, he swam in the creek, then walked the last four miles to Chillicothe.

The situation of the town, which is the capital of the state, is on an elevated plain of nearly ten thousand acres of as fine a soil as any in America, partly in cultivation and partly covered with its native forests. . . .

There is a remarkable Indian monument in Mr. Watchup's garden in the very heart of the town.—Like that at Grave creek [West Virginia, at that time part of Virginia], it is circular at the base, about seventy or eighty feet diameter, but differs from that, by being round, instead of flat on the top, which has an elevation of about thirty feet perpendicular from the level of the plain. It is formed of clay, and though it has been perforated by the proprietor, nothing has been found to justify the common opinion of these mounts having been barrows or cemeteries. They talk of having it levelled, as it projects a little into Market street, but I think it a pity to destroy any of the very few vestiges of aboriginal population, which this country presents to the curious and inquisitive traveller. . . .

Colonel [Duncan] M'Arthur[9] coming to town was polite enough to invite me to take a bed at his house [Fruit Hill], which I had passed about two miles back in the morning. I found the situation surpassed what I had thought of it then, when I only saw it from the road, it commanding a beautiful and extensive prospect including the town of Chilicothe, which, however is now seen rather indistinctly on account of the foliage of some trees on the brow of a small projecting hill, which will probably soon be cut down.

Next morning, Friday, 14th August, I walked before breakfast half a mile through the woods to the northward to an elegant seat [Adena] belonging to Col. [Thomas] Worthington.[10] It will be finished in a few weeks and will be one of the best and most tasty houses not only of this state but to the westward of the Allegheny mountains. . . .

Cuming took the next leg of his journey by stagecoach and horseback.

New Lancaster is a compact little town of one wide street, about six hundred paces long, containing sixty houses, amongst which is a neat little court house of brick, forty-two by thirty-six feet, just built, with a cupola belfry. There are six stores and nine taverns. There is but one brick house, all the rest being of wood, amongst which conspicuously the best is that of Mr. Bucher [probably Philemon Beecher] a lawyer. In most towns in the United States, the best houses are chiefly inhabited by gentlemen of that profession.

After supping at the inn where the stage stopped, I was shewn to bed up stairs in a barrack room the whole extent of the house, with several beds in it, one of which was already occupied by a man and his wife, from the neighbouring country, who both conversed with me until I feigned sleep, in hopes that would silence them, but though they then ceased to direct their discourse to me, they continued to talk to each other on their most private and domestick affairs, as though there had been no other person in the room. In spite of their conversation I at last fell asleep, but I was soon awoke in torture from a general attack made on me by hosts of vermin of the most troublesome and disgusting genii. I started from the bed, dressed

---

9. Duncan McArthur was a wealthy Ross County land speculator who served in the War of 1812, became a general, went to Congress, and in 1830 was elected governor of Ohio.
10. Thomas Worthington, who built this beautiful house, was a U.S. senator during the War of 1812, and was elected governor in 1814 and 1816.

Adena, Thomas Worthington's home near Chillicothe, Ross County. Fortescue Cuming described it in 1807 as "one of the best and most tasty houses . . . to the westward of the Allegheny mountains." Courtesy of the Ohio Historical Society.

myself, spread a coverlet on the floor, and lay down there to court a little more repose, but I was prevented by a constant noise in the house during the whole night, beginning with church musick, among which some sweet female voices were discernible, and ending in the loud drunken frolicks of some rustick guests, who kept Saturday night until late on Sunday morning.

Cuming soon arrived in Zanesville.

I crossed the ferry to Zanesville, and dismounted at an inn where the stage generally stops. On entering I walked into a room, the door of which was open, where the first object that met my eye was the corpse of a female, laid out in her shroud on a bier. There was no person in the room but another female who was seated near the corpse, and to whom I apologized for my abrupt entrance, explaining my reasons as being in advance of the stage. She answered by wishing she had some mode of preventing the stage from driving up to the house, as her sister had died that morning, and it would be inconvenient to accommodate travellers that night, on which I remounted, rode to the post office, where I found the stage delivering the mail. . . .

On August 17th, Cuming left Zanesville in the morning and crossed Salt Creek by breakfast time.

From Salt Creek, I ascended half a mile of a steep road to the highest hill which I had been yet on in this state, and keeping two miles along its ridge, I had there to ascend a still higher pinnacle of it, from whence there is a most extensive view in every direction, of ridges beyond ridges covered with forests, to the most distant horizon; but though grand and extensive, it is dreary and cheerless, excepting to a mind which anticipates the great change which the astonishingly rapid settlement of this country will cause in the face of nature in a few revolving years. Such a mind will direct the eye ideally to the sides of hills covered with the most luxuriant gifts of Ceres; to valleys divested of their trees; . . . while the frequent comfortable and tasty farm house—the mills—the villages, and the towns marked by their smoke and distant spires, will cause the traveller to ask himself with astonishment, "So short a time since, could this have been an uninhabited wilderness?"

He continued east on the 18th, passing through present-day Old Washington to Morristown.

On the road I met in straggling parties above fifty horsemen with rifles, who had been in Morristown at a militia muster, for the purpose of volunteering, or of being drafted to serve against Britain, in case of a war with that country, now much talked of. Most of them were above half seas over, and they travelled with much noise—some singing, some swearing, some quarrelling, some laughing, according to their different natural dispositions, which are always most manifest when in that unguarded situation.

I found Morristown, where I arrived just before dark, all in a bustle from the same cause, many of the country people remaining to a late hour, drinking and fighting.

My host Morrison who is a justice of the peace, and a major of the militia, had shut his house against them, but there was another tavern, where squire Morrison, while commanding the peace, during an affray, came in for his share of the blows, and had his shirt torn. . . .

Cuming continued on to the Ohio River, following Wheeling Creek, which he calls Indian Wheeling, down to where it joins the Ohio at Wheeling Island, which was then called Zane's Island because of Mr. Zane's large farm on it, "some of whose apples, pulled from the orchard in passing, were very refreshing to us, while we sat on the bank nearly an hour awaiting the ferry boat."

A Businessman's Perspective:
The Travels of John Melish, 1811

John Melish traveled extensively around the United States from 1807 to 1811, mainly in pursuit of commercial connections between America and Britain. In 1811, he came to Ohio, traveling by way of Pittsburgh and the Ohio River with a couple of companions. He went to Cincinnati and beyond to the Indian territories of Indiana and Illinois, then back to Kentucky and Tennessee. Like Cuming, he crossed the river at Maysville and traveled northeast to Zanesville. He met some of the same characters Cuming did. Then he turned north up the Muskingum and through the Western Reserve. He visited Cleveland and left from there for Canada via the south shore of Lake Erie.

August 26th, [1811] we left Steubenville about 8 o'clock; the morning was foggy; the temperature of the atmosphere 60°. We proceeded down the river three miles, when, Mr. Ward having some inquiries to make, we stopped at a very handsome plantation, situated on the Ohio side, on an extensive bottom, which raised corn, oats, barley, hemp, wheat, and rye, in great abundance; and there was a peach orchard literally *loaded* with fruit. . . .

We dined by the way on broiled chickens, which we purchased at Steubenville for six and a quarter cents each; and after a very agreeable sail we reached Wheeling, 23 miles from Steubenville, at five o'clock in the evening. . . .

By August 28 they were on Long Reach.

As we proceeded along this delightful *reach*, the afternoon became very sultry, and, seeing a fine peach-orchard on the Ohio side, we pulled towards it, to get into the shade of the trees. The people were *mashing* peaches, preparing to make peach-brandy, and one of them, learning that a *New England man* was in company, saluted us with great cordiality, and led us through the peach-orchard. And such an orchard I never saw before; the trees were figuratively *groaning* under their burden, and hundreds of bushels were lying on the ground. It was no sin to eat peaches here; and they were really delicious.

The proprietor told us he was from Connecticut, that had been a considerable time settled here, and could maintain his family as well on the labour of one day in the week, as he could in Connecticut in all the six. Those who were industrious, he said, could not fail to lay up a comfortable stock for old age, and for posterity. . . . The first settlers were selling their improvements, and moving off; while men of capital were coming in, and making elegant improvements, and, in 10 years more, the banks of the river here would be beautiful. The Ohio side, he said, was thriving remarkably; the Virginia side not near so well; and he assigned the operation of slavery as the principal reason, which I believe to be correct. . . .

Melish left Marietta on September 1. At Buffington's Island (called here Buffentin's) the Frenchman who traveled with them tried to buy milk from Mrs. Buffington, but she refused him. He said it was just as well because she was a "dirty-looking hussy."

On September 7 they arrived at the mouth of the Scioto, where stood Portsmouth on one side of the river and Alexandria on the other.

As the latter is an old settlement, we meant to have stopped at it all night; but, on making inquiry for a tavern, we found there was none, and that the town was going to decay. It appears, it is liable to be flooded, although it is on a bank 60 feet high; but Portsmouth, on the east bank of the Scioto, is not subject to that inconvenience, and is progressing very fast. Being at the outlet of the Scioto, one of the finest rivers in the state of Ohio, I presume it will become a place of very considerable importance. We were told that the banks of the Scioto were very rich, though a little unhealthy; but, as the country was clearing up, the sickness was diminishing every year. . . .

On September 10, at dark, they arrived in Cincinnati.

The streets of Cincinnati are broad, crossing one another at right angles, and, the greater part of the houses being of brick, it has a very handsome appearance. The streets, however, are not yet paved,

Cincinnati, about 1810. From Emilius O. Randall, *History of Ohio*, vol. 2 (1912).

except the side walks, on which account they are unpleasant in muddy weather, but that is an evil which will soon be remedied. Cincinnati was laid out about 21 years ago, since which it has made rapid progress, and now contains about 400 houses, and 2283 inhabitants. . . .

This is, next to Pittsburg, the greatest place for manufactures and mechanical operations on the river, and the professions exercised are nearly as numerous as at Pittsburg. There are masons and stone-cutters, brick-makers, carpenters, cabinet-makers, coopers, turners, machine-makers, wheel-wrights, smiths and nailors, coppersmiths, tinsmiths, silversmiths, gunsmiths, clock and watchmakers, tanners. . . .

As the people are becoming wealthy, and polished in their manners, probably a manufactory of pianofortes would do, upon a small scale. . . .

This place, like Marietta, is mostly settled by New Englanders; and the state of society is very excellent. Education is well attended to, and the people are very correct in their morals. [T]here are three newspapers printed here, and they get papers from every state in the union.

In October, after going to Indiana, Illinois, Tennessee, and Kentucky, Melish re-crossed the Ohio River and pursued the same route up Zane's Trace that

Fortescue Cuming had two years previously. He arrived in Zanesville on October 7.

I found a large thriving town, with a great number of handsome brick houses, the buildings going rapidly on; and every thing wearing a flourishing aspect. The ground around it was well cleared, the neighbouring hills were getting into a state of cultivation, mills were erecting; and bridges, banks, and manufactures were projected. . . . The Muskingum river is navigable to this place, and beyond it, to near its head, from whence there is a communication with lake Erie, by a small portage. There are fine falls in Zanesville, and mills may be erected to almost an unlimited extent. . . .

In point of commerce, Zanesville is likely to become a considerable place. The banks of the Muskingum and its waters upward are settling rapidly; and the quantity of produce that will come down the river will encrease every year. At present, almost the only article of surplus produce is flour. . . . Other articles are raised in abundance, but the great influx of emigrants consumes nearly the whole. . . .

Melish went from Zanesville to Coshocton and on towards New Philadelphia.

From [Newcomerstown] is about 4 miles, through a pretty muddy road, to Yankee-town, where there are a number of thriving settlements; but, owing to its being an Indian reservation, the settlers cannot become possessed of the land and they move off as soon as they get land of their own; so that the place will probably not soon be of much importance.

Beyond Yankee-town I again crossed the river, about knee deep, and stopped at Gnadenhutten, a small town, consisting of 3 or 4 houses, a post-office, tavern, and store. The people are mostly Germans from Bedford, Pennsylvania, and appear to be very poor. This is also an Indian reservation. Two miles and a half from Gnadenhutten I again crossed the river. . . . to Shoenbrun, an Indian town, consisting of a few houses only. The Indians look wretchedly poor.

In New Philadelphia, Melish made a traveling companion of a young "Dutch" farmer from Cleveland. The young man was, of course, Pennsylvania Dutch, meaning German, not a Dutchman from Holland. Melish and the farmer followed the Tuscarawas River as it took a sharp bend to the east.

This is the seventh time that I forded this river since I left Zanesville, and I always found nearly the same result—clear water, knee deep, and gravelly bottom; and I have no hesitation in pronouncing it the most beautiful river I ever saw, except the Ohio; and the scenery on its banks is even more beautiful than on the Ohio. . . .

After crossing the river we called at the house of a Dutch farmer, who told us he had settled here 10 years ago, at which time there was no house between him and Gnadenhutten, and there are now numerous settlements, a proof of the rapidity with which this country is settling up. . . .

The Dutch people make excellent settlers in a new country: they are a plodding, slow, sure-footed, sober race; and have an excellent knack at finding out the rich places. The only foe they have to encounter is the ague, but they seem to be *used to it* . . . .

Melish continued on to Canton, located in an area that had only recently been bought from the Native Americans. His route still followed the Tuscarawas to a tavern about ten miles beyond Canton.

After leaving the tavern about a mile, we saw a tent pitched in the woods a little off the road and turned aside to make inquiries. This was an emigrant family, consisting of a man, his wife, and two children. They had travelled far in quest of a settlement, and their means being exhausted, they were obliged to stop short at this place, where they meant to *sit down* and clear and cultivate a piece of land. In the language of the country, they were *squatters*. The only visible substance they had, was a tent, a waggon, a horse, a cow, and some bedding. The tent and bedding had been drenched by the rain, but they had a large fire before the door, at which the bedding was hung up to dry, and they sat round it apparently very contented.

Soon Melish was in the Western Reserve, where the settlers were mainly from Connecticut. He was told that Hudson was a thriving town with "a number of handsome *frame houses*," so he headed north from Canton. He never got to Hudson. The road went through swamps "in some of which my horse sunk to the knees." He spent a night shivering in a poor house "literally like a riddle" with holes in the chinking and broken panes in the windows. "And there was an opening almost close by my bed-side, that would have let in a horse."

I reached Cleveland; but, without stopping to examine the city, I rode on to the bank, where, from an eminence about 70 feet high, I beheld the lake in all its glory. To the northward, no land was to be seen; and to the east and west, the banks were high, and the scenery very picturesque; the view was really sublime. I was delighted with

it; and, full of the pleasing sensations which such a view was calculated to excite, I pursued my way to the tavern. But, O! what a con-
trast was there! the people looked pale, sickly, and dejected. I learned
that they had been afflicted with a very severe sickness this season.
It was periodical, they said, and generally fever and ague; but this
season it had been worse than usual, and accompanied with some
very severe cases of bilious fever. I found that this had proved a complete check upon the improvement of Cleveland, which, though dignified with the name of a CITY, remained a paltry *village,* containing
a few houses only.

Some Pioneer Memories: Henry Curtis's Youth in Licking County, 1809-1815

Henry B. Curtis shared memories of pioneer days in Licking County, including
a public whipping, in a speech he gave to the Richland County Historical and
Pioneer Society in 1885. He died shortly afterward at his home in Mount
Vernon. He came to Newark, in Licking County, with his family in 1809.

The war of 1812, occurring as it did in the pioneer day of Ohio, the
proximity of the settlers to the Indian villages and the Canada border brought them in direct connection with many of its painful
events, and added greatly to their sufferings and privations. There
was an Indian village on the upper waters of the Raccoon branch of
the Licking, near where the village of Johnstown now stands; another, called Greentown, near Perrysville, in this county; and then
the Wyandottes at Upper Sandusky. Although these several Indian
Pueblos professed to be friendly, yet their friendship was unreliable;
many young braves of the tribes, as well from their natural hate towards the whites, as also from British bribes and influence, were co-
vertly hostile; and these villages gave shelter and harbor to emissar-
ies from other tribes openly hostile. Indians that had been peaceful
in our villages, as traders with their cranberries, pelts, and mocca-
sin-work, became a terror to the settlers; and the massacre of the
Copus family in this county, and the Snows in Huron, and other depredations, added to the alarm.

There was a block-house at Fredericktown, another at Bellville;
also one at this village [Mansfield], and at other exposed places. And
often on signal of danger, all the inhabitants of a village or settlement would gather in these places of security for protection of their

wives and children, against apprehended night attacks of the savages. These alarms were often without just cause—sometimes perpetrated as practical jokes. . . .

The return of peace was hailed with joy, and the little eight-by-ten windows of the cabins, as well as of the more pretentious dwellings that had grown up in our villages, blazed with added lights, and music and rejoicing filled our streets and our dwellings. . . .

I do not know that this beautiful city, Mansfield, was ever adorned with a *whipping-post;* but I remember very well that interesting feature on the public square in Newark. It was a centre for our games, to us school boys, and afforded the test of agility in our trials to reach the great staple near the top. It was in 1812, I think, that a poor fellow of the name of John Courson was convicted of stealing some bags of flour from a mill, and perhaps some other articles. He was sentenced by Judge Wilson to receive fifty "stripes," well laid on (as the law then required),—five the next morning, fifteen at noon, and thirty the following day at noon. George Alliston was high sheriff and Andy Beard deputy. The flagellation was performed by the latter under the oversight of the chief. A circle of about sixty feet diameter was drawn and a cordon established that kept back the crowd that pressed to the line. The prisoner was brought out from the log jail and secured by his upraised hands to the big staple. The first blow of the "cowhide" simply left a welt. "A little harder," said the sheriff, and Andy marked the four succeeding blows in distinct red lines on the poor fellow's naked back. He received this first installment of his sentence without an audible groan; but when returned to the same position for the second, his utterances and screeches from the first stroke were heart-rending, and when returned to the prison, his audible lamentations and prayers for annihilation before another day were fearful and most painful to be heard. Yet he stood the whole punishment, receiving the following day the heavy remainder of the infliction, and returned to his prison with his back lacerated and bleeding from his shoulders to his hips. It was a painful and disgusting sight, the first and last of the kind in Licking county.

Cleveland in Infancy: Isham Morgan
Remembers the Village, 1812-1813

Isham A. Morgan remembered Cleveland as a raw new town on the lake, before it prospered and grew. This account is from 1890.

My first distinct recollection of Cleveland dates back to 1812, when I rode behind my father on horseback to Cleveland, which, possibly, then contained twenty families. On the Public Square, near where the lower fount now is, I saw the gallows standing, on which the Indian murderer, John Omic, was hung a few days before.[11] Then there were many large stumps on the Square, and clumps of bushes which extended to the lake, and all along the bank of the lake, from the summit to the beach, the trees were all standing. . . . On the south side of Superior street, from the Square to near where the American House now is, was woods, except some four or five spaces cleared adjoining the street for as many houses and gardens. Where Prospect street is now, next to Ontario, was the old cemetery, surrounded by bushes and blackberry briers. Outside of the cemetery, west, south and east, the forest stood in its native grandeur. Only a narrow strip had been cut out for a road where Ontario street is. On Ontario street, a little south of the old cemetery, was a large mound, supposed to be the work of the Mound Builders of prehistoric times. It stood several years after we came before it was made level with the surrounding earth. It has passed away, probably to be forgotten that such a structure ever existed there. . . .

James Fisk and his brother Moses were the first settlers at the center of Brooklyn [now a suburb of Cleveland]. They went there in the Spring of 1812. Not a tree had been cut before they went there to clear a spot for their log cabins. The following Winter, my father, mother and myself went there in a cutter by the way of the Cleveland hamlet, not as big as Newburgh in those days. When we arrived at the foot of Superior street we were ferried over the river. Then a few rods took us to the woods, where the trees were marked for guides through the woods. These, by skillful driving, my father followed, crooking this way and that way to get through among the trees.

After the Fisks had got to raising cereals, in order to get it ground, they put as much in bags as a horse could carry, with a boy to ride and guide the horse and sent the boy with it to the Newburgh mill, by the way of the ferry, and always on arriving at the mill, the considerate miller knowing that wolves, at night, were liable to attack a single horse and rider, ground the boy's grist first of any, so that he could get home before dark. . . .

---

11. Po-ka-haw, or Omic, or John Omic, was the first person legally convicted of murder in the Western Reserve. He and a companion named Semo killed two white traders on Pipe Creek in Cuyahoga County. Tecumseh ordered them turned over to the white authorities. Semo committed suicide before he was tried.

The Cuyahoga river, with its late superb bridges over it, is not what it used to be, when a drink from its gentle running water would not poison the thirsty woodman. I remember how we used to catch delicious fish in the river in our boyhood. That finny tribe, which in favorable days brought joy to the angler, has left for parts unknown. And they say that even the catfish have become disgusted with the oil and filth allowed to contaminate the river, causing them to abandon their old favorite haunts under protest.

In the early times of Cuyahoga county, there were bears, wolves, deer, a few elks, wild turkeys, coons, porcupines, opposoms, squirrels, wild ducks, wild geese, and pigeons innumerable. They too have nearly all left. I have often seen pigeons flying when from the zenith to the horizon, in every direction, they were as close together as could be and not prevent their flying, and it took the fast flyers not less than ten minutes for the flock to pass by, and smaller flocks would follow. One day they would fly in one direction and perhaps the same day, or a day or two after, they would fly in the opposite direction. . . .

The Maumee Settlement and the War of 1812: Philothe Clark Recalls Her Family's Flight to Urbana, 1811-1812

Philothe Clark recalled the early days along the Maumee River, where her father, Isaac Clark, moved the family in 1811.

They [the Clark family and their fellow travelers] stopped at the Wapakonetta, an Indian village at the head waters of the Auglaise River. There they made two flat-bottomed boats by halving two basswood logs, dug out and securely put together in the middle in a manner that they would not leak. He [Isaac Clark] was a natural mechanic, and could turn his hand to almost any kind of business.

There was one white man living with the Indians there. We left in our boats, gliding down the Maumee by day, and nights fastened our boats to the shore by a tree and pitched our tents to sleep under and cook our victuals, for which we had good appetites. Wild onions were plenty, and were deemed quite a luxury by us pioneers.

The country was an unbroken wilderness, excepting now and then an Indian village; but the journey was not devoid of interest and pleasure to a lover of nature. Child as I was, the wilder the scenery the more attractive to me. We stopped at Fort Defiance [present-day city of Defiance] and took in my uncle Squire, father's mother, and an-

other family; they had spent the winter there. There was a Frenchman living there with a squaw; he was an Indian trader, and the only
white man living there.

When we got down to Wolf Rapids, our men, not being acquainted
with the river, took the wrong side where the water was not deep
enough to carry our boats over, and they stuck about midship. The
men dashed into the water up to their armpits and carried the children to the shore. Two men would take one woman (of which there
were six) between them and wade them sighing to the bank. Not
one of them thought it was fun. In a short time the Indians came
flocking over in canoes from the small town on the opposite side of
the river. Quite a scene ensued; the Indians, four in number, agreed
to take our boats over and land them for a quart of whisky, but on no
other terms. Father did not like to let them have any; we had but a
small quantity. Not being able to make the Indians do it any other
way, they finally agreed to let them have it. They soon landed the
boats and took their whisky; but, true to their custom, they insisted
upon having more. Quite a number of Indians and squaws collected
and did not leave the ground that night. They cried and sang, smoked
and told stories, alternately, till morning. In a love scene which they
enacted that night, one truant squaw got her nose bit off by her in-
dignant spouse.

We reached the Maumee settlement [Perrysburg] the 1st of May;
raised some crops that season. The new comers suffered dreadfully
from malignant fevers that season. Several heads of families died.
My father's only sister died the 10th and his mother the 12th of August. There were no boards to be had, so he took his broad-axe, and,
with two other men, went into the woods and felled a basswood tree,
split out puncheons, hewed and planed them, and with his own hands
made their coffins and helped to bury them, where Fort Meigs was
afterwards built. . . . His own family suffered very much—many days
not one of them being able to help themelves for several hours at a
time. He was sick with ague and fever. All the water that we could
have for twenty-four hours was two pails of river water brought in
every morning by a kind neighbor. His youngest child died, aged two
years.

In the spring of 1812 he planted potatoes and corn on the island
in the river. The army made use of it, and he got his pay from the
Government. There was a company of soldiers stationed near us, but
they left immediately after we heard of Hull's surrender. A British
officer, with a few soldiers and a band of warriors, came to take pos-

session of what public stores there were at that place. The Indians plundered a few houses, took all the horses and mules they could find, and left. The inhabitants had to leave, some of them in open boats. Father, in company with twelve other families, left by land. They took the road cut through by Gen. Hull's army to Urbana. After a toilsome journey of two weeks through the mud of the Black Swamp, nearly devoured by mosquitoes—sometimes no water, only what stood in the ruts and cattle tracks—we arrived safely at Urbana.

Early Child Labor: Royal Taylor Works for His Weight in Sugar, circa 1813

Colonel Royal Taylor was born in 1800. He became a prosperous land agent and attained the rank of colonel during the Civil War. In 1887, five years before he died, he wrote some memories of his early years in the Western Reserve.

We were four days on the road from Warren to Aurora, a distance of less than thirty miles, where our journey of forty-five days [from Massachusetts] terminated, June 22, 1807.

When we built our first log cabin the nearest neighbor on the north was thirty miles away, on the west, sixty miles, on the east, about eight miles, and on the south of Aurora about ten or eleven miles to a house in Franklin township.

At that time northern Ohio was a vast wilderness, with but a few inhabitants, except the Indians, who outnumbered the whites two or three to one. . . . The Indians were generally peaceable and kind, and supplied us with honey, sugar, venison, turkeys, and various other necessary articles which we could not obtain from any other source; but when the Indians had visited some trading post and had procured a supply of bad whiskey, they were noisy, and gave us a sample of the Indian yell and war whoop. . . .

My father died of camp fever when I was about thirteen years old, leaving my good old mother with a large family of nearly helpless boys and girls to feed, clothe and educate as best she could, with only a few acres of poorly improved land, filled with stumps and roots and surrounded with a dense forest. In the spring of 1813 she hired me to a neighbor for the sugaring season, of five or six weeks, and was to receive for my services my weight in sugar at the end of the term. My employer was a careful man and kept me as busy as possible, so that my avoirdupois weight should not be greatly increased during the term. At the close of my service my weight was just seventy pounds, and the sugar was delivered and sold for nine dollars and fifty cents, and the proceeds applied to the support of the family. By strict economy and untiring industry my mother kept the family together and accomplished more for our education and support than the mothers of the present day would be willing to undertake.

Those persons who came to this part of Ohio after the war of 1812 can have no just conception of the hardships and privations endured by those who were here before and during that struggle. . . .

News from the Frontier: A Letter from Cynthia Barker to Julia Buttles, 1813

Cynthia Andrews married Eliphalet Barker in 1813. The letter excerpted here was written by Cynthia to her friend Julia Buttles on September 19, 1813. Cynthia and her husband and Julia all had left Worthington, Franklin County, Ohio and were in New England, so Cynthia referred to news that had just arrived of friends in Ohio. Julia Buttles, daughter of an early Ohio settler, married Job Case, also of Worthington and went back there to live.

Dear friend
. . . Noah had a letter this day from his father Griswold. . . . Emily Griswold is taken again with the fever, Nancy Taylor lay at the point of death; Hezekiah Benedict's wife is dead; Henry Willcox had moved down from the forks of Whetstone for fear of the Indians; his wife was taken stone blind, and lay at the point of death. Luther Case's wife sent for the Doctor the day before he wrote—he says that Doctor Wills has more business than he can do—The Indians are getting to be thick very near them; they have come as near as Lewis Settlement on Allum Creek not ten miles from Worthington (3 nights before he wrote, which was August 30th) guns have been fired on both sides but not any of our people killed, it is supposed that one or two of the Indians were killed by the appearance of blood, the days after for there were two different times, and places that they were fired at; but [Ezra?] G. says that our people are in full chase after them, and he believes they will soon be glad to clear out; just as he had finished his letter, news arrived of the defeat of our fleet on the lower lake with the loss of two of our vessels sunk and two taken—"WORSE & WORSE" . . .

Squatters on Indian Land:
A Letter from Benjamin Stickney to
Major General John Gano, 1813

Soon after Cynthia Barker wrote her letter, in October, 1813, Tecumseh was defeated and killed at the Battle of the Thames in Ontario, Canada. After that, the settlers had no more to fear from Indians in Ohio. Many natives left the state. Those who stayed behind were pushed onto reservations. And from then on their reservations were constantly invaded by the surrounding whites. The Indians complained repeatedly to the government of these trespasses but little was done to protect reservation boundaries, and the Indians no longer could protect them by force. It was an old story (see Ensign Armstrong's expedition against the squatters in 1785).

The following letter was written by Benjamin F. Stickney, the United States Indian agent in Fort Wayne, Indiana, to his superior, Major General John S. Gano, Governor of Michigan Territory, Superintendent of Indian Affairs.

Upper Sanduskey Decr. 1813
Sir
Prior to the present war there being no Officer in this part of the country whose proper business it was, to keep the reserves of land made by the Treaty of Greenville for the purpose of managing Indian affairs, clear from intruders, who had become (at Lower Sanduskey) considerably numerous and a Lawless set indeed. In the bustle of the war, this set of people have had great additions to their numbers, and appear to have lost all ideas of Law or equity (if they ever had any.) Possession in their estimation, is as good a title as a Deed, or a bill of sale.

When I arrived, I found that a gathering had commenced here likewise. The Indians complained to me of the settlement upon their lands. When the setlers came to be told that they were intruders, and that their intrusions could not be permitted, they appeared surprised, and took it as an offense. And I find, further, that in consequence of those being permited to remain unmolested, that very considerable arrangements are making by many others to move into the Public Reserves, and into the Indian Country, since now, they are not afraid of the Indians killing them. As the fear of Indian hostility has now ceased in this quarter, something decisive appears to be necessary at this time, to convince those disposed to intrude themselves, that it will not be winked at. . . .

Will you be pleased to order off from Lower Sanduskey all such as you may not consider of immediate utility to the Division of the

Army under your command. By doing so, I think you will be meeting the views of the Gen. Government for I am justified—from Orders I received while at Fort Wayne,—that they wish to keep the Indian Country intirely clear of white setlers.

Since I have acted as an Agent for Indians affairs, I have had more
difficulty with the White Settlers in their interfering with the Indians, and Indian Affairs, than all other difficulties put together. Indeed, it is none but the refuse of society who will intrude themselves
in this manner. . . .

PART THREE

The Passing of the Frontier
1816-1843

The inherent energies and resources of the land will be developed.
—Baltimore American, 1841

After the War of 1812 ended in early 1815, Ohioans returned to the business of populating and taming the wilderness. As settlements turned into cities and forests into farms, a sense of community began to spread over the land. Slowly, people began to leave their isolation in the forest and work and play in groups with their neighbors. The struggle to survive began to give way to the struggle for better conditions.

The state became divided into two cultures. Where the forests still dominated, pioneer life was almost as tough as it always had been. Livvat Böke describes the hardships as late as the 1830s in western Ohio. But in second-generation settlements, such as thriving Cincinnati, urban life took on the trappings of civilization. While Fortescue Cuming could entertain a cabinful of young men with a violin in 1807, Frances Trollope noted that Cincinnatians organized formal balls for young people of quality twenty years later.

By eastern standards Ohio remained crude and backwoodsy, however. Its people were materialistic, opportunistic, usually uneducated, and too sure of the superiority of their kind of democracy. To more sophisticated visitors, such as Trollope, Zerah Hawley and Cyrus P. Bradley, Ohioans often were the objects of amusement and contempt. After all, as everyone noticed, one of the most common sights on city streets in Ohio was an abundance of pigs.

There was no more urgent need for the new state, if it ever was to hold up its head as a civilized place, than improved transportation. Many of the voices in this section complain about the terrible roads. They were hard-packed ruts in dry weather and muck to the hubcaps in wet weather. People's efforts to travel on them sometimes were almost comical. It was not so comical to live on a farm in the hinterlands of Ohio and have no good roads to transport produce to market, however. This drawback hindered the growth of such places as Columbus for years.

In 1822 a canal board was established, and in 1825 a canal fund. On the Fourth of July, 1825, a day celebrated then with more patriotic fervor than it is

Map of Ohio about 1840, showing the canals, the National Road, and
Zane's Trace. Courtesy of the Ohio Geological Survey.

today, work was officially begun on the first canal. It would connect the Ohio
River to Lake Erie via the Scioto, Muskingum, and Cuyahoga Rivers. It was
the canal that Joseph Suppiger and his family, newly arrived from Switzerland,
took from Cleveland to the Ohio River in 1831. The canal system finally vaulted
Ohio from a frontier state to a center of commerce.

Improved roads and the construction of canals sped up immigration into
Ohio, but they also sped up a process that had begun even earlier—the migration further westward. Ohio was the first state of the Old Northwest and the
earliest area to be populated by settlers, but soon it acted as a funnel to the great
beyond—Indiana, Illinois, and points west. Americans never ceased dreaming
of the paradise beyond the rainbow. Many a land speculator was ruined who
ignored the truth that land was only as valuable as the cheapest sod the most

adventurous settlers could bust in the next county or state. As soon as land prices rose in eastern Ohio, brothers and sons moved their families to western Ohio, then to the new states being created further west. While Cincinnati and other towns along the Ohio River were stopping places for all sorts of folk going downstream, the overland migration pattern upstate was fairly predictable. Historians Oscar and Lilian Handlin write in *Liberty in America: 1600 to the Present*: "Migrants followed routes that kept them in contact with the homes they had left, preferring neighbors like themselves. The foreign-born formed their own clusters; and the natives maintained lines of continuity with the places of their origin." New Englanders usually joined their fellow Yankees in the Western Reserve and Firelands in northern Ohio, then swept west across northern Indiana and Illinois. As the large Pennsylvania German families outgrew their acreage in Columbiana County, they moved west into Stark, Portage, or Jefferson Counties and eventually to Indiana and Illinois, often leaving behind family members, like footprints, as they moved across the plains.

Innumerable families were like that of Daniel Lower, an early pioneer settler of Jefferson County, which began to be settled only in 1827. According to a county history, Lower had come to Ohio from Pennsylvania, where he first lived in Columbiana County. After a time he moved on to Jefferson County, but he didn't stay permanently. Finally, with many of his friends and neighbors, he helped populate Wabash County, Indiana. The Thomson brothers, whose letters appear in this section, are another variation on the pattern: some of them stayed in Massachusetts; some emigrated to Ohio and settled down, and some stayed in Ohio only until a better opportunity arose in Indiana.

Ohio was the beginning of this great migration, not the end of the road. It is not an accident that many genealogists in Indiana, Illinois, and Iowa look back to Ohio to trace their roots. Ohio's history made further western settlement possible; and many of its people were the settlers.

The Suppigers were among the early immigrants who came straight to Ohio from Europe, without spending a generation or two east of the Alleghenies first. They joined a recent migration of Germans and Irish who came to farm, work at skilled trades or, in the case of the unskilled Irish, toil as laborers on the canals. It is difficult now to think of these long-assimilated ethnic groups as foreign immigrants, but that's what they were in early nineteenth-century Ohio. Often they joined their countrymen in small ethnic communities, such as the German settlements in Auglaize and Mercer Counties, where Livvat Böke and her family lived. There they could be with people like themselves. More established groups felt free to make fun of their accents, steer them to less desirable jobs, and generally get along with them only as long as they kept their place.

Not surprisingly, African Americans had far more serious problems than other settlers. Ohio had been established as a free state under the Northwest Ordinance of 1787. With its substantial population of Quakers, who had moved

west from Pennsylvania and other eastern states, its tendency was to be an actively anti-slave state. With Kentucky on one border and Virginia (now West
Virginia) on another, and traffic from the Ohio River passing through Cincinnati, Ohio was a center for the Underground Railroad, which spirited escaped
slaves north to Canada. But no escaping slave could count on universal good
will. The law allowed fugitive slaves from slave states to be returned to their
owners. Many whites were sympathetic to slavery or simply were willing to turn
in an escapee for the reward money. William Wells Brown's account of his escape to freedom across Ohio, the suicide of the escaped slave in Cincinnati, and
Cyrus Bradley's encounter with a couple of slave hunters give several sides to
this story.

Ohio also had a population of free blacks from the beginning. There were
4,723 "Free Negroes" listed on the 1820 census. This number grew as job opportunities increased in the growing cities. One of their number was John
Stewart, the zealous missionary among the Wyandots of Upper Sandusky.

Stewart's missionary work represents one strand of a tough religious thread
that runs through the history of Ohio. Religion was such a basic need on the
frontier that, as the preceding sections have shown, clergymen often were the
first arrivals in the new land. And despite the scoffers and drunks that the Reverend Paul Henkel complains of, religion was an essential component of most
pioneers' lives. Except for hardened backwoods reprobates, the pioneers were
firm in their various faiths. Religion also led to quarrels and bigotry, however.
Even the peaceable Quakers almost came to blows, as William Cooper Howells
describes, over the politics of religion. Several degrees of religious enthusiasm
and modes of worship are represented in these pages.

With all the excitement of the land rush to Ohio, where the acreage was
cheap and the possibilities for the good life seemed limitless, there was, however, a reaction to what was called "Ohiomania." John Stillman Wright and Zerah
Hawley both tried to dampen the enthusiasm of their friends and neighbors in
the East for this new land. Hawley wrote that he considered it his "duty to
undeceive the community, respecting a portion of the Western country, which
has been represented as an *earthly Paradise*."

Ohio flourished despite Wright's and Hawley's disclaimers. The forests receded and the towns grew. The wolves and bears that had threatened early settlers disappeared, the squirrels were depopulated. The lands were fenced and
plowed. Newspapers, institutions of higher education, and other elements of
white culture sprang up. By 1837, the first railroad had been laid from Springfield to Sandusky.

In the meantime, however, the original inhabitants shrank in population
and receded from the land. By 1818 the Indians' remaining lands were mere
reservations. In the 1820s, many individuals and families slipped away from an
Ohio they no longer knew. By 1825 only some 2,350 Native Americans were

left in Ohio from the Shawnee, Seneca, Wyandot, Ottawa, and Delaware tribes. In 1826, 250 Senecas and Shawnees, including Tecumseh's brother and son, left their Wapakoneta reservation for Kansas. In 1829, the Delawares gave up their last tract of land and moved west. Pressure mounted on the Wyandots of Upper Sandusky to do the same. They held out until 1843. When they were gone, no Indian tribes remained in Ohio.

Interestingly, as they disappeared, the attitudes of white people toward them changed. First, whites ceased to be frightened by the Indians. Then the sight of Native Americans became rare enough that they were regarded as colorful tokens of the past. In short, they were sentimentalized. By the time the Wyandots left Ohio, the white townspeople who watched them leave felt them to be symbols of a passing era, as indeed they were.

The Hard Life of the Small Farmer: Recollections of William Cooper Howells

William Cooper Howells, the father of novelist William Dean Howells, came to Ohio in 1813 at age five. His father was a Quaker who lost that faith soon after he came to Ohio, and then became an enthusiastic Methodist. William Cooper's father never was a good provider. First the family lived in Mount Pleasant, a Quaker community. Then they moved near Steubenville. The elder Howells bought or leased small farms in the vicinity, and commuted to work in the woolen mill at Steubenville. William Cooper attended school only for a short time, and otherwise was tutored at home by his mother. The family's life demanded that he work from an early age around the farm.

William Cooper Howells wrote his memoirs in the 1870s. They are noteworthy for describing the independence, dangers, responsibilities, and pleasures of childhood on an early Ohio farm. Despite the risks, childhood offered good times and wonderful memories to carry into old age.

Among the glories of the place I remember unlimited crops of peaches that, at that period, grew to great perfection in the new soil of the country. . . . These orchards were set with apple trees as the principal crop, but the rows were interalternated with peach trees, which grew more rapidly and were expected to die out by the time the apple trees came into good bearing. At this time the peaches had reached their prime, and almost every year they bore abundant crops, of which any one could gather for the asking. Cherries were of slower growth, and had not come forward every-where, but they were planted along the fences on the roads and soon became common property. Besides these there were wild plums, grapes and nuts, that helped to make the country charming to a boy.

The Quaker meeting house in Mt. Pleasant, Jefferson County.

As a less agreeable incident of our life there, I remember my sister getting her arm broken, with great risk of being killed. They were hauling timber for our new building, dragging one end of the log on the ground, while the other rested on the wagon. She got on the log to ride, and falling off, was drawn under it, and was saved from death by father's lifting the log as it passed over her. . . .

After father left for Steubenville he would remain there about two weeks at a time, coming home each fortnight. The distance was twenty-one miles—seven to Warren, on the bank of the river, and fourteen up the bank from that point. The day he was first to return, I was started off very early to meet him with a horse, which he and I were to ride back. I was a little over nine years old; the horse was much older, and safely lazy. It was a great enterprise for me, and my directions were to go fourteen miles of the way, which brought me to Wellsville (then Charleston), where I was to wait for father at the tavern and ferry house. The people here happened to know him, and treated me very kindly and talked encouragingly. I waited until afternoon and then began to grow very uneasy. I fretted, and looked up the road till two o'clock, and then got out the horse and went a mile or so up the river bank, where the hill and rocks came down almost to the water, and it was then gloomy and wild enough to add much to my perturbed state of mind. But he was not in sight as I looked wistfully through my tears, and in my despair I concluded father would not come that day and started back, taking a hearty cry as I passed back along that narrow road, lined on each side with paw-paw thickets, where I had the whole forest to cry in by myself. I jogged on home alone (with many a long look behind me), and arrived at dark. I had hardly got fairly housed and eaten my supper, when father came, having walked the whole way. Had I been told properly to wait at the tavern till he came, and that it would be late, I should have managed well enough. The Monday following I went with him about the same distance and returned alone very well. . . .

One of our great sports in the street, at that time, was bon-fires made of shavings from the new houses building. To add to the excitement some boys were engaged to gather a great quantity, that is to say, sundry hatfuls of buckeyes—wild horse chestnuts—that grew in great abundance along the river. These were saved up till Saturday, when the carpenters would throw out the rubbish for the bon-fire. When the fire was nearly burned down, and the flame began to lose its splendor, the buckeyes were thrown into it by the boys who surrounded the fire, when, as they became hot there was a gas generated in them that exploded them with a report like a pistol; and thus a fusilade would be kept up as long as the supply lasted; after which sticks and stones would be thrown into the coals to brighten them up. It was wonderful what a crowd of boys would gather, and how little mischief would be done.

The Howellses bought a twenty-five acre farm in 1818 and moved into one of the cabins on it that winter.

Father got some repairs done on the one we were to occupy, so as to make it a little more habitable, by the addition of glass windows; for it had previously been lighted by leaving the door open in addition to a four-light window with greased paper for glass, and the opening of the great chimney at the end of the single room, down which the daylight flowed in goodly quantity. . . . A very common event was for these chimneys to take fire, in which case it was necessary to use water bountifully or pull them down. Ours had so settled away from the house that we steadily expected it to pull itself down. But like the tower of Pisa it stood against all the gravity that affected it, I suppose, till the house went also. The repairs delayed our moving till after New Year's, 1819. . . .

This was the period when steamboats were beginning to take their place in the navigation of the Ohio, and when the stream was full they made occasional trips up and down the river. Their appearance would create a great excitement along the banks, and at the towns and villages their arrival and landing were great occasions. The citizens turned out, and civic ceremonies were observed between those in command of the boat and those in command of the town. At Steubenville they had a little cannon, with which they always fired salutes on these occasions. . . .

In the spring of 1821, my uncle Powell left Mingo Bottom to settle in Coshocton county, on the Tuscarawas river, near White Eyes Plains, then a wild and only partially settled country. He was not able to buy land, but took a lease of a tract for seven years, the conditions of which were, that he was to reduce the land to cultivation and have the produce for his compensation—the quantity of land that he should clear being a matter of his own choice. The occasion of their family's moving was an event for me, particularly as I was engaged to assist in driving their farm stock a part of the way. . . .

We worked along till night, when we put up, about seven miles from the starting point. We stopped at a tavern, as was then the custom, only hiring the use of one room, on the first floor, known as the movers' room, and the privilege of the fire to make tea or coffee or fry bacon. It was very much like camping out, and, except that we were housed, was soldiers' quarters. This night two of the horses were taken with homesickness and, as they were not well secured, went back to the old place. The wagoner started after them at daylight, but it was noon before they were brought back, after which the line of march was taken up. This was Sunday, and though they were very strict about the Sabbath in that Presbyterian country, movers were tolerated in traveling on that day from an admitted necessity. . . .

The next day we got along pretty well and reached Cadiz, in Harrison county, about three o'clock; and here they concluded to let me return with Paddy [the horse].

By this time the Howells family had left the first farm and leased a second, closer to Steubenville.

Our new place suited father better than the other place, as he could come home almost any evening from his business in the town, whilst it enabled him to go with the family every Sunday to meeting.

Among the Methodists at that time there was a very steady suc-

cession of meetings of one kind or another, and those who belonged
to the church found abundant entertainment, if nothing else, in the
continual round of preaching, class and prayer meetings. There were
then very few public entertainments, and religious meetings took
the place of these for nearly all the people. A consequence of this
was, that meetings were carried to an extreme, and religious enthusiasm and extravagant experiences were cultivated at the expense of
propriety. There was a class of people who really made a dissipation
of their religion, and were never satisfied unless going through the
most powerfully agitating experiences.

In 1825 the family moved once again, this time to a farm they bought in Harrison
County. Howells was eighteen years old.

Where the country had only been a few years settled, and where the
farms were still being opened up, the families were mostly young;
that is, the children nearly all in their minority, so that the farmer
himself and one or two big boys made up the laboring strength of
the farm; and for an extra lift at any time, the wife or older daughter
would be called on to help, and sometimes they would assist in planting and hoeing the corn, raking the grain or hay in harvest. The rule
was, that whoever had the strength to work took hold and helped. If
the family was mostly girls, they regularly helped their father in all
the lighter farm work.

Once again the family gave up the farm, which never did well, and this time
moved to Wheeling. Young Howells went to Mount Pleasant, looking for a job
in a Quaker-run printing office. There was no job, but the town was full of
trouble as the Quakers were splitting into two factions.

The Yearly meeting of the Quakers was in session. The sect had not
yet divided, and they had endeavored to ignore the fact that they
were composed of two irreconcilable parties, and go on together, each,
however, striving for the ascendency. When they came to organize
the meeting by the election of a Clerk, who is the presiding officer,
and who really controls the proceedings if he will, the two factions
came into collision, and a strife ensued, which, with any body but
Quakers, would have been a fight. Instead of striking, they gave vent
to their passions, and sought to conquer by pushing and jamming
each other as they pressed towards the Clerk's table with their re-
spective candidates. In this way some of them got pretty badly hurt,
and Jonathan Taylor, the [Elisha] Bates, or Orthodox candidate for

Clerk was nearly killed by being jammed against and under the table. The accident broke up the meeting, and to this day it is not known which candidate was chosen. . . . After this farce, the Society of Friends were two societies.

Howells lived to the age of 87, always earning a precarious living, sometimes as a printer, a publisher, a house painter, and even a small farmer like his father. His son, William Dean Howells, finished his memoirs for him.

John Stewart and James Finley Preach to the Wyandots: A Memoir by William Walker, and the Reverend James Finley's Accounts of the Upper Sandusky Mission, 1816-1825

According to the tiny book of memoirs published after his death, John Stewart was a free man, the child of free blacks from Virginia. On his way to Marietta in the teens, Stewart was robbed of everything he owned. In despair, he tried to drink himself to death, but was stopped by his Marietta landlord, who refused to serve him more liquor. Finally, Stewart found God, then Methodism, and set off from Marietta to preach among the Indians. He arrived at Pipetown, a Wyandot village on the Sandusky River, in 1816. There he met William Walker, an Indian sub-agent, who befriended him and later collected Stewart's memoirs, which were published in 1827. Stewart never learned the Wyandot language and never became a full-fledged Methodist minister, but clearly he had a profound, and controversial, effect on the Wyandots.

The Reverend James Finley was a fiery Methodist circuit-riding minister in an age of evangelism. As a young man he had been converted at a revival meeting, and he in turn converted others. In 1819 the Methodist Church voted to send a missionary to the Wyandots at Upper Sandusky. Finley was in charge of the effort and eventually was designated the superintendent of the mission, where he continued the work Stewart had begun.

The doctrine of repentance was not well received by Jonathan [Pointer], (who at this time and afterwards acted as Stewart's interpreter,) and supposing as he did, that the congregation would be of the same mind, he would sometimes, whilst interpreting, after stating the substance of Stewart's discourse, add and say, "so he say, I do not know whether it is so or not, nor do I care; all I care about is to interpret faithfully what he says, to you; you must not think that I care whether you believe it or not. . . ."

A few white traders who had been permitted by the Officers of the Indian department to settle amongst and trade with the Indians having heard Stewart preach, either from a real suspicion which they entertained that he was a runaway slave and an imposter, or from malicious principles, advised the Indians to drive him out the country; stating that he was not a licensed preacher; but a runaway slave, a villain, &c. and that he had only come among them for protection. This was readily believed by many. . . .

At a certain meeting, Stewart, in the course of his sermon, made some pointed remarks against their old system of heathenism, and added, that instead of their mode of worship being pleasing to the Lord, it was on the contrary, displeasing to him, and that although in the time of their ignorance, God winked at their conduct; yet now, the gospel having reached them, and in such a manner as to be understood by them, they were all required to repent. At the close of this discourse, he informed the congregation that if any one present had any objection to his doctrines, they were then at liberty to speak. Whereupon, John Hicks, one of the chiefs, arose and spoke as follows, ". . . I, for one, feel myself called upon to rise in defence of the religion of my fathers;—a system of religion the Great Spirit has given his red children, as their guide and the rule of their faith, and we are not going to abandon it so soon as you might wish; we are contented with it, because it suits our conditions and is adapted to our capacities. Cast your eyes abroad over the world, and see how many different systems of religion there are in it—there are almost as many different systems as there are nations—say this is not the work of the Lord. No, my friend, your declaiming so violently against our modes of worshipping the Great Spirit, is in my opinion, not calculated to benefit us as a nation; we are willing to receive good advice from you, but we are not willing to have the customs and institutions which have been kept sacred by our Fathers, thus assailed and abused."

Whereupon Manoncue [Mononcue], another chief, arose and said, ". . . I do not doubt but what you state faithfully what your book says; but let me correct an error into which you appear to have run, and that is, your belief that the Great Spirit designed that his red children should be instructed out of it. This is a mistake, the Great Spirit never designed this to be the case; he never intended that they should be instructed out of a book, a thing which properly belongs to those who made it and can understand what it says; it's a plant that cannot grow and flourish among red people. Let me call your attention to another important fact.—Where did the Son of God first make his appearance? According to your book he first made his appearance away in the East, among the white people. . . . The Son of God came among the white people and preached to them, and left his words written in a book, that they when he was gone, might read and learn his will concerning them; but he left no book for Indians, and why should he, seeing we red people know nothing about books? If it had been the will of the Great Spirit that we should be instructed out of this book, he would have provided some way for us to understand the art of making and reading the books that contain his words. Ours is a religion that suits us red people, and we intend to keep and preserve it sacred among us, believing that the Great Spirit gave it to our grand-fathers in ancient days. . . ."

One thing is here worthy of remark, and that is, that not a single instance occurred during the time Stewart laboured among them, of their treating his per[s]on with any indignity or violence. Notwithstanding his doctrine was so offensive to many of them, yet in his intercourse with them, he was always treated in a friendly and decorous manner. . . .

They were a very intemperate people, so much so, that on actual investigation, not twenty really sober men could be found in the whole nation, which consisted of about seven hundred, young and old. Stewart's preaching produced a reformation in regard to this particular vice; drunkenness seemed to have flown from their border, and many other vicious practices were abandoned. . . .

Stewart had to go to Marietta in the late winter of 1817. He returned the following summer. Once again he experienced opposition, especially from Chiefs Mononcue and Two Logs.

Summer was with them, a season of amusement and great happiness. Feasts, dances, ball-plays, foot-races, horse-races, &c. were their chief delight, and it will not be wondered at, that they should with great reluctance give up the things which afforded them so much pleasure. . . .

Two Logs began a general argument about Stewart's ideas of proper behavior versus the Indians'. Stewart tried to support his view by quoting a poet declaiming against dancing and frolic.

> Now Hail! all hail! ye frightful ghosts,
> With whom I once did dwell,

> And spent my days in frantic mirth,
> And danced my soul to hell.

At this Two Logs raised a great hoarse laugh, and inquired whether the persons who made those bitter lamentations were Indians, and added "I do not believe the Great Spirit will punish his red children for dancing, feasting, &c. yet I cannot say that he will not punish white people for doing these things; for to me it looks quite probable the Great Spirit has forbidden these things among the whites, because they are naturally wicked, quarrelsome and contentious; for it is a truth they cannot deny, that they cannot have a dance, a feast, or any public amusement, but some will get drunk, quarrel, fight, or do something wrong. Now, my friend, you have been present at several of our dances and feasts, and did you see any of these bad things going on? No, we have our public amusements in peace and good will to each other, and part in the same manner. Now, where is the great evil you see?!" It is not known what Stewart's reply was.

Two Logs would sometimes tell the people, it was really derogatory to their character, to have it said, *that they had a Negro for their preacher*, as that race of people was always considered inferior to Indians. "The Great Spirit," said he, "never created Negroes, they were created by the Evil Spirit. . . ."

However, other preachers arrived to help out, including Moses Henkle, Sr., and James B. Finley. Considering that "much good seed had been sown by the preaching of Stewart," they made great progress among the Wyandots. Finley officially established the Methodist mission there and built the mission church in 1824. Mononcue, Two Logs, and John Hicks, among others, were converted. In 1823, at age 37, Stewart took ill and died at the mission.

This was a period when Christianity was being attacked by traditionalist Indians as a threat to Indian culture. The Reverend Finley told the following story of one of his attempts to preach in 1822.

The head chief, De-un-quot, and his party, at one time, came on Sabbath to the council-house, where we held our meetings, dressed up and painted in real savage Indian style, with their head bands filled with silver bobs, their head-dress consisting of feathers and painted horse hair. The chief had a half moon of silver on his neck before, and several hanging on his back. He had nose-jewels and earrings, and many bands of silver on his arms and legs. Around his ankles hung many buck-hoofs, to rattle when he walked. His party were dressed in a similar style. The likenesses of animals were painted on their breasts and backs, and snakes on their arms. . . .

After the sermon, De-un-quot rose and said that while the sermon was not bad, it had nothing to do with Indians. And he told a parable proving that Indian magic was more powerful than white religion. Finley responded.

"[Y]our being a red man, and I a white man, is no argument at all that there are two Gods. And I again say, that this book is true in what it states of man having a bad heart, and being wicked; and that my friend has a proud heart, is evident from his dress, and painting himself. God made me white, and that man [Pointer, the interpreter] black. We are contented. But my friend does not think the Great Spirit has made him pretty enough—he must put on his paint to make himself look better. This is a plain proof that he is a proud man, and has an evil heart."

Finley wrote that he never again was troubled during one of his sermons by the traditionalist Indians.

Although most Indians had kept their tradition of subsistence farming supplemented by seasonal hunting, with the disappearance of their hunting grounds they were more and more aware they had to change their lifestyle in order to survive in the new order, as Finley wrote.

The Indians turned their attention, this spring, to the improvement of their farms, and to the building of comfortable houses. A number of hewed log-houses were put up, with brick or stone chimneys; and great exertions were made to inclose large fields, for raising grain and grass. Many purchased sheep; and means were taken to improve their breed of cattle and hogs. With the means in their hands, I believe they did do all they could to provide for the future, without following the chase; for they clearly saw that the vast influx of white population would soon fill up all their hunting-ground; and that they must starve, unless they could procure the means of living at home. The mission furnished all the means in its power to facilitate this good work. Their wagons, oxen, plows, and all that could be spared, were lent freely; and the missionaries themselves took all the pains they could, to show them the best methods of cultivation. They even went in person to house-raisings, and log-rollings, and took hold and said, *"Come on, my friends."*

In 1825, the government, under the pressure of white expansion and greed for the last remaining Indian land in Ohio, began to talk of moving the Indians west of the Mississippi River. Finley opposed the idea, and wrote the following letter to Lewis Cass, the U.S. government's spokesman for the Wyandots.

HONORED SIR,—I take this opportunity of writing to you on the claims of the Indians under my care, at this place; and am happy to state that the work of civilizing this nation is progressing as fast as can be reasonably expected. . . . In making these people an agricultural people, it is to be hoped that all the necessary aid, both in money and advice, will be furnished. And, I think, it will not be doubted or disputed that this handful of Indians have great and lasting claims on this Government.

1. As a conquered, subdued enemy, who were once a strong and powerful nation, to whom the pleasant homes we now enjoy once belonged, they have strong claims on our generosity. They contended for their country—as we would have done had we been in their places—as long as they could. But the overwhelming population of whites has well-nigh swallowed them up. They have given up their whole country, except a small reserve, on which the bones of their fathers sleep. This they would never have done willingly, but because they could not help themselves; and it would seem as though we were making a contract with them, but they must submit to our proposition in view of their helpless, forlorn, and dependent state. In view of what they have been, they possess some strong claims.

2. Since Wayne's treaty at Greenville, the Wyandotts have been faithful friends to our Government; and, in the last war, did their part in resisting, as agents, the combined power of Indian and British warfare. Many of their men fell in battle, or died with sickness, and left their families and friends destitute.

3. They have claims from this consideration, 'Blessed are the merciful, for they shall obtain mercy.' The Wyandotts, although not behind the first in battle, were more merciful than their neighbors. They saved more prisoners, and purchased many from other Indians, and adopted them into their families, till they are much mixed with white blood; and some of the best families in our country are allied to them; namely, the Browns, an old Virginia family; the Zanes, another well-known family; Walker, of Tennessee; Williams, Armstrong, M'Cullough, and Magee, of Pittsburg. This handful of Indians are mostly the descendants of our own people. Their fathers were citizens, and why not their children? Shall we not show mercy to our own?

4. Their present prospect for civilization is very promising; and little doubt can be entertained but, in a short time, these people will

be well prepared to be admitted as citizens of the state of Ohio; and
to remove them just at this time, contrary to their wishes, would be,
in my judgment, a most cruel act. It would be undoing what has
been done, and throwing them again into a savage state.

5. The promises made by the commissioners, in the name and
faith of the President and Government, that if they would cede all
their fertile lands but this spot, the Government would never ask
them for a foot more, or to sell it and move; but that the Government would build a strong fence around their land, which should
never be broken; and this promise was one strong inducement to
them to sell their lands. Such strongly-plighted faith ought to be most
sacredly observed.

My dear sir, these are some of the reasons why I think these Indians have strong claims on the Government. I have done as you requested. I have spoken fully and freely my mind. May the blessings
of Heaven rest upon you and your labors for the good of the red man!

"Ohiomania": John Stillman Wright's
Cautionary Tale, 1818

John Stillman Wright was just one of many Easterners struck with "Ohiomania,"
the overpowering desire to sell up and move west where the climate was better,
the land cheaper, and the opportunities limitless. He sold his land near Saratoga,
New York, and went to Ohio in December, 1818, to reconnoiter and buy a
farm. But the scales fell from his eyes while he was there, and he wrote his
book, Letters from the West, from a duty to warn others: "Should this warning be
the means of saving one family, from the cruel disappointment and vain regret,
which so many thousands are now enduring, the work which I intrude on the
public will not have been written in vain."

Cincinnati, Jan. 6, 1819
. . . In certain parts of this country, there are poisonous roots or
weeds, which frequently kill the cattle that eat much of any of them:
and should a hog, dog or wolf, make a feast of the carcase, it inevitably proves his last. Poisoned milk, too, is quite common, of which,
if people eat they sicken immediately, and will need medical aid before they are restored to health. Another of the evils of the "garden
of the world," is what is termed sick wheat: This is most frequently
found on the rich bottom lands, and is supposed to be owing to the
fogs, which often prevail there. It is only to be distinguished, while

growing, by the fuzzy end of the berry containing a small red speck: in all other respects, it appears like healthy wheat: it is said to be certain death to any creature that eats of it: consequently, whenever a crop is found to be infected, the whole must be destroyed. While on the subject of poisons, I will mention snakes, which are rather numerous; especially the copper-head and rattle snake, which annoy the happy inhabitants of this *terrestial paradise*. . . .

Wherever, in my tours, I saw a situation that was desirable, I was naturally led to inquire for the owner: the answer was almost invariably the same: it is the property of the capitalist, the speculator, the resident of some adjacent village or large town, and cannot be had at a fair price: if there is even a lot of wild land worthy the attention of the farmer, depend upon it the speculator has his clutch upon it, and you cannot buy it short of, perhaps, three times the government price. . . .

Zanesville, Muskingum Co. Ohio, March 2d, 1819.

. . . The number of my weary steps has, in all my rambles, been much augmented by the difficulty of keeping the direct road: this difficulty, sufficiently perplexing in the inhabited country, is painfully increased in the woods, where, if a tree happens to fall aross the road, no one thinks of disturbing it: . . . To add to his distress, he cannot find one person in five who can direct him three miles from their own doors; nay, more, I have met with numbers, who could not tell me the name of the county or town they lived in, or even that of the Governor of the state. . . .

I have more than once mentioned the ancient mounds, but neglected to describe one, which is entitled to particular notice. Circleville, a town on the Sciota, Pickaway Co. Ohio, is enclosed with two circular walls of earth, about sixteen feet apart, perhaps twenty feet at the base and ten in height: the open space contains about four acres of ground: there is no appearance of the earth having been removed, within or without the walls; But between them it is somewhat depressed; a circular mound once stood in the centre which is now removed, and a Court-house erected on the spot. Adjoining the circle on the east, is what might be termed a fort; it is square, larger than the circle, with gateways at each corner, and two mounds within the square on the east side: the whole bears marks of design and skill. . . .

Cleveland, March 10th, 1819.

. . . These countries, collectively, have been long and loudly extolled, as exeeding all others, in point of soil and natural productions, and in a limited sense, perhaps, the boast is not altogether

false; for if any reliance can be placed in my judgment, many, very
many thousand acres of river bottom land, equal, if not surpass, the
best lands in the state of New-York. These bottoms, in their natural
state send forth an astonishing growth of vegetation; and when cultivated as they should be, generously repay the hand that tills them.
. . . The soil of the upland, is almost every where the same, consisting of a whitish clay mixed sometimes with gravel, though usually
with sand, insomuch, that when brick are wanted, they generally
find the materials as completely mixed as the most skilful brickmaker
could desire. This mixture, however, is very inconvenient to the
farmer; if the season is a little too wet his lands are a bed of mortar,
if too dry it is so baked as to be almost impenetrable. . . .

Its waters are almost universally impregnated with lime, more or
less; its taste is extremely unpleasant, and its effects are almost always felt by the new settlers, especially among the little ones; it
usually produces a dysentery which sweeps away the poor innocents
by hundreds, before they have been a year in the country. . . . I now
add, that *generally,* where the land is best, there the water is worst.
. . . One of the bad effects, perhaps the most pernicious, of the insalubrity of the water, is, that it forms an apology for drinking ardent
spirits, commonly whiskey; . . . the demand for it is so steady that if
a person wants only half a barrel he must bespeak it some time before it is called for. . . .

Cleveland, March 16th, 1819.
. . . One may travel here an hundred miles without finding a bridge:
a school-house is rarely to be seen; a church more seldom still. . . .
Although every county has its *seat of justice,* as they are termed,
yet people, most frequently, depend on their own personal powers,
for the redress of their real or imaginary grievances. . . .

[A]fter reviewing every circumstance on both sides of the question, I have no hesitation in saying, that I would rather have a con-
veniently situated farm in one of the New-England states, or in New-
York, than almost any that could be offered in the south western
country. . . .

Wright actually liked some of the land in Portage County, although it was
swampy and cut up by lakes, and he felt a kinship with the people of the Western Reserve, "an industrious, enterprising people." His last days in Cleveland
were delightful and restored his spirits. However, he hastened back to the state
of New York, where he found land near Chatauqua and extolled its virtues.

An English Farmer Follows his Curiosity:
William Faux's Memorable Days
Traveling in Ohio, 1819

William Faux called himself a farmer. He traveled to America to visit the Birkbeck settlement in Illinois and to figure out why so many of his country-men were emigrating to the New World. He arrived in Ohio from Wheeling in October, 1819.

At four this morning, on the driver getting down to lock the wheel, the horses started, and instantly struck a stump of a tree, and upset the mail with a crashing fall, which bruised my side, cut my face, and blackened my eyes; the two leaders escaped into the forest, and we saw them no more. The driver went in pursuit of them, and left me to guard and sleep one hour and a half in the damaged vehicle, now nearly bottom upwards. When I awoke it was daylight, and I walked up to a farm log-house, the people of which put their heads out of the window and thus addressed me,—"Stranger come *into* the fire!" and I went in, without being burned. At five, the driver re-turned, and with two horses only, we got under weigh, and moved on through Cambridge and Washington to breakfast, and at sun-set reached our inn at Zainsville, where I determined on resting a few days to repair the damages of the past day. . . .

[October] *14* [1819]. . . . I wandered in the fields shooting pigeons, which is here fine sport; they fly and alight around you on every tree, in immense flocks, and loving to be shot. They are rather smaller than English pigeons, and have a lilac breast; but in other respects are blue, or blue grey. They breed in the woods, and seem to court death by the gun, the sound of which appears to call them together, instead of scaring them away; a fowling-piece well charged with dust shot might bring down a bushel of these willing game dead at your feet.

Sunday, 17th—At Chilicothé to breakfast, where I rest for the day and night. This town is situated on the beautiful Sciota river, in a rich valley of plantations. Its population is 3,000, and its age 20 years. Many houses and town cots are deserted for migration further west. The American has always something better in his eye, further west. . . .

18th—. . . . Six miles west of Chilicothé, the land is remarkably rich. Here I met and passed General M'Carty[1] to whom my friend

---

1. General Duncan McArthur, 1772-1839 (see p. 122, n. 9). His "seat" was called Fruit Hill, not far from Thomas Worthington's house, Adena.

nodded and said, "How do, General." The General looks dirty and butcher-like, and very unlike a soldier in appearance, seeming half savage, and dressed as a back-woodsman. . . . We passed his seat, very little bigger and no better than my kitchen at Somersham. . . .

19th— . . . . I now pass many farm log-houses along the road; miserable holes, having one room only, and in that one miserable room, all cook, eat, sleep, breed, and die, males and females, all together. . . .

An Unhappy Visitor: Zerah Hawley Travels from Old to New Connecticut, 1820-1821

Dr. Zerah Hawley traveled to the Western Reserve from his home in Connecticut late in 1820 and worked there for a year as a doctor. He was not a happy visitor. The following year he published the letters he had written to his brothers out of a "duty," as he explained it, "to undeceive the community, respecting a portion of the Western country, which has been represented as an earthly Paradise." He complained of the muddy roads, the ignorant inhabitants, the wretched living conditions, the poor soil, and even weather so changeable it couldn't be forecasted. Like John Stillman Wright, Hawley liked almost nothing of what he saw. In some places, his description of the drawbacks of Ohio is so similar to Wright's he may have used him as a source. Hawley arrived by way of Erie, Pennsylvania, crossing the state line near Salem and Ashtabula.

Sept. 30 [1820]—Crossed the State line and entered Ohio, the *fabled region* of the West. I say *fabled region*, because more, much more has been said about the State, than has any foundation in truth. . . .

I was much disappointed upon my arrival in this State, to find it so much more thinly settled, than from all accounts I had heard, I had reason to expect, and to discover so few marks of wealth, and so frequent and great appearances of poverty and distress.

Austinburgh, Oct. 1st. 1820

DEAR BROTHER,

I arrived in this part of the country the last day of September. This day rode to Harpersfield to see a sick woman, through the woods about a mile; the road so bad in consequence of the abundance of stumps, roots and mud, that I could ride only upon a slow walk; and entered for the first time in my life into a log-house with one room without any fire-place, the log being laid against the logs of the house and the fire built in front.

In consequence of this manner of building the fire, some of the logs were entirely burnt in two, and many were much injured by the fire. The furniture of the house consisted of a bed, laid upon a bedsted made of saplings of suitable size, (having bark on) with holes bored to receive the legs which were made of the same materials.—Three or four indifferent chairs, a chest or two, a few articles of hollow ware, two or three shelves made by boring holes into the logs of the house, into which were inserted pins of wood upon which rough boards were laid, forming the whole pantry of the house, containing a few articles of crockery. . . . A large hole through the roof, answered the two-fold purpose of a vent for the smoke, and the admission of light. The house was also lighted and ventilated by many large cracks or spaces between the logs, which in winter are sometimes filled with clay, and many times are left without filling through the year, for the purpose (perhaps) of preventing pestilential diseases, as in many cases little pains is taken to keep their habitations cleanly, and in all it is utterly impossible that neatness should exist in consequence of the continual falling of clay from the crevices between the logs, and of bark with which the roof is in many instances covered, and the constant accumulation of mud which is brought into the only room in the house in great profusion. . . .

October 7.—Rode to a part of H[arpersfiel]d, to see a child sick of the intermittent fever, whose parents with two children, lived in what is here called a *Shanty*. This is a hovel of about ten feet by eight, made somewhat in the form of an ordinary cow-house, having but an half roof, or roof on one side. It is however, inclosed on all sides. . . .

October 25.—. . . On the 20th I was called from A[ustinbur]g to R—g, to see a man who had been much injured by a limb falling from a height of about seventy feet, directly upon the top of his head, and who it was feared would die before I should have an opportunity to see him. The messenger urged me forward, and I came very near breaking my own neck, by riding a dark night in full speed through one of the worst roads in this country. I bled the man, and examined his head and found it most awfully fractured.

Next morning assisted in trepanning the patient above-mentioned, removed *forty-six* pieces of bone, and found the membranes inclosing the brain perforated by the small fragments of the bone in many places. The man died two days after the operation, having been insensible from the time the accident happened. . . .

On the whole there is no difficulty in procuring enough to eat, if people are industrious; but in many towns here, industry is not so much the order of the day, as it is generally in the Eastern States. . . .

Geneva, (Ohio) Dec. 5th, 1820.

DEAR BROTHER,

. . . In New-England and the Atlantic States generally, a person can, with a good degree of certainty, prognosticate from certain appearances, what kind of weather may be expected for a day or two, or perhaps a week, as when the sun sets clear, we foretel with confidence, that the next day will be fair, if it sets clear with a red atmosphere, that the succeeding day will be fair and warm, &c. but here there are no appearances in the least to be depended upon. . . .

The weather here very frequently changes from fair and warm to cloudy and cold, in the space of two hours, then within another hour it will rain, hail, snow and blow a tremendous gale, which will last perhaps for fifteen minutes, and then die away, the sun will make his appearance with considerable warmth, and every prospect of fine weather; but instead of this, in a few minutes, rain, hail, and snow, with tremendous wind, succeeds, and the changes will many times take place from six to twelve times in the twenty-four hours. . . .

The climate is not the only thing respecting this part of the country, about which people are deceived. They are told that the society is *good*: "As good," say those who are interested in the assertion, "as in any of the country towns in the New-England States." Nothing can be more untrue than this assertion. . . . Excepting a few respectable families, the society is such as is considered the most indifferent in the Eastern States, being ignorant, unpolished, and extremely anxious to pry into the concerns of others with whom they have no business, but merely to gratify curiosity. . . .

[Geneva, February 1, 1821.]

I will give you a description of the dress of the females in this part of the country. It is of necessity almost all home-spun, and comfortable enough; (when whole) which is not too frequently the case, but the fashion thereof is very ancient, similar to the fashion of our grandmothers. . . .

The men generally dress in home-spun cloth, and in many cases appear quite decent on days of exhibition; but their every day wardrobe is most miserably deficient. It is much the custom here to overlay pantaloons on the seat and the inside and front of the legs with sheep-skin. Some wear a semi-leathern apron ending in half legs, covering the fore part of the legs, and fastened behind by leathern straps and buttons.

Some females, sixty years old or more, wear their hair platted, and depending behind, very much in the manner of the Chinese gentlemen. . . .

Others who are very gray, comb the hair in front from one side to the other perfectly smooth. Many of the young females twist the hair, and fasten it on the top of the head with nicely polished brass combs, and others, for the want of these or any other combs, dock the hair square behind, leaving it about six inches long, which gives them a very uncouth and forbiding appearance. . . .

A small part of the community, both male and female, dress with some good degree of taste and neatness. . . .

[Wrightsburg, February 5, 1821.]

. . . In general, the manners of the inhabitants are very rude and uncultivated. To this remark there are a few exceptions, though not numerous. . . .

Whether they do not know enough to think it is proper to take off their hats when they enter an house, or suppose that the head is the most convenient place to hang their hats, is not for me to determine. . . .

When persons have got within the door, it is common for them to stand as near it as they can, till they are invited forward, staring wildly upon every article in the house, some, especially of the children, turning quite round to see if there is nothing behind them which they have not already discovered. . . .

When females enter a room, it is in much the same manner, frequently coming in without knocking, especially on the Sabbath after meeting, when half a dozen come in upon you without any previous notice, or being bid to enter, huddling in and standing behind each other, till you have time to dispose of them in some orderly manner. They have the same stare of astonishment as the male part of the community. . . .

These manners and customs, perhaps you will say, are innocent and harmless, as they do not affect the morals of the people. To this I agree; but there are others not so free from censure. One custom in particular I shall mention, which cannot be denied or excused, which is very indelicate, and has a very demoralizing tendency. It is this. Sleeping *promiscuously* in one room. In almost every house, parents and children, brothers and sisters, brothers and sisters-in-law, strangers and neighbours, married and unmarried, all ages, sexes and conditions, lodge in the same room, without any thing to screen them from the view of each other. . . . And this is done in some cases which I could particularize, where there is not the least shadow of necessity. . . .

[Jefferson, April 10, 1821.]

. . . Schools in this part of the country are taught, (if kept up at all,) by females about three months for the Summer term, who teach merely the rudiments of reading, writing and plain sewing. In many cases these schools are not taught more than eight weeks, and some not more than six, and compensation for teaching is made in almost all cases in such articles as the country affords, and not in money, so that teachers of much erudition, cannot be prevailed upon to undertake the business of teaching the rising generation.

In the winter term, men teach the same branches as are taught by the females in the summer, with the addition of a little Arithmetic, and the exclusion of sewing during about three months.

From this method of teaching, and the short time the Schools are kept, and the long intervals that intervene between the terms, it will readily be conceived, that the children forget nearly as much as they learn, and it is very common to meet with young men and women, who cannot read, better than children in Connecticut, of six years of age, and even with less propriety than some with which I am acquainted. . . .

It may farther be remarked that many families are without the Word of God, and are groping in almost Heathenish darkness, and are unable to procure the Word of Life to make them wise unto Salvation. This is not all; at least eleven months in twelve, the great body of the people have no better oral instruction, than what they receive, from the most uninformed and fanatical methodist Preachers, who are the most extravagant Ranters, of which any one can form an idea, who bawl forth one of their incoherent rhapsodies in one township in the morning, in another township in the afternoon, and a third in a third place in the evening. Thus they run through the country, "leading captive at their will, silly women," and men equally unwise.

. . . The future prospect respecting Literature, Population, and Religion, is very unpromising. There appears to be no reason to suppose, that either will improve or increase much for a long time yet to come.

Emigrations to this part of the country are almost entirely at an end, or at least at a stand; so that the increase of population will only be a natural augmentation, which cannot be very rapid, because of the small number of the present inhabitants. . . .

It may be said that Ohio will have a good market when the canal is completed, and then these difficulties will be done away.

Undoubtedly this in some degree, will be the case; but it will for ever be expensive to transport all heavy agricultural articles the distance of from four hundred and fifty to six hundred miles, to Albany or New-York, which are the nearest markets to which the inhabitants of this part of the country can ever have access.

The above remarks will apply to the transportation of articles from the Atlantic to the lakes.

Hawley left Ohio for Connecticut on August 27, 1821. In an afterword to his book, entitled "Advice to Immigrants," he encouraged emigrants to buy land in New York instead of going further west. But he added: "Above all, I would recommend to all, before moving on with their families, to go and view the country for themselves, as in the nature of things it is scarcely possible, that any two person would be equally pleased with the same place, consequently no man can see for his neighbour, or friend."

The Death of Charles Brady: Charity Osborn Tells of Early Widowhood, 1824

Charity Osborn moved to Greenwich, Huron County, with her first husband, Charles Brady, in 1823. She was 31. They were joined the following year by her father and family. The Bradys had lived there less than two years when Charity became a widow.

Early the morning of the 18th of December, my husband took what proved to be his final leave of our earthly home. He took his gun and after loading it went to the Center, where, joined by my brother Benjamin Kniffin, he started with an ox team to take a load of grain to Washburn's mill. The track lay through the woods, which then reached the entire distance. When they had passed about one-third of the distance, Charles took hold of his gun which lay upon the load and pulling it towards him, it discharged, killing him instantly.

Benjamin was obliged to leave him alone in the woods while he went back to the Center for father. He with others went immediately back to the spot and made a rude bier of poles, bound together with bark. They laid him on and brought him back to the Center. A messenger came running to bring me the heart rending intelligence. In two short hours what a change! He went out full of life and vigor, and now the word came that he was a lifeless corpse. . . .

Thus was I left with a family of small children, none of them old enough to render me much assistance. Our house was a mere shelter right in the woods, without door, chimney, hearth, or window.

A Quaker Woman on the Frontier:
Letter of Anna Briggs Bentley, 1826

Anna Briggs Bentley came from a prominent Maryland Quaker family. In 1812 she married Joseph Bentley and moved with him and their six children, including a babe in arms, to Columbiana County, Ohio, near present Lisbon, in 1826. The following is one of the earliest letters she wrote back to her family after they arrived. Bentley dates her letters in the Quaker style. Sunday is 1st day, Monday is 2nd day, and so on, the months being numbered likewise.

The Cabin 8th Mo 17th 1826
5th day night [Thursday]

My dear friends
     . . . This has been a most laborious week to me washing, baking, scouring, cooking & I have been constantly on my feet. I feel very tired now and look forward to tomorrow as a *treat* for I have a great pile of *patching* to do that I can sit down to—and I have 4 and 1/2 loaves baked and pies enough. I have had many calls from neighbors since 1st day [Sunday]. . . . It is customary here for neighbors to go out and help at what they call a logrolling, that is rolling in long heaps with levers the largest size logs and then piling on the brush and firing it[.] All their pay is to go home and take supper with them
     3rd day [Tuesday] the 22nd [of August]
Well I get on slowly with my letter but you can have no idea of the constant variety of engagements I have and I now know how to make allowances for the poor black people who can not keep awake when they sit down of an evening. But I sometimes shead tears of thanksgiving when I find how much I am *made capable* of doing *cheerfully*. My beloved mother, thy prayers have been heard—the hearts of strangers have inded seemed to be turned toward us in a manner wonderful to me, not in empty professions but in real substantial acts of kindness I will give some instances[.] [M]y cow in jumping a low fence tore open one of her teats the whole length[.] [W]e could not milk her at night In the morning I went over to friend Millers (1/4 of a mile) for a little tallow to grease it and to know what to do. Friend Miller was very busy but she immediately left all and came through the dew to milk her, which she accomplished in spite of her kicking, by making a kind of pew in a fence corner[.] One of the girls came and milked her in the evening[.] Friend Miller says let them know whenever I have more work to do than I can easily get through with and some of them will come and help[.] They supply me with

beans, potatoes, cucumbers in abundance, also apples, and peaches, and roasting ears. This is the way she talks[:] "now do send over for any vegetable and any thing thee stands in need off[.] Thee must not be any ways backward with us more than thy own *people* I know just how it is with you, new beginners have all to buy till they can make for themselves and I want thee to feel welcome and always at home here[.] I want our intercourse to ripen into a friendship, not of a day but permanent. Come, that is thy hen and chickens I will have them a rooster caught and sent over and I have a tub of soap for thee when I can get it over. . . ."

1st day 27th [August 27]
6th day was our mo[n]thly meeting[.] I attended for the first time and was surprised to find it considerably larger than yours[.] It was much crowded about *30 babies attended* [and] there were more monstrous fat women than I ever saw at once. . . .

Joseph went down to the clearing (i.e. our land) today and found some person had stolen our hive which was nearly full of honey botheration to them. We cannot raise [our house] till next week and Ah then the work to cook for these pie eating people[.] S Holland and Hannah Miller will help and I shall bake in friend Holland's oven. . . . How I have feasted on plum's for 2 or 3 weeks past so large and delicious[.] They grow in the greatest abundance about 50 yds from the house larger trees almost breaking down with them—And wild cherries are here used for pies[.] [T]hey grow larger here than with you and resemble black heart cherries in taste. I make a great many pies and puddings and try some experiments with them[.] I mostly bake 18 or 20 a week[.] I stir peaches not dried or apples and make a custard and mix with them seasoning it nicely and make puff paste and bake them in[.] I do all my baking in a dutch oven and spider [a frying pan with legs]. . . .

We have heard there was a house raised a mile from here day before yesterday[.] A man got his head between the logs[.] When it was extracted he was bled and he soon conversed with those arround telling them he was not seriously injured they need not have sent for the Dr[.] When the physician examined his head he instantly pronounced it fractured and no hope of saving him. He died yesterday—ours will be such a *heavy* raising that I dread accidents—

I believe my account of the children might as well be stuck in here as I am so bothered I can hardly think of anything[.] I am at this moment and have been all the time I have been writing this side, singing "bye O baby" as loud as I can bawl and D[eborah] wont go to sleep. She is a sweet good babe it has been some time since she could get up in the floor and stand alone but she does not walk yet. . . . She had 4 teeth and our little indian looking Hannah is as fat and hearty as need be[.] She will not wear a bonnet and her neck is like a mulatta. . . . What shall I say for Maria she is very useful and I would be glad to say she strove to conquor her temper, was always respectful to me, and did not tease her brothers and sisters but she gives me a great deal of trouble by teasing them and disputing with them and they follow her example with each other. I hope I shall have a better account next letter. . . .

Dear sister Mary was there any thing more than a jokeing in thy talking of paying us a visit sometime it would be almost *too much* for me to bear. . . .

Oh all of your dear faces come so plain before me that [I] closed my eyes and kept them before my mental view, forgetting that it is past midnight and a toilsome day approaching, trying to forget the mountains, the long long road, but I must no[t] cherish useless regrets. . . .

An English Lady in Cincinnati:
Frances Trollope's Book about Cincinnati, 1828

Frances Trollope and her children arrived in Cincinnati in February, 1828. They came to pursue her husband's harebrained scheme to open a bazaar to sell English goods to the settlers. That business venture failed miserably, but Frances Trollope went back to England with material for a book, *Domestic Manners of the Americans*, which earned her a tidy sum of money and launched her literary career. Later her son, Anthony, became famous as a novelist. Maybe it was that she was under tremendous financial stress while she lived in Cincinnati, but Trollope was not always charitable about Americans or the discomforts of frontier society.

The greatest difficulty in organising a family establishment in Ohio, is getting servants, or, as it is there called, "getting help"; for it is more than petty treason to the republic to call a free citizen a *servant*. The whole class of young women whose bread depends upon their labour, are taught to believe that the most abject poverty is preferable to domestic service. Hundreds of half-naked girls work in the paper-mills, or in any other manufactory, for less than half the wages they would receive in service; but they think their equality is compromised by the latter, and nothing but the wish to obtain some particular article of finery will ever induce them to submit to it. A kind friend, however, exerted herself so effectually for me, that a tall stately lass soon presented herself, saying "I be come to help you." The intelligence was very agreeable, and I welcomed her in the most gracious manner possible, and asked what I should give her by the year.

"O Gimini!" exclaimed the damsel, with a loud laugh, "you be a downright Englisher, sure enough. I should like to see a young lady engage by the year in America! I hope I shall get a husband before many months, or I expect I shall be an outright old maid, for I be most seventeen already: besides, mayhap I may want to go to school. You must just give me a dollar and a half a week, and mother's slave Phillis must come over once a week, I expect, from t'other side the water, to help me clean. . . ."

This young lady left me at the end of two months; because I refused to lend her money enough to buy a silk dress to go to a ball, saying: "Then 'tis not worth my while to stay any longer." . . .

I cannot imagine it possible that such a state of things can be desirable, or beneficial to any of the parties concerned. I might occupy a hundred pages on the subject, and yet fail to give an adequate idea of the sore, angry, ever-wakeful pride that seemed to torment these poor wretches. In many of them it was so excessive, that all feeling of displeasure, or even of ridicule, was lost in pity. One of these was a pretty girl, whose natural disposition must have been gentle and kind; but her good feelings were soured, and her gentleness turned to morbid sensitiveness, by having heard a thousand and a thousand times that she was as good as any other lady; that all men were equal, and women too; and that it was a sin and a shame for a free-born American to be treated like a servant. . . .

I never saw any people who appeared to live so much without amusement as the Cincinnatians. Billiards are forbidden by law, so are cards. To sell a pack of cards in Ohio subjects the seller to a penalty of fifty dollars. They have no public balls, excepting, I think, six, during the Christmas holidays. They have no concerts. They have no dinner-parties.

They have a theatre, which is, in fact, the only public amusement of this triste little town; but they seem to care little about it, and either from economy or distaste, it is very poorly attended. Ladies are rarely seen there, and by far the larger proportion of females deem it an offence against religion to witness the representation of a play. It is in the churches and chapels of the town that the ladies are to be seen in full costume: and I am tempted to believe that a stranger from the continent of Europe would be inclined, on first reconnoitring the city, to suppose that the places of worship were the theatres and cafés of the place. No evening in the week but brings throngs of the young and beautiful to the chapels and meeting-houses, all dressed with care, and sometimes with great pretension; it is there that all display is made, and all fashionable distinction sought. . . .

It seems hardly fair to quarrel with a place because its staple commodity is not pretty, but I am sure I should have liked Cincinnati much better if the people had not dealt so very largely in hogs. The immense quantity of business done in this line would hardly be believed by those who had not witnessed it. I never saw a newspaper without remarking such advertisements as the following:

"Wanted, immediately, 4,000 fat hogs."

"For sale, 2,000 barrels of prime pork."

But the annoyance came nearer than this; if I determined upon a walk up Main Street, the chances were five hundred to one against my reaching the shade side without brushing by a snout fresh dripping from the kennel; when we had screwed our courage to the enterprise of mounting a certain noble-looking sugar-loaf hill, that promised pure air and a fine view, we found the brook we had to cross, at its foot, red with the stream from a pig slaughter-house; while our noses, instead of meeting "the thyme that loves the green hill's breast", were greeted by odours that I will not describe, and which I heartily hope my readers cannot imagine; our feet, that on leaving the city had expected to press the flowery sod, literally got entangled in pigs' tails and jaw-bones; and thus the prettiest walk in the neighbourhood was interdicted for ever. . . .

Our walks were, however, curtailed in several directions by my old Cincinnati enemies, the pigs; immense droves of them were continually arriving from the country by the road that led to most of our favourite walks; they were often fed and lodged in the prettiest valleys, and worse still, were slaughtered beside the prettiest streams. Another evil threatened us from the same quarter, that was yet heavier. Our cottage had an ample piazza (a luxury almost universal in the country houses of America), which, shaded by a group of acacias, made a delightful sitting-room; from this favourite spot we one day perceived symptoms of building in a field close to it; with much anxiety we hastened to the spot, and asked what building was to be erected there.

"'Tis to be a slaughter-house for hogs," was the dreadful reply.

As there were several gentlemen's houses in the neighbourhood, I asked if such an erection might not be indicted as a nuisance.

"A what?"

"A nuisance" I repeated, and explained what I meant.

"No, no" was the reply; "that may do very well for your tyrannical country, where a rich man's nose is more thought of than a poor man's mouth; but hogs be profitable produce here, and we be too free for such a law as that, I guess." . . .

At Cincinnati there is a garden where the people go to eat ices, and to look at roses. For the preservation of the flowers, there is placed at the end of one of the walks a sign-post sort of daub, representing a Swiss peasant girl, holding in her hand a scroll, requesting that the roses might not be gathered. Unhappily for the artist, or for the proprietor, or for both, the petticoat of this figure was so short as to show her ankles. The ladies saw, and shuddered; and it was formally intimated to the proprietor, that if he wished for the patronage of the ladies of Cincinnati, he must have the petticoat of this figure lengthened. The affrighted purveyor of ices sent off an express for the artist and his paint pot. He came but unluckily not provided with any colour that would match the petticoat; the necessity, however, was too urgent for delay, and a flounce of blue was added to the petticoat of red, giving bright and shining evidence before all men, of the immaculate delicacy of the Cincinnati ladies. . .

In noting the various brilliant events which diversified our residence in the western metropolis, I have omitted to mention the Birthday Ball, on the 22nd of February, in every town and city throughout the Union. It is the anniversary of the birth of General Washington, and well deserves to be marked by the Americans as a day of jubilee.

I was really astonished at the *coup d'oeil* on entering, for I saw a large room filled with extremely well-dressed company, among whom were many very beautiful girls. The gentlemen also were exceedingly smart; but I had not yet been long enough in Western America not to feel startled at recognising in almost every full-dressed *beau* that passed me, the master or shopman that I had been used to see behind the counter, or lolling at the door of every shop in the city. The fairest and finest *belles* smiled and smirked on them with as much zeal and satisfaction as I ever saw bestowed on an eldest son, and I therefore could feel no doubt of their being considered as of the highest rank. Yet it must not be supposed that there is no distinction of classes; at this same ball I was looking among the many very beautiful girls I saw there for one more beautiful still, with whose lovely face I had been particularly struck at the school examination I have mentioned. I could not find her, and asked a gentleman why the beautiful Miss C— was not there.

"You do not yet understand our aristocracy," he replied; "the family of Miss C— are mechanics."

"But the young lady has been educated at the same school as these, whom I see here, and I know her brother has a shop in the town, quite as large, and apparently as prosperous, as those belonging to any of these young men. What is the difference?"

"He is a mechanic: he assists in making the articles he sells; the others call themselves merchants."

Otto-wau-kee Speaks for His People

Lewis Cass Aldrich edited a history of Henry and Fulton Counties in 1888. In it he told of his youth among the Indians who lived in his area. During the 1830s, many Indians who had stayed in Ohio after Tecumseh's defeat drifted west, pressured to leave their reservations by settlers, land speculators, and the state and federal governments. In the following memoir, Aldrich writes of a treaty with the Ottawas he attended opposite Fort Meigs in 1831. The U.S. Indian commissioner had just painted a rosy picture of the land the Indians were being encouraged to go to. Clearly, Otto-wau-kee was skeptical. Aldrich, telling the story late in life, possesses the romantic idea of the noble Indian that grew up after the Ohio Indians had been defeated and reduced to poverty on their small, vulnerable reservations.

After closing his eloquent address, and taking his seat, amid a profound silence throughout the council, all eyes were turned upon the stoical and dignified countenance of Otto-wau-kee (Che-ot-tire-wan-kee), the great O-taw-waw chief, who sat with his gaze riveted upon the earth, seeming unconscious of the wild throbbing of the thousand anxious hearts of the assembled council. Many minutes passed in silent suspense, when he rose to his feet, and with that majestic dignity born to the North American savage, scarcely equaled by the cultured prince or statesman, folded his arms across his breast, his eyes now riveted upon the face of the commissioner, and flashing with the inward emotion of his bosom, he spoke as follows: "The ears of my young men are open: they have heard what the pale-face chief has said: his voice is like the bird, and the land is as beautiful as the flowers, among which it builds its nest and feeds its young;

land of the great Man-i-too, beyond the setting sun. Their heads are young, and they are not wise; they may go, but the old and the wise, will stay where the graves of their fathers are; where the council fires of their people have never gone out; the land and the water given to them by the Great Spirit, so long ago that no one lives who remembers the time—the land of the beautiful Me-au-me, and when the Great Man-i-too calls, we will answer—'here!' My pale-face brother is wise; his beautiful daughters from the sun-rise love the shade and the flowers, and the beautiful land toward the sun-down, that he sings in the ears of the red children; will he not go there with his pale-face children? There is no enemy of my brother on the long trail, and no one to molest him; he need not be afraid; the Great Spirit of his fathers, will protect him. Go to the wigwam of the great father (the President of the United States), and tell him that his red children will give the 'beautiful land' to their pale-face brothers, and they will sleep where their father's sleep, and their last council fire shall go out on the banks of their beautiful Me-aw-mee. Go, tell this to the great father."

Swiss Immigrants on the Ohio Canals: The Diary of Joseph Suppiger, 1831

In 1831 a group of Swiss immigrants arrived in America from their homes near Lucerne. Among them was Joseph Suppiger, who had left prosperity in his homeland to seek religious freedom in America—specifically Illinois. He and his fellow travelers came to Ohio via canal boat and lake steamer to Cleveland. They arrived at midnight and immediately signed on to a canal boat bound for Dresden, Ohio. Suppiger's diary was translated from German by Leo Titus, the husband of a Suppiger descendant.

The prices on this canal are higher than on the New York canal. By the mile one and a half to two cents fare was demanded, for food one-half dollar per day, and freight for the effects, one half dollar per hundredweight. This canal is not yet finished, so far only something over 168 miles.

There is so little competition here that we could find only one good arrangement. For freight, passage and food for eleven persons, it was $50 to Dresden, 151 miles from here; then we must detour toward Zanesville. At three o'clock at night all our possessions were loaded and we lay down to sleep in our new quarters. Our canal boat belonged to the Farmers Line and was named "Citizen," with Captain Timothy Capen.

Our present steward speaks only English and we have to try to understand him as well as possible. Awake at daybreak, we could now try to see this place. A steep street washed by a heavy shower, led upward. Only small warehouses stand along the water. The city, already laid out regularly has a magnificent view over the Lake. It has only one important, wide, main street bordered on both sides with brick houses. On the adjoining streets already laid out there are only a few buildings. There is a population of 1000. After the completion of the Ohio Canal business will boom. So far there are 60 canal boats. When we came back to the boat our goods had to be unloaded and weighed for the assessment of tolls. At first everything was carefully brought to the scales, but whenever the Inspector turned away, much was shoved back in the hold and the Captain had to pay tolls on less than half the goods.

We left during breakfast. No attendant has yet been placed at the lock and the boat people have to operate the gates. All day we went through a wooded region, with only a log cabin to be seen here and there. The heavy growth of the trees showed good soil. . . .

Sunday, 14 August.

. . . In the morning we passed Bolivar and in the afternoon, Soir or Zoar, lying on the right side of the canal. Here there are many Germans and Swiss, and vineyards from which wine is sold at forty cents a bottle. . . .

It is strange that we could not get exact information anywhere about the waterways in the interior. All is new and under development and changes every year. . . . The keel boat had left for Zanesville just before our arrival, but this morning there was still expected the steamer, new since the connection between Dresden and Zanesville was completed fourteen days ago. The distance is 18 miles which is covered in about three hours. The fare is 25 cents a person and freight costs 10 cents per hundredweight. The little steamer really came but did not want to leave until morning. However, there seemed to be enough load with our effects and so we made an agreement at $8 with the understanding that the steamer would go today. As the locks are not yet ready we had to have our effects carted to the steamer. I mention this because only in a new world is such conveyance possible. The bank of the canal, still without stone paved streets, was softened by rain storms and cut into diagonal ruts, and still the cartman with four horses in three trips brought our effects happily aboard, all for the low price of $1. Who among us would lead four horses over such a route for that? . . .

At half past six o'clock the loading was finished. We reached Zanesville at nine. The effects remained on the ship with a watchman while the others went to look for Herr Brak, who lodged us in the National Hotel where we lived like princes, but cheaply.

Tuesday, 16 August.

. . . The city of Zanesville, some 25 to 28 years old, is already very important because of its many industries and manufactures, such as iron foundries, nail machines, glass works, weavers, saw and flour mills, etc. The great national highway from Pittsburg and Wheeling goes through here. A boat trip on the Muskingum River will also be more popular when the steamer can come up all year. This is possible now only in spring time during high water, but the state locks already started can make the river passable the year around.

Towards two o'clock we again had our goods under shelter. I need not say that they just about filled the floating palace for it is scarcely 20 feet long and some 8 feet wide. We only let the two rowers and the tillerman go. Happily but laboriously they came along and we all climbed aboard. The most dangerous place was found right here. Like many American rivers, the Muskingum has the fault that it is too shallow and wide. . . .

At Marietta, they took a paddle steamer down the Ohio River.

Saturday, 20 August.

. . . Our ship, named "Emigrant," which is commanded by Captain H. Thomson Baylett, has twenty sleeping places for men and eight for women. In the men's cabin a table is used in common.

The steamers are usually well painted and the interiors most beautifully decorated and hung with tapestries. Each bunk has its own small window that can be closed or open according to the weather and over those are venetian blinds. . . .

They arrived in Cincinnati at midnight and explored the town on Sunday.

Sunday, 21 August.

. . . Last year alone, 1500 new buildings were started and this year even more would have been built had there not been a shortage of workers. It is unbelievable that a place can grow so fast. The canal from Dayton will lead into the heart of the city. It is still under

construction inside the city and will lead down into the Ohio. Hills
were leveled and gullies filled. Above the second rise everything will
be leveled clear to the hills lying behind. Next to these opens the
valley of the Miami. It is a noble location and must be very healthy.
There are several Germans here, yes, even from the Canton Luzern,
which was a great surprise to us. . . .

The Suppigers and friends ended their journey in western Illinois, where they
founded the community around Highland known as New Switzerland.

The Capture of a Fugitive Slave:
A Newspaper Report

Many slaves escaped to or through Ohio in the years before the Civil War. Under the federal laws of that time, slave owners could pursue their slaves, reclaim
them, and take them back to slave territory. Feelings about runaway slaves and
their right to freedom were mixed in Ohio. Some white people, believing in the
abolition of slavery, worked actively on the Underground Railroad, hiding runaway slaves and helping them escape to freedom. Others turned them in, either
for the reward or because they believed in the property rights of the slaveholders.
But the capture of a fugitive slave in Ohio often stirred up people. This story
from the *Dayton Journal* in 1832 conveys the heartbreak of the slave being re-
captured and the compassion and indignation the event aroused.

A short time ago a negro man, who had lived in this place two or
three years under the name of Thomas Mitchell, was arrested by some
men from Kentucky, and taken before a justice under a charge of
being a slave who had escaped from his master. The magistrate, on
hearing the evidence, discharged the black man, not being satisfied
with the proof brought by the claimants of their rights to him. A few
weeks afterward some men, armed and employed by the master,
seized the negro in our main street, and were hurrying him towards
the outskirts of the town, where they had a sleigh in waiting to carry
him off. The negro's cries brought a number of citizens into the street,
who interfered, and prevented the men from taking him away without having legally proved their right to do so. The claimants of the
negro went before the justice again, and after a long examination of
the case on some new evidence being produced, he was decided to
be the slave of the person claiming him as such. In the meantime a
good deal of excitement had been produced among the people of the
place, and their sympathies for the poor black fellow were so much

awakened that a proposition was made to buy his freedom. The agent of the master agreed to sell him, under the supposition that the master would sell him his liberty, and a considerable sum was subscribed, to which, out of his own savings, the negro contributed upwards of fifty dollars himself. The master, however, when his agent returned to Kentucky, refused to agree to the arrangement, and came himself the week before last to take the negro away. Their first meeting was in the upper story of a house, and Tom, on seeing those who were about to take him, rushed to the window and endeavored, but without success, to dash himself through it, although, had he succeeded, he would have fallen on a stone pavement from a height no less than fifteen feet. He was prevented, however, and the master took him away with him and got him as far as Cincinnati. The following letter, received by a gentleman in this city, gives the concluding account of the matter:

POOR TOM IS FREE.
CINCINNATI, Jan. 24, 1832.
DEAR SIR:—In compliance with a request of Mr. J. Deinkard, of Kentucky, I take my pen to inform you of the death of his black man Ben, whom he took in your place a few days ago. The circumstances are as follows: On the evening of the 22d inst. Mr. D. and company, with Ben, arrived in this city on their way to Kentucky, and put up at the Main Street Hotel, where a room on the uppermost story (fourth) of the building was provided for Ben and his guard. All being safe, as they thought, about one o'clock, when they were in a sound sleep, poor Ben, stimulated with even the faint prospect of escape, or perhaps pre-determined on liberty or death, threw himself from the window which is upwards of fifty feet from the pavement. He was, as you may well suppose, severely injured, and the poor fellow died this morning about four o'clock. Mr. D. left this morning with the dead body of his slave, to which he told me he would give decent burial in his own graveyard. Please tell Ben's wife of these circumstances.
Your unknown correspondent,
  Respectfully,
R. P. SIMMONS.

Tom, or, as he is called in the letter, Ben, was an industrious, steady, saving little fellow, and had laid up a small sum of money; all of which he gave to his wife and child when his master took him away. A poor and humble being, of an unfortunate and degraded race, the same feeling which animated the signers of the Declaration of

Independece to pledge life, fortune and honor for liberty determined him to be free or die.

The Escape of a Fugitive Slave:
The Memoir of William Wells Brown, 1834

On January 1, 1834, the slave William, age 21, escaped from his master, a steamboat captain, when the boat docked in Cincinnati. He walked the length of Ohio to Cleveland, where he hoped to sail to Canada and freedom. He got his freedom but never got to Canada. Brown dedicated his book, *Narrative of William W. Brown, a fugitive slave*, published in 1847, to a Quaker, Wells Brown, who gave him help when he desperately needed it and provided him a new name as a free man.

At last the time for action arrived. The boat landed at a point which appeared to me the place of all others to start from. I found that it would be impossible to carry anything with me, but what was upon my person. I had some provisions, and a single suit of clothes, about half worn. When the boat was discharging her cargo, and the passengers engaged carrying their baggage on and off shore, I improved the opportunity to convey myself with my little effects on land. Taking up a trunk, I went up the wharf, and was soon out of the crowd. I made directly for the woods, where I remained until night, knowing well that I could not travel, even in the State of Ohio, during the day, without danger of being arrested.

I had long since made up my mind that I would not trust myself in the hands of any man, white or colored. The slave is brought up to look upon every white man as an enemy to him and his race; and twenty-one years in slavery had taught me that there were traitors, even among colored people. After dark, I emerged from the woods into a narrow path, which led me into the main travelled road. But I knew not which way to go. I did not know North from South, East from West. I looked in vain for the North Star; a heavy cloud hid it from my view. I walked up and down the road until near midnight, when the clouds disappeared, and I welcomed the sight of my friend,—truly the slave's friend—the North Star!

As soon as I saw it, I knew my course, and before daylight I travelled twenty or twenty-five miles. It being in the winter, I suffered intensely from the cold; being without an overcoat, and my other clothes rather thin for the season. I was provided with a tinder-box, so that I could make up a fire when necessary. And but for this, I

Williams Wells Brown fled slavery
in 1834 and took the name of a
Quaker who helped him escape
across Ohio. By permission of the
Ohio Historical Society.

should certainly have frozen to death; for I was determined not to go
to any house for shelter. I knew of a man belonging to Gen. Ashly, of
St. Louis, who had run away near Cincinnati, on the way to Washington, but had been caught and carried back into slavery; and I felt
that a similar fate awaited me, should I be seen by any one. I travelled at night, and lay by during the day.

On the fourth day, my provisions gave out, and then what to do I
could not tell. Have something to eat, I must; but how to get it was
the question! On the first night after my food was gone, I went to a
barn on the road-side, and there found some ears of corn. I took ten
or twelve of them, and kept on my journey. During the next day,
while in the woods, I roasted my corn and feasted upon it, thanking
God that I was so well provided for.

My escape to a land of freedom now appeared certain, and the
prospects of the future occupied a great part of my thoughts. What
should be my occupation, was a subject of much anxiety to me; and
the next thing what should be my name? I have before stated that
my old master, Dr. Young, had no children of his own, but had with
him a nephew, the son of his brother, Benjamin Young. When this
boy was brought to Doctor Young, his name being William, the same
as mine, my mother was ordered to change mine to something else.

This, at the time, I thought to be one of the most cruel acts that could be committed upon my rights; and I received several very severe whippings for telling people that my name was William, after orders were given to change it. Though young, I was old enough to place a high appreciation upon my name. It was decided, however, to call me "Sandford," and this name I was known by, not only upon my master's plantation, but up to the time that I made my escape. I was sold under the name of Sandford.

But as soon as the subject came to my mind, I resolved on adopting my old name of William, and let Sandford go by the board, for I always hated it. Not because there was anything peculiar in the name; but because it had been forced upon me. It is sometimes common at the south, for slaves to take the name of their masters. Some have a legitimate right to do so. But I always detested the idea of being called by the name of either of my masters. And as for my father [a white man], I would rather have adopted the name of "Friday," and been known as the servant of some Robinson Crusoe, than to have taken his name. So I was not only hunting for my liberty, but also hunting for a name; though I regarded the latter as of little consequence, if I could but gain the former. Travelling along the road, I would sometimes speak to myself, sound my name over, by way of getting used to it, before I should arrive among civilized human beings. On the fifth or sixth day, it rained very fast, and it froze about as fast as it fell, so that my clothes were one glare of ice. I travelled on at night until I became so chilled and benumbed—the wind blowing into my face—that I found it impossible to go any further, and accordingly took shelter in a barn, where I was obliged to walk about to keep from freezing.

I have ever looked upon that night as the most eventful part of my escape from slavery. Nothing but the providence of God, and that old barn, saved me from freezing to death. I received a very severe cold, which settled upon my lungs, and from time to time my feet had been frost-bitten, so that it was with difficulty I could walk. In this situation I travelled two days, when I found that I must seek shelter somewhere, or die.

The thought of death was nothing frightful to me, compared with that of being caught, and again carried back into slavery. Nothing but the prospect of enjoying liberty could have induced me to undergo such trials, for

"Behind I left the whips and chains,
Before me were sweet Freedom's plains!"

This, and this alone, cheered me onward. But I at last resolved to seek protection from the inclemency of the weather, and therefore I secured myself behind some logs and brush, intending to wait there until some one should pass by; for I thought it probable that I might see some colored person, or, if not, some one who was not a slaveholder; for I had an idea that I should know a slaveholder as far as I could see him.

The first person that passed was a man in a buggy-wagon. He looked too genteel for me to hail him. Very soon another passed by on horseback. I attempted speaking to him, but fear made my voice fail me. As he passed, I left my hiding-place, and was approaching the road, when I observed an old man walking towards me, leading a white horse. He had on a broad-brimmed hat and a very long coat, and was evidently walking for exercise. As soon as I saw him, and observed his dress, I thought to myself, "You are the man that I have been looking for!" Nor was I mistaken. He was the very man!

On approaching me, he asked me, "if I was not a slave." I looked at him some time, and then asked him "if he knew of any one who would help me, as I was sick." He answered that he would; but again asked, if I was not a slave. I told him I was. He then said that I was in a very pro-slavery neighborhood, and if I would wait until he went home, he would get a covered wagon for me. I promised to remain. He mounted his horse and was soon out of sight.

After he was gone, I meditated whether to wait or not; being apprehensive that he had gone for some one to arrest me. But I finally concluded to remain until he should return; removing some few rods to watch his movements. After a suspense of an hour and a half or more, he returned with a two horse covered-wagon, such as are usually seen under the shed of a Quaker meeting-house on Sundays and Thursdays; . . .

He took me to his house, but it was some time before I could be induced to enter it; not until the old lady came out, did I venture into the house. I thought I saw something in the old lady's cap that told me I was not only safe, but welcome, in her house. I was not, however, prepared to receive their hospitalities. The only fault I found with them was their being too kind. I had never had a white man to treat me as an equal, and the idea of a white lady waiting on me at the table was still worse! Though the table was loaded with the good things of this life, I could not eat. I thought if I could only be allowed the privilege of eating in the kitchen, I should be more than satisfied! . . .

The fact that I was in all probability a freeman, sounded in my

ears like a charm. I am satisfied that none but a slave could place
such an appreciation upon liberty as I did at that time. I wanted to
see mother and sister, that I might tell them "I was free!" I wanted
to see my fellow slaves in St. Louis, and let them know that the
chains were no longer upon my limbs. I wanted to see Captain Price,
and let him learn from my own lips that I was not more a chattel,
but a man! I was anxious, too, thus to inform Mrs. Price that she
must get another coachman. And I wanted to see Eliza [his sweet-
heart] more than I did either Mr. or Mrs. Price!

The fact that I was a freeman—could walk, talk, eat and sleep as
a man, and no one to stand over me with the blood-clotted cowhide—
all this made me feel that I was not myself.

The kind friend that had taken me in was named Wells Brown.
He was a devoted friend of the slave; but was very old, and not in the
enjoyment of good health. After being by the fire awhile, I found that
my feet had been very much frozen. I was seized with a fever which
threatened to confine me to my bed. But my Thompsonian friends[2]
soon raised me, treating me as kindly as if I had been one of their
own children. I remained with them twelve or fifteen days, during
which time they made me some clothing, and the old gentleman
purchased me a pair of boots. . . .

Before leaving this good Quaker friend, he inquired what my name
was besides William. I told him that I had no other name. "Well,"
said he, "thee must have another name. Since thee has got out of
slavery, thee has become a man, and men always have two names."

I told him that he was the first man to extend the hand of friendship to me, and I would give him the privilege of naming me.

"If I name thee," said he, "I shall call thee Wells Brown, after
myself."

"But," said I, "I am not willing to lose my name of William. As it
was taken from me once against my will, I am not willing to part
with it again upon any terms."

"Then," said he, "I will call thee William Wells Brown."

"So be it," said I; and I have been known by that name ever since
I left the house of my first white friend, Wells Brown.

After giving me some little change, I again started for Canada. In
four days I reached a public house, and went in to warm myself. I
there learned that some fugitive slaves had just passed through the

---

2. Probably a reference to followers of the medical theories of the nineteenth-century
practitioner and herbalist Samuel Thomson, who preached the efficacy of herbal rem-
edies. He had many disciples in Ohio.

place. The men in the bar-room were talking about it, and I thought that it must have been myself they referred to, and I was therefore afraid to start, fearing they would seize me; but I finally mustered courage enough, and took my leave. As soon as I was out of sight, I went into the woods, and remained there until night, when I again regained the road, and travelled on until the next day.

Not having had any food for nearly two days, I was faint with hunger, and was in a dilemma what to do, as the little cash supplied me by my adopted father, and which had contributed to my comfort, was now all gone. I however concluded to go to a farm-house, and ask for something to eat. On approaching the door of the first one presenting itself, I knocked, and was soon met by a man who asked me what I wanted. I told him that I would like something to eat. He asked where I was from, and where I was going. I replied that I had come some way, and was going to Cleaveland.

After hesitating a moment or two, he told me that he could give me nothing to eat, adding, "that if I would work, I could get something to eat."

I felt bad, being thus refused something to sustain nature, but did not dare tell him that I was a slave.

Just as I was leaving the door, with a heavy heart, a woman, who proved to be the wife of this gentleman, came to the door, and asked her husband what I wanted? He did not seem inclined to inform her. She therefore asked me herself. I told her that I had asked for something to eat. After a few other questions, she told me to come in, and that she would give me something to eat.

I walked up to the door, but the husband remained in the passage, as if unwilling to let me enter.

She asked him two or three times to get out of the way, and let me in. But as he did not move, she pushed him on one side, bidding me walk in! I was never before so glad to see a woman push a man aside! Ever since that act, I have been in favor of "woman's rights!"

After giving me as much food as I could eat, she presented me with ten cents, all the money then at her disposal, accompanied with a note to a friend, a few miles further on the road. Thanking this angel of mercy from an overflowing heart, I pushed on my way, and in three days arrived at Cleaveland, Ohio.

Being an entire stranger in this place, it was difficult for me to find where to stop. I had no money, and the lake being frozen, I saw that I must remain until the opening of navigation, or go to Canada by way of Buffalo. But believing myself to be somewhat out of danger, I secured an engagement at the Mansion House, as a table waiter, in payment for my board. The proprietor, however, whose name was E. M. Segur, in a short time, hired me for twelve dollars per month; on which terms I remained until spring, when I found good employment on board a lake steamboat. . . .

It is well known, that a great number of fugitives make their escape to Canada, by way of Cleaveland; and while on the lake, I always made arrangement to carry them on the boat to Buffalo or Detroit, and thus effect their escape to the "promised land." The friends of the slave, knowing that I would transport them without charge, never failed to have a delegation when the boat arrived at Cleaveland. I have sometimes had four or five on board, at one time.

In the year 1842, I conveyed, from the first of May to the first of December, sixty-nine fugitives over Lake Erie to Canada. In 1843, I visited Malden, in Upper Canada, and counted seventeen, in that small village, who owed their escape to my humble efforts.

Early Oberlin: Marianne Dascomb Arrives at Oberlin College, 1834

Marianne Parker Dascomb was in her early twenties when she arrived in Oberlin with her husband, James, who had been appointed professor of chemistry, botany, and physiology at the new college, as well as town physician. The couple became integral to the Oberlin community, where Dr. Dascomb taught for forty-four years. Mrs. Dascomb for many years was principal of the college's Ladies Department. She died in 1879. She wrote the following letter home to her friends in Dunbarton, New Hampshire, shortly after she arrived in Oberlin.

. . . Next morning at five o'clock we took stage for Elyria, which is ten miles from Oberlin—road very bad from ruts and mud. We were in constant danger of overturning. Once when we came to a ditch in the road the gentlemen got out and took down a fence, so that we could turn aside into the adjoining field and ride around the obstacle. At Elyria we dined, and obtained a two-horse wagon to transport us, and two gentlemen from new England going to the Institute as students, to our journey's end. We found the wagon a very comfortable conveyance, and I was in no fear of being turned out into the mud, for the driver assured us it could not turn over. You cannot conceive of a more miserable road than we had, the last two miles especially, but still I enjoyed the ride, and our party were all very cheerful. When passing through the woods I was so delighted with the black squirrels, the big trees, and above all the beautiful wild flowers, that at

Marianne Parker Dascomb traveled to Oberlin from New Hampshire in 1834 and later became principal of the Ladies Department of Oberlin College. From James H. Fairchild, *Oberlin: The Colony and the College, 1833-1883* (1883).

times I quite forgot to look out for the scraggy limbs that every now and then gave us a rude brush, till a warning from Dr. D. that I would get my eyes torn out, seconded perhaps by an unceremonious lash from a neighboring bough, would call me to the duty of self-preservation. Glad were we when an opening in the forest dawned upon us, and Oberlin was seen. That, said our driver, is "the city." We rode through its principal street, now and then coming in contact with a stump, till we were set down, not at the coffee house or tea house, but the boarding house. . . .

We have now been here two weeks, health and spirits good, and Oberlin already looks to us like home. Things about us are all going on so briskly, one cannot well feel sleepy. The colonists work with all diligence, and students too, at working hours. You hear great trees falling, see fires blazing, and new houses going up in all directions. There are a few log-houses, which were put up at first, but now they are all building framed houses. . . .

Do not let me forget the food, or mother will not forgive me. It is plain, but palatable. We shall have more variety when the land is cultivated. We shall have good bread, and milk, much of the time this summer. We always have good wheat and brown bread, and generally good butter. Can have meat twice a day if we choose, but it is not very good, and I generally prefer vegetable food. Our potatoes, which we have for a rarity, are not like yours, but rather heavy. Puddings and nut-cakes are made sometimes, but no pies. Cheese we have now and then, and very good. We have hot water with milk and sugar if we choose, but most prefer cold. . . .

I spend three or four hours a day hearing classes recite. Mrs. Waldo also assists in school. The females are very interesting; most of them are from other States, and many from a distance. . . .

Charles Hoffman's Winter in the West: A New Yorker Goes West, 1834-1835

Charles Fenno Hoffman, born 1806, was a novelist, poet, and magazine editor in New York. Although he had lost a leg as a young man, he remained physically active, and undertook a tour of what is now the Midwest in the winter of 1834-35. In November, Hoffman traveled from Pittsburgh to Cleveland by stagecoach, following the Ohio River, then angling off through Beaver, Pennsylvania. Later, he went to Michigan Territory, St. Louis, Prairie du Chien, and Chicago, among other places in the Midwest. He seemed to be interested in the plight of the Indians he met, and was critical of government policy toward them. "It is destructive to them as a people to remove them from their homes, and scatter them among hostile tribes, over strange hunting-grounds, and it is destructive to them individually by keeping them continually on the frontier, and in contact only with the most lawless portions of society—it is destructive, too, to furnish them with the means of idleness, to enrich them for others to prey upon," he wrote.

For his book, *Winter in the West*, he used the pseudonym, "A New-Yorker."

Awaking with the sun, I found that we were in the midst of new clearings, the road leading through a level country as far as the eye could reach, and having its sides faced beyond the fields with trees, which, with tall stems and interlacing summits, stood like giants locking arms along the highway. I must now be in Ohio, thought I; and I was right. The effect of this magnificent vegetation was striking even at this season; but after riding for half a day along such a wood, with not a valley to break the view, nor a hill to bound it, it could not but be monotonous. We passed two lakes in the course of our ride, approaching one of them near enough to see that it was a clear sheet of water, with a pretty yellow sand-beach. But, though shut up by woods, it wanted entirely the wild yet gentle picturesqueness of the lakes I have seen among and near the Highlands of the Hudson; much less could it boast of the savage grandeur of those which form the sources of that princely river.

The most interesting objects on this route are decidedly the growing towns and hamlets which abound along the road. Some of them
have been manufactured only this season; and it is really surprising
to see rude log huts of two years' date standing side by side with
tasteful edifices of yesterday, like the old and new branches of one
flourishing tree; brick churches and hotels, with handsome porticoes,
surrounded by the stumps of recently-felled forests. In one village,
called Hudson, particularly,—where, by-the-way, much good taste is
exhibited in the private houses,—the progress of improvement is said
to be as perceptible as the rise of the tide at the seaboard. I could
not, however, discover a palpable growth in the place from the time
we sat down to dinner till hurried away from table by the call of the
stage-driver.

We reached Cleaveland during a heavy shower long after night-
fall. The roar of the surf reminded me of Rockaway; and the first
view of Lake Erie, the next morning, was really grateful to my eyes.
I felt, while walking along the high esplanade of turf which here forms
its banks, and upon which the town is built, like one who has just
come out of a pent-up chamber into the full and free air of heaven.
The effect of coming on such a wide expanse of water when just
emerging from the forest is much greater than when, after long riding
through an open country, you view the ocean stretched beyond its
shining beach.

Cleaveland is very prettily situated upon the lake. The Cayuhoga
makes a bend around a high bluff as it passes into the inland sea
which receives its waters, and on the level peninsula thus formed is
built the town. The harbour, naturally an indifferent one, has been
much improved by running out a pier from either side of the river,
where it debouches into Lake Erie; and there being now few better
ports on this side of the lake, Cleaveland must become one of the
most important places on its waters. . . . The town, which can already boast of a public library, a fine church, two capital taverns,
and many handsome private dwellings, is laid out with broad streets
and a spacious square in the centre. The business part is as yet beneath the bluff, where a single winding street runs along the bank of
the river towards the lake; but the main street above is already the
scene of much bustle, and bears about the same relation to that below as Broadway does to Southstreet in your city. . . .

I had just left the reading-room of the Franklin Hotel, in
Cleaveland, and was making myself at home for the rest of the
evening, in my own neat chamber, when the sound of a steamboat-

bell, about nine o'clock, gave note that one of these vessels, which at this stormy season cannot navigate the lake with any regularity, had touched at Cleaveland on her way to this place. No time was to be lost, and huddling my clothes, &c. into my trunk as quickly as possible, I jumped into a vehicle, waiting at the tavern door, and in a few minutes was upon the quay. Here I witnessed a scene of indescribable confusion. The night was dark and somewhat gusty, and the boat and the wharf were both crowded with boxes, bales, and the effects of emigrants, who were screaming to each other in half as many languages as were spoken at Babel. Lanterns were flashing to and fro along the docks, and hoarse orders and countermands, mingled with the harsh hissing of the steam on every side. At length we pushed from the shore, and escaping in a moment from the head of the mole, stood fairly out into the lake, while the bright beacon of the Cleaveland lighthouse soon waned in the distance, and was at last lost entirely. I found myself, upon looking around, on board of the fine steamboat "New-York," Captain Fisher, to whose politeness I was much indebted for showing me about the boat before turning in for the night. Taking a lantern in his hand, and tucking my arm under his, he groped about among the motley ship's company like Diogenes looking for an honest man.

Our course first led us through a group of emigrants collected around a stove, mid-ships, where an English mother nursing her infant, a child lying asleep upon a mastiff, and a long-bearded German smoking his meerchaum on the top of a pile of candle-boxes, were the only complete figures I could make out from an indefinite number of heads, arms, and legs lying about in the most whimsical confusion.

In March, Hoffman took a boat down the Mississippi and up the Ohio from St. Louis to Cincinnati. He arrived April 3, 1835.

It was a still sunny morning, when, in rounding one of those beautiful promontories which form so striking a feature in the scenery of the Ohio, we came suddenly upon a cluster of gardens and villas, which indicated the vicinity of a flourishing town; and our boat taking a sudden sheer from the shore, before the eye had time to study out their grouping and disposition, the whole city of Cincinnati, imbosomed in its amphitheatre of green hills, was brought at once before us. It rises on two inclined planes from the river, the one elevated about fifty feet above the other, and both running parallel to the Ohio. The streets are broad, occasionally lined with trees, and generally well built of brick, though there are some pretty churches and noble private dwellings of cut stone and of stucco. Of the latter there are several with greater pretensions to architectural beauty than any which I remember in New-York. The first impression upon touching the quays at Cincinnati, and looking up its spacious avenues, terminating always in the green acclivities which bound the city, is exceedingly beautiful; and your good opinion of the town suffers no diminution when you have an opportunity to examine its well-washed streets and tasteful private residences. . . . Verily, if beauty alone confer empire, it is in vain for thriving Pittsburg or flourishing Louisville, bustling and buxom as they are, to dispute with Cincinnati her title of "Queen of the West."

The population of the place is about 30,000. . . . There is a common phrase in the new settlements of the West—"We all come from some place or another,"—which you may imagine to be particularly applicable to a place that only dates from the year of our Lord 1808; . . .

The principal buildings of Cincinnati, besides more than twenty churches, some of which are very pretty, and several fine hotels, one of which, the Pearl-street House, would rival the best in New-York, are the Cincinnati college, a couple of Theatres, four Market-houses, one of which is five hundred feet in length, a Court-house, United States' Branch Bank, Medical College, Mechanics' Institute, the Catholic Atheneum, the Hospital, and High-school, and two Museums. The collection of one of these museums is exceedingly interesting, from embracing a number of enormous organic remains among its curiosities, with antique vases and various singular domestic utensils, excavated from some of the ancient mounds in Ohio. In the upper story of the same building there is another exhibition, which, from the accounts I have had of it, I should hardly expect to be patronised in so enlightened a community:—it is nothing less than a nightly representation of the final place of torment in the other world, with all the agreeable accompaniments that the imaginations of the vulgar delight in conceiving as belonging to it. . . .

The most remarkable, however, of all the establishments of Cincinnati are those immense slaughter-houses, where the business of butchering and packing pork is carried on. The number of hogs annually slaughtered is said to exceed one hundred and twenty thousand; and the capital employed in the business is estimated at two millions of dollars. . . .

A Young Man's Travels:
The Journal of Cyrus P. Bradley, 1835

Cyrus Parker Bradley was a sixteen-year-old Dartmouth student on leave for his health when he traveled to Ohio in 1835, taking a steamer down the Ohio River from Pittsburgh to Cincinnati. Not a young man of means, Bradley managed to spend only about $100 during his six months on the road. He returned to his brilliant college career afterwards, but died only two years later. Obviously very bright and articulate, Bradley also possessed many of the harsh judgments and strong opinions of youth, which he turned on the crude life in frontier Ohio.

[June, 1835] 1. Mon. . . . Blannerhasset's splendid mansion is nothing but a heap of ruins; what was once the abode of beauty, taste and hospitality, is now a sad monument of the folly of human ambition. Coming down, I peeped into the place where are stowed the deck passengers. I was astonished at their number—black, and white, men, women and children lolling about on the floor, the trunks, couches, etc. they carry their own supplies with them, and feast or starve as they choose. My throat being quite sore, I applied to the waiter for some ginger tea—no ginger on board. He, however, recommended stewed vinegar and the barkeeper told me to tie my stocking round my throat—both certain cures. With the greatest docility I followed both prescriptions, and retired early to my berth.

2. Tues. . . . Said my negro doctor [the waiter from yesterday], as he cleared the table for lunch, "I do begrudge your education," and to-night, "I would steal your learning, if I could." Poor fellow—there is little opportunity for one of his color, however disposed. . . .

3. Wed. NOON . . . Have just returned from a perambulation about the streets of Cincinnati. Yes, I am actually writing in a tavern in this queen of the West. The steamboat arrived here about midnight, but I did not know it till morning. . . .

We walked up to the canal—the Miami canal—which comes up in the northerly part of the city, and here are furnished with seven locks, excellent specimens of durable workmanship. Only freight boats come up through the locks, the packets remaining below. The canal was crowded with boats. We looked in upon the celebrated Buckeye fire engine, owned and manned by lads. They are very proud of it, and it is the most effective engine in the city—the earliest on the ground. Passed Mrs. Trollope's folly—her celebrated Bazaar— which she planned and built, but failed before it was quite finished, and never paid for it. The profits of her book doubtless compensated her for her disappointment. . . .

Bradley then took the ferry across the river to Covington.

We entered one of the rolling mills, an extensive, open shed, under whose roof were going on all sorts of manufacture of iron. It was indeed a curious scene. The laborers were almost in a state of nudity, their brawny limbs covered with a glowing perspiration and their blackened features and hideous, naked deformity reflected from the raging furnaces and the white-hot masses of hissing steel; combined with the curious operations they were engaged in performing, the oaths and imprecations so freely employed, and the suspicious looking instruments which they handled, gave this much the appearance of a portion of the kingdom of the Arch Fiend, populous with devils, imps and the paraphernalia of torment. I watched many of their operations with great interest. . . . There were many very little boys employed in this horrible business, whom I pitied exceedingly. They nearly forfeited all claim to my commiseration, however, by their impudence, amusing themselves in the intervals of their occupation by throwing lumps of coal at the strangers. I suppose they knew no better. The huts of these workmen of course add little to the beauty of the villege.

[A]propos of swine, it is giving them a grain too much liberty to allow of their running at large in the streets. In a morning paper I saw a notice of one of these ravenous beasts seizing a young child by the arm, tearing him from his mother's doorstep into the gutter, where, had it not been for the child's screams and the interference of a gentleman, he would inevitably have devoured it. This was a little too bold. . . .

Bradley left Cincinnati and traveled by steamer back up river to Portsmouth. He was alarmed to hear of cholera in Maysville, where the boat planned to stop.

6. Sat. We stopped this morning two hours at Maysville, landing and taking in passengers, freight, etc. Those who join us report five new cases of cholera. Some of the deaths happened in a shockingly brief period after the first attack. Yet, although surrounded in this way by disease and death, the center of our cabin supports a gambling table, around which sit four respectable looking men, with cards in their hands, oaths on their lips, cigars in their mouth, liquor on the table, and heaps of silver before them. . . .

7. Sunday. [Portsmouth] . . . The Front street, facing the river, is the business street; here every other door is a tavern or a grocery; the character of the population is that of a community of drunkards, at least that part of it which has fallen under my observation, and the whole town seems to be contaminated with it. Then, the back streets—they are nothing but lanes—and every house, whether stone, brick or wood, bear symptoms of decay. But this isn't the worse feature—the filth, the nastiness, is perfectly disgusting. The soil is hard clay, impervious to everything. Pools of stagnant water, and swine, their hides encrusted inch deep with putrefaction, infest the ways— the yard or lane under our winder [window] (private, too) is a stinking nursery of pestilence. No wonder the cholera makes dreadful havoc when it enters such a place. . . .

Later that day Bradley booked passage on a canal boat traveling up the Scioto to Columbus.

Freight is scarce here, a greater part of the produce of the country being carried toward Cleveland, and by the way of the Erie Canal, to the New York market. The boats come down not more than half loaded, and back again with hardly any freight at all for the first hundred miles. They have more passengers down than up, by far, however. They have here no packet boats exclusively for passengers. The forward part of the boat is the gentlemen's cabin, about 10 feet by 12; next, the ladies' cabin, about 10 by 5; then the main part of the boat for the freight, where are also stowed the midship passengers; then, in the after part of the boat, the dining room, perhaps 10 feet square, with a kitchen closet adjoining. . . .

8. Monday . . . This kind of traveling is undoubtedly pleasant enough for a short time, when one doesn't feel in a hurry, so as to be impatient at the delay of the plaguey locks. There are a great many of them on this canal in its whole extent—no long levels, as in the great New Yorker. They go very slow, advancing about sixty miles a day. Were the roads decent, we should have tried the stage, but they are horrible. The mail has been due many hours at Portsmouth, but cannot cross Beaver Creek. Why? exclaims a New Englander. Because, friend, they have no bridges in the south and west over fordable streams, and this fact explains what I have wondered at—newspaper notices of the failures of mails because they cannot cross such and such a stream, or creek, as they call them here. . . .

Occasionally we pass a log hut or two, sometimes situated on a road, frequently surrounded only by rocks and stumps, but all alike in one particular—the abundance of little tow-heads which lay sunning about the door.

At one of these houses, where is a fine spring and where the boat stopped for water, we landed and obtained a glass of milk, or rather a dipper of milk. We asked the woman what was the name of the township or the county in which she lived. She giggled, hardly seemed to understand the question, but at length replied that it was "an out-in-the-woods place, she reckoned." That was all the name she knew, and that was enough for her purposes. But these children, they are growing up in ignorance, perfect darkness, intellectually. . . .

Towards evening in company with most of the passengers, went ashore at one of the locks and walked to the next one about a mile, where we waited for the boat. Here about a dozen Irishmen were at work digging and filling up an excavation, which the water had worn around the gate. Two old canalboats, their dwelling house, were moored near. Noticing rather an inviting room in one of them, I went, in company with another, and entered it, making an errand for a glass of water. An Irish girl, very comely and neat in her appearance was busily engaged in baking two tempting loaves of bread in a commodious cookstove. Everything had an air of cleanliness and comfort which one would hardly expect to find in such a place. . . .

9. Tues. Our little cabin was fitted most ingeniously with berths, for ten persons, but so contracted were the limits appropriated for each that he could only draw himself onto his shelf lengthwise and there lie, without stirring for fear of a fall or a broken head. We did not wish the windows open on account of the unhealthy miasms from the canal, and of course were uncomfortably hot. I had a good nap, on first crawling in, and a late one in the morning. . . .

Awoke. Looked out of my window upon a block of stores, which it seemed I could almost touch. . . . [W]e were in Chillicothe, the ancient seat of government of the Ohio, and the canal runs directly through it and is lined on either side with shops and stores. Took a long walk round the town, and am much pleased with it, but there is displayed much of the same negligence in building and the outskirts are filthy. . . .

Bradley and three other canal boat passengers hired a wagon for the next stage of their journey to Circleville.

One extent of rich, fertile bottom, and such glorious farms, 'twould make a New Englander farmer's mouth water to see them. They raise a vast quantity of beef and pork of the finest quality in this region. . . .

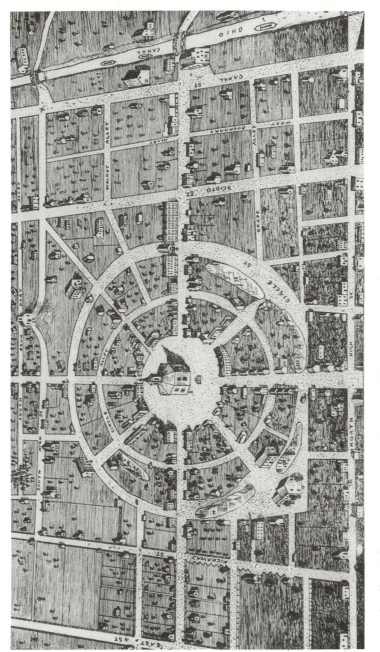

Circleville, Pickaway County, as it looked in 1835 when Cyrus P. Bradley traveled through on his way from Pittsburgh to Cincinnati to Sandusky. From Henry Howe, *Historical Collections of Ohio in Two Volumes,* vol. 2 (1902).

We passed through Jefferson [about three miles south of Circleville, and once considered a possible site of the county seat], a small *town* in the *township* of Pickaway, and forming the seat of justice of the *county* of Pickaway. It is now all in ruins, their decline entirely brought about by intemperance and dissipation, for which it was long notorious.

The dilapidated state of the houses is truly deplorable. "Somehow," said the drunken landlord of a tottering tavern, "the people seem to have all moved off to Circleville."

Arriving in Circleville, Bradley explored the huge Indian mound that the town was built on and around. The work of the prehistoric Indians was so reduced in size by plowing and building, Bradley remarked: "Our descendants of the second generation will know nought of them, except from description." He continued on to Columbus, where he found the city filled with legislators and others involved in a battle with Michigan over the boundary between the two states.

I went over the capitol. It is a small, square, temporary, brick building, with two entrances, and surmounted with a patriotic extract from [Joel] Barlow—a thing which struck me as in bad taste—a few energetic words might have answered—but twenty or thirty lines make an undignified appearance.

They will, however, ere long, erect a building more consonant with the wealth and power of the state. . . . Near the State House is a long building, containing the public offices and state library, and directly beyond is the court house, surmounted with a handsome dome. . . .

These buildings form one side of Capitol square, a public reservation, containing ten acres of fine clover, in which were rioting at pleasure somebody's pigs, perhaps the State's. . . .

11. *Thursday.* Were disappointed in our expectations of leaving Columbus today. The stage came in full from the south and we were obliged to give way, although we had engaged and paid for our passage. There being no opposition, the proprietors are perfect tyrants, absolutely uncivil in speech—they do not care to accommodate—if the stage is full, you must wait, even if it be a case of life and death—"we have no extras here, sir." I visited the legislature. They had a short session and did nothing. . . . Many of the members were smoking, and a great portion rested their legs and part of their bodies on the desks before them. . . .

12. Fri. Bid adieu with some regret, to this pleasant little village, or city, as the inhabitants in anticipation, persist in terming it. . . .

At Delaware, a very pleasant and thriving village, we tarried about an hour. This is the seat of the celebrated White Sulphur Springs, said to be fully equal to the noted Sulphurs of Virginia. We visited the principal spring. Near it, is erecting a most splendid hotel for the accommodation of visitors, whose convenience demands it and whose number it will doubtless greatly increase. . . .

Bradley went north by stagecoach via Marion to Sandusky across the swamps and prairies of the middle of the state. The roads got worse and worse.

The road in the afternoon was, if possible, worse than before dinner. Besides the usual depth of mud, we would occasionally, without warning, dive into a hole of unknown depth, filled with black mud, whose murky consistency effectually concealed the mysteries of the interior—and there stick. This they call being stalled—and on such occasions we were obliged to take a fence rail and help along. . . .

No attempt to cover the natural shaky, sticky black soil with anything of a firmer nature has ever been made, and where there was once a ditch at the side of the road, it is now obliterated. In one instance we turned from the road and waded through the long grass of the prairie for miles, prefering a foot of unadulterated water, for it stood to that depth on the surface of the ground, to a great or greater depth of mud. In another, we walked three long miles at one stretch, each one with his boots filled with water and holding up his pantaloons with both hands, as boys play in the puddles, and this because the state of the road was such the horses could not draw us. . . .

Bradley then discovered that three of his traveling companions were slave hunters from Virginia pursuing runaways across Ohio.

The three negroes were all, they said, first rate—one a good scholar, and remarkably intelligent. His master was then very sick, and could not live. Not long since, he expected to die immediately, having had a relapse, and sent for this slave, who had been hired out on another plantation. The faithful negro came, watched upon his master, and for a week never left his bedside except on his business and at his bidding. Yet this master, in expectation of a speedy departure, must rob this poor slave of his liberty that he may leave a larger inheritance to his children. These runaways went by stage to Chillicothe, and were so unwise as to enter their usual names on the waybills. At Chillicothe, the keeper of the principal house sent them to the negro tavern and this is the last they have been heard of. The hunters did not dare to go to the negroes on such an errand, but they are confident they have steered for Canada, as the runaways invariably do, and they expect to find them on the lake, detained by certain men they have stationed at the prominent places to watch or capture suspected negroes. They did not dare to make any inquiries on the road, because they say, they never get any satisfaction, and complain bitterly of the disposition the Ohio people show to cheat them out of their inalienable rights. . . .

In Sandusky, Bradley noticed two things: the unhealthiness of the location and climate and the size and number of the flies.

I was struck with one singularity—the air was filled and every sunny wall or building was covered with myriads of a disgusting fly, about an inch long, with large wings and feelers. They are sluggish in their movements and perfectly harmless—nobody seemed to notice them. When flying, if they strike an object, they either cling to it or fall, and 24 hours is the extent of their brief existence. Like mosquitoes, they breed on the water and generation daily follows generation in inconceivable numbers. The inhabitants did not appear to notice them, and gentlemen and ladies as they passed the streets were covered with these reptiles. They find their way into the houses and infest everything; even the table where we dined swarmed with them. A gentleman assured me, that he was on board a steamboat last week which ran aground at the mouth of the Detroit river in the night, and they were obliged to remain till daylight. In the morning, vast heaps of these vermin were found on deck, particularly congregated about the funnels, being either dead or nearly so, and that the quantity shoveled overboard was variously estimated by the passengers at from 6 to 8 bushels.

Almost immediately upon arrival in Sandusky, Bradley boarded a steamboat bound for Detroit. And thus ended his visit to Ohio.

A German Woman on the Ohio Frontier: The Memoir of Livvat Böke, 1835 and After

Livvat Knapke came to the United States from Neuenkirchen, a village near Osnabruck, Germany, during a wave of immigration in the 1830s. She came from an area that had been made desperately poor by the introduction of machine weaving, which had destroyed a major cottage industry, but her German village was a highly civilized place compared to frontier Ohio. In 1835, when she was about 28, she joined Bernard (Natz) Böke, her fiance, who had come over in 1833. They were married in Cincinnati, and settled on the land he bought near St. John (now Maria Stein), Mercer County, Ohio.

Livvat Böke was unusually well educated for a peasant. She could read and write, had been trained as a midwife and was skilled at drawing. Her memoirs of life in the German settlement in western Ohio are enlivened by her sketches of people, places, and frontier implements. She also was a woman of strong personality and firm convictions who wasn't afraid to take on authority, even the local priest, to whom she took a disliking.

She raised three children to adulthood. Her husband, Natz, died in 1857, three years after he fell from a tree and was crippled. She died in 1882.

The following selections are from her memoirs detailing her earliest years on the frontier. They were preserved by the family, unread, for some eighty years before a descendant, Vincent Boeke, began the job of sorting and translating them from Low German. After his death, the task was finished by Luke Knapke.

The memoirs were not organized chronologically. Böke wrote them by topic, or in essays or as instructions on how to make or do something. So the following pieces cannot be dated exactly but are from roughly the period 1835 to 1845.

How different I and Natz seem in those first times, how we struggled to overcome the dense, ominous, wet, silent forest, the streamlets, the creeks, the stones, the solitude . . . just we two against time, need and trees. The trees were strong-limbed and Natz is strong-boned.

It is indeed an important notion to describe how hard and tedious it was, the time it took to clear the land of all these trees and underbrush. The forest is a vast, attractive, wonderful sight to see and enjoy, but that one cannot eat or wear. Natz and I are thankful about our decision to emigrate to America. It is the best situation to live in the forest, also much better married to a nice fine man whom I love. Mary Joseph, I am so very thankful. . . .

Often there is no meat in the house, so that Natz goes out early in the morning in the dark with an empty stomach and his gun and powder. He says that his hunger and the thought of his hungry family forces him to try harder, and continually reminds him of his need and of our family's need, whereas with a full stomach he is more easygoing, negligent and lazy, all the time thinking about his house, and he wastes his time to no purpose. . . .

If he is not back home again by ten o'clock, then we eat hardtack or rye and cornmeal mush. Cornmeal pancakes with honey are the best. We know many different ways to prepare corn.

The Bökes had to make almost everything they used, including their cooking oil, clothing, bedding, and crockery.

Because people know that I am a midwife, I get many questions. The usual cause of the sicknesses and of the unsound outlook is that the people here do not use enough soap. Each time they have been in the woods, or with animals of any kind, or use the toilet, they must wash their hands thoroughly with soapy water and a clean hand towel. Once a week wash their bare bodies all over with soap and dry well with another clean body towel. People in the forest can be filthy and live untidily and think nothing of it. To sweat is good, to wash is better, particularly little children, else they become sore with raw buttocks. Health here is in danger. I told the community that all the water we drink must first be boiled, then covered with a clean lid so the flies and lice cannot get in. Let the water cool off, and drink from a proper clean cup held with clean hands. . . .

The wives worry themselves half to death with complaints. Many are without hope. Always and all the time they are in the dismal forest. Their husbands are usually outside in the woods, sawing and chopping down trees and gathering and burning the underbrush. . . .

Houses lie far apart from each other here in the forest. Right up to our doorsill and to those of our neighbors reaches the huge, somber and vaulted forest. There are no openings to break up the overshadowy wolf-haunted woodland. The great trees tower heavenwards until their individual crowns are lost among the many branches at the top, and the lower branches disappear under the wild growth that chokes the open places between the trunks. . . . The sunlight cannot get through the arches of the murmuring leaves. Through the grayish shadow and down the pathways in the forest men walk, continually in a kind of midday gloom. . . .

Life is a long struggle. We must fell the trees, but also cope with droughts, deep snow, sudden flooding, cloudbursts, forest fire, swarms of deerflies and mosquitos and midges, snakes, wolves, and twice the wolves were mad. If men meet mad wolves, it is certain that they will be bitten and that they will die with hydrophobia. There are many wild hens. Pigeons sometimes fill the woods here like clouds so that the sun is hidden! And they break the branches down. Squirrels in swarms eat up all the cornfields. In time, some people here go completely mad, change, commit suicide. Countless people do not talk with their spouses; many women have miscarriages, their pregnancy lost. . . .

Now finally we must especially push aside our Saxon cautiousness, sensitiveness and mysticism, and must let ourselves go with laughter and singing and fun. Afterwards we will better be able to clean, to build, and to try to fit in a new concept, namely, that the real need here in St. John or in our houses is *building of a new mental attitude*. There is more in life than gear for keeping warm, and clean, and for eating, drinking, bathing, sleeping, working and praying. There are also visiting, looking in on others with troubles. Everyone can contribute something. . . .

Everyone suffers, today, yesterday, or the day before, or whenever, with asthma, hay fever, allergies affecting the skin, grippe and that painful toothache. I have extracted many teeth with string and pliers. St. John is almost toothless. From bending and lifting trees and heavy work there are many men with hernias and I make for them a leather binding that fits tight. Some men, and the women in pregnancy, get piles and bleeding from the rectum (Latin). Yeast mixed with sheep liver oil into a salve applied outside and inside reduces the swelling. Used 3 or 4 times a day it brings relief. One must rub it into the rectum. Sore throat, rheumatism, dropsy, bad eyes, foot troubles, and on and on. This land is so different compared to Germany, and there are new sicknesses. The European body has not yet learned what it must watch out for and cannot resist. . . .

In the forest they say, "Death is always waiting to touch, intentionally and decisively, the trees and animals and plants that one likes." Hardly a day goes by without something dying, and then we must cut it down, or root it up, or bury it. Every day! . . . In some cases there is then a moment when a tiny little living thing gasps a little, squirms a little bit, and it is gone—so completely gone one wonders if it ever really existed! There it is—that extraordinary, that marvelous little organism, yes, it is already almost cold and stiff; and if one does not quickly bring a shovel there are promptly maggots! . . .

The immigrants here are mostly young folks. When something bad happens, it is to a young one—the old people stayed in Europe. In time, 20-30-40 years, there will also be old folks here and old folks must die; the young might. Because of the violent deaths of men and sometimes women, either in the forest, or from tools, or from guns and powder, or from bulls or other wild animals, or from lightning, the expectation for violent death is a little more natural here than it is in cities.

In the St. John-Stallostown vicinity: the first year here - 1835.

. . . We had to walk everywhere and used the Indian path north and south. The path to St. John village we made with logs and branches. We used wheelbarrows—back and forth—for fetching and carrying. Wheat, corn, and all things we carried or hauled by pack-saddle on a horse, to the mills or other businesses, to Sidney, Dayton, or Cincinnati, there and back. Riding horses were costly and scarce. One day each week Natz had to work for Marion Township, building bridges, culverts, roadways, dirt roads, dams; also half a day for building the church and school. That was precious time to give up, but not wasted.

During the winter Natz built us a *sundial,* and in the spring we set it up in an open space between the trees. Underneath he built a good foundation, solid and strong and level, of brick and mortar. Before he could make it level he also had to assemble an exact and accurate water level. He has the skill, patience and interest to figure it out. With so many needed tools and handmade things, he must think it out himself with minimum help from me. The neighbors are too far away and are not inventive. They are not interested until the time Natz had finished, built, or made something . . . and then they praise him greatly so that he will lend the item. . . .

In spring the children play in the warm forest, scurrying around and looking about, and carelessly they get turned around, don't recognize the surroundings, are *lost!* They feel as if they are in a tunnel, in great fear, alone and inept in the limitless forest. Then we parents uncertainly and fearfully search with stomach-wrenching worry. Often then the parents, unthinking and so badly upset also become lost in their urgent haste. Each neighborhood learns the vastness of the treacherous forest. . . .

At the beginning of summer the barns, cribs, cellars and stalls stand empty. There is only game to eat, no home-killed smoked meat, no sausage, no bacon. There is no milk in the pot, no butter in the dish, no cream in the churn, and many times there is no bread in the cupboard. We should and must help one another for the entire community's needs are our concern. The support of a neighbor would console us were we in a similar case. Onto our faith we must hold fast, for we farmers here in St. John depend above anything and everything on God's blessings. We know sympathy for the little man, helping when the shoe pinches. We must be patient for as Natz says, "By 1860 this will be a paradise. . . ."

Nevertheless, self-concern is more common each succeeding summer and is now almost epidemic. The people, men and women, are locked in the solitude of their own hearts and minds. The men want to chop down the forest in a short time, and it is not possible. The men fall short in their undertakings and, in their dissatisfaction, they are silent and sulky, sullen and pouty. Such behavior smothers the women's spirits, and they feel themselves alone, apart from the community, without friends and female companions. . . . Also the loneliness brings on drinking and suicide here. . . .

We all had our start under Europe's feudal system, but the forest here is a savage wilderness, and many people cannot adjust themselves. Their acceptance does not sit well. Their worth, and their patience strained, they don't know the how, why or when of the forest, of the work, or of adjusting to the lifestyle.

America is entirely different than we had imagined formerly. . . . [T]he American culture puts emphasis on things, acquisitions, possessions and status. . . .

In America, personal freedom, knowing one's own worth, and self-determination have great value. You are answerable to yourself alone. Here in America the Yankee culture places high value on being left alone, and one must not interfere with another or come between others. Yet self-culture or individualism is a terrifying demand or challenge which contains the elements of loneliness. . . .

The *Yankees* here were born in America. Their outlook and expectations are naturally more realistic; they can accept the reality of our forest. Their attitude is most positive, the highest. They read English newspapers. I can understand them well since I am studying English in order to speak and write it. (This is something for all Germans here to learn immediately.)

Following the Dream: Letters of the Thomson Family in Ohio and Indiana, 1818-1836

The Thomson brothers emigrated to Vinton County, Ohio, from Massachusetts with their families, leaving brothers, sisters and an elderly mother behind in Massachusetts. Thereafter the brothers intermittently kept in touch with the family back in New England, mainly by letter. The mother lived into her nineties, dying in 1836. The Thomson family followed a typical American migration pattern of the time: Joseph stayed in the East, Dan and Ziba emigrated as far as Ohio and stayed, and after a time in Ohio Seth and Eli picked up and went even further west, looking for better land and opportunities. Indiana and Illinois were usually first stops for migrants, such as Eli and Seth Thomson. Eventually, of course, as the far west opened and the land in the Midwest filled up and became more expensive, second and third generations moved on once again, as did Dan Thomson's son, George.

Before roads and canals made it easy to ship produce to markets outside the Midwest, farmers often had to turn their grain and fruits into alcohol to market them. Many settlers, such as Dan Thomson, and Job Phittiplace, a neighbor, thereby earned a living they couldn't have earned from the raw produce.

Wilksville, Ohio [Vinton County] November the 15, 1818.
Brother Ziba Thomson
   . . . I understand you have sold your farm[..] I want you to Come and build Mill on my farm for I have more business than I can attend to[.] I have bought one half of a Still wich is now running and all of a Sawmill in town which Cost me twelve hundred Dollar[.] [W]e run Six Bushel of Grain per Day and expect to run 18 after new year[.] [W]e find reddy Market for all the whiskey we make[.] Mill is wanted the most of any thing in this place . . . This Country looks a little [more] prosperous than it Did last fall five familys come in with a Month and three or four more Coming all Settled within a Mile of Seths [Thomson's.] Eight years ago not a house in the township and now about Six hundred inhabitants[,] a post road through the town. . . . if you think of Coming the Sooner you Come the better. . . . So I remain yours the Wilksvill November the 15 1818 Job Phittiplace

Wilksvill February the 6 1825
Brother Joseph Thomson
   I this day Stay at home from Meating to rite a few Lines to you once more to inform you we are all well as can be expected and I hope these lines will find you all reapeing the Same Blessing. . . . Seth has Swaped his farm for Town Lots in Wilksvill he is now building him a house on them to move in Soon he has found a hill of Stone of Sea Coal on his Lots in town but unbenown to any but his family and my Self the way he found it was by a Small Brook or spring that comes out of the hills and runs togeather that had washed the ground about as Deep as my head off the Coal it being not Cleaned Land[.] George one day hunting along the Brook he discovered Something black[.] Jumping down he began to dig out the coal with his fingers[.] I expect [t]he coal will be valuable in this place. . . . Your Brother and friend Eli Thomson

Dear Brother
   it is more than four years Since I left Bellingham [Massachusetts] and I have not wrote to you nor received any from you[.] I have no excuse to make only negligence and I thought I would not neglect it any longer[.] I would inform you that my Self wife and familey are all well[.] [W]e have had Some Sickness Since we lived in Wilksville though for the most part healthey[.] [L]ast year was very Sickley hear

The grave of Job Phettiplace (or Phittiplace) above Wilksville, Vinton County.

more than ever was known before[.] There was a number of our neighbours died of the bilous fever, George was Sick and his life dispared of for Sometime but he got well and has had his health Since[.] [W]e have ben blest with two more Sons in adition to our family the oldest we Call Charles and the youngest Stephen he has the title of Doctor being the Seventh Son[.] [T]here has been a great alteration in Wilksville Since I lived hear[.] [W]hen I first Came here there was but three houses that familys lived in round the publick Square or Common and now there is fifteen beside two[-]Story[.] one blacksmiths Shop one waggonmakers Shop one hatters Shop and a number of other buildings[.] Brothers Job and Seth and Ziba have got large two storey houses round the Common[.] I live about one hundred rods from them at the Same place where I first moved to[.] I live on one of the first Settled farms in Wilksville Sixty acres in the farm and more than half of it cleared with a good orchard and three houses one I use for a Shop[.] I plant four and a half acres of Corn this year my Orchard does not bean full this year but year before last if I had made all the apples into Cider I think I Could have made fifty barrels but I only made eighteen on account of there being no Cider mill Short of two miles from here[.] [M]y work has been Cabinet making principly Since I have ben here except I finished one Small Organ the first Summer that I lived here at Galipolis and now I have just begun a Small Organ that I am to have three hundred and twenty dollars for[.]

[M]y Son George has ben a School master the three first winters that he lived here and Since then he has tended Store for one of our merchants here[.] [H]e has built him a two Storey house with two Stacks of Chimneys the largest house in the vilige except one he was married last fall to Sophia Strong. . . .

Give my love to my Mother if She is alive[.] She is in her eighty fifth year of her age and is an old woman[.] I don't no that I Shall ever See her again[.] [W]hen I went away I expected to Come Come [*sic*] back and take my leave of her and crave her blessing but I presume I have her blessing now as she is a dutiful Mother. . . . I remain your friend and Brother
Dan Thomson
Wilksville July 14th 1831

Wilksville June the 19 1833
Brother Joseph Thomson I feel it a Grate pleasure to write a few lines by way of communicating our thoughts unto you and our knews what we have to write although we are so far distant we cant se each other Yet we can talk with Each other in writing. Brother Job Phettiplace has Left us to be with us no more he Died the Last Day of May with the Consumption. . . . the rest of our Relations are all well. . . . Seth moved from Wilksvill last Summer to the State of Indiany on the St. Joseph River, him and his family are well pleased with the country we expect him back this Summer I have Sold to Ziba and have made my Calculations to go back with Seth this Summer

. . . Joseph fail not to write me a letter and you will oblige Your Brother and friend Eli Thomson

Mishawaka St. Joseph County Indiany
August 17 1836
Brother Joseph Thomson
I feel myself under the necesity of of takeing my paper pen and ink to rite to you after So Long time absent from hering anything from you for I know not whither—I am riting to the Dead or Living but I trust to providence this Letter may find you all alive[.] Brother Joseph I have neglected riting to you So Long I hardly know where to begin or Leave of[f] but I mus tell you I am In good health and brother Seth and his family are well Seth and his family and myself are all of our connections in this Country[.] Brother Seth was back in the Ohio Last June and all our brothers and sisters all well and I hope these Lines will find you all enjoying the Same Grate blessing of health . . .

Brother Joseph I am now workeing here at Mishawaka on the St. Joseph River at one Dollar per Day Carpentering 3 miles above the southernmost bend in the river and 8 miles below where Seth lives[.] Mishawaka is a Lively thriving place on the St Joseph river with grate water power[.] Iron works are established here and a Large Cotton factory is now to be built and money plenty and Land raising fast[.] Seth owns a farm of 120 acres and I have got 120 acres close by Seths and Horace Thomson owns 160 acres and Seths George has not bot any land yet . . .

· This is the finest country of Land I ever saw. . . . we are 30 miles from lake Michigan[.] Steam boats come up the river to this place in high water.

George W. Thomson [son of Daniel] has moved from Wilkvill Ohio on to the Missippy near St. Louis, he moved in Consequence of going bale for a merchant in Ohio and failed and run off[.] We had a letter from George W. Thomson about 4 weeks since he rote they were all well and he was comeing here this fall I believe Dan makes a Living in Ohio and that is about all and Ziba is Doeing verry well when I came from there 2 years since I left here and Nancy Phettiplace and the Boys are Doeing well[.] Seth is Doeing better in this Country than he ever did in any other place. . . . brother Joseph I have not much more to rite at preasant that will be much interesting to you as this is a new Country here is much to be made in speculation. . . . my best respects to you all[.]
Eli Thomson

Disease and Death on the Frontier: Judge Fowler Remembers the Death of His Family, 1836

Judge Harvey Fowler emigrated to Margaretta Township near Venice in the Firelands in 1818. He still lived there in 1867, when he told the following account of the deaths of four members of his family of milk sickness or sick-stomach. Many other families could tell similar stories on the frontier.

August 8th, 1836, my third daughter, nearly eight years old, was taken sick. The second day she was prostrated and seemed to be sinking rapidly, but revived by the help of medicine. She was taken vomiting in the evening of the second day and died on the morning of the fifth day, having had medical attendance during her entire sickness. On the 10th of August my second daughter, a remarkably robust girl nearly eleven years old, was taken with vomiting, attended with high fever and the most intense restlessness, that continued for three days, when her case assumed a more sinking form and her life was only kept up by the use of the most powerful stimulants and chafing the extremities, which continued for several days when she revived and seemed better. Her physician thought there was no further use of medicine, and for several days she seemed doing well, but began to complain of soreness in the throat, which resulted in the rupture of a blood vessel and a profuse discharge of blood from the nose and mouth, which prostrated her very much, and on the 27th of August she breathed her last. On the 8th of September my only son, a little over five years old, was taken sick with the same disease and died in two and a half days.

My wife, who was much worn down by fatigue, was taken with the same disease on the 7th of September, and her case was promptly attended by three skillful physicians, but without success. She died on the 21st of September, being the fourth member of my family consigned to the grave in the short space of six weeks and three days.

The Battle of the Bridge: Oren Wiley Tells of Early Commercial Competition, 1836

Oren Wiley emigrated from New England to Ohio City, Ohio, in 1836. He worked in a tin shop there and later became a partner in the store. He eventually returned to Massachusetts in the mid 1850s. "The Battle of the Bridge" is his account of a quarrel between the residents of Cleveland and the inhabitants of Ohio City, across the Cuyahoga River, over the building of a bridge across the river that diverted traffic from the farmers and merchants of Ohio City.

In the course of the fall months of Oct. and Nov. of this year [1836] a controversy arose between Ohio City and Cleveland. The difficulties arrose from a bridge that was built across the Cuyahoga River at the most southerly point of the City of Cleveland, on the principal road leading to the state's capital, and was every [sic] calculated to take the travel from Ohio City and forward it to Cleveland. This was too much for the infant city to endure.

It was soon ascertained that fair means was to no purpose. Foul followed next. It was on a pleasant afternoon in the month of Oct. All the bravest wariors being assembled and after lending a listening ear to a number of stump speeches from the greatest talent that the city could produce, gave a war whoop and imediately repaired to the

so much accursed bridge for the purpose of entirely battering it from
its foundation. I think about one hundred men volunteered their services. Among the number was the presbyterian Priest and [he] could
be seen urging the wariors on to battle.

They commenced their work of destruction by hewing off the
principal timbers and thus let the bridge fall from its foundation to
the water below. Perseverence universally prevailed. The fate of the
bridge for a time looked like inevitable ruin. Entirely destitute of all
opposition and backed up in their glorious cause by all the farming
interest in the back part of the town, nought but success appeared to
attend their victorious arms.

Thus things for a time went on, but their prosperity was of short
duration. The war bugle's note was sounded clear and shrill throughout Cleveland. All were in arms, as much so as if the fate of the city
had depended on [the] bridge for its salvation. A formidable force was
immediately raised, armed with rifles, pistoles, dirks, boaknives, axes,
clubs, and brickbats. Thus led on by the Sheriff of the county, Ohio
City forces were ordered to disperse instantly, which they promptly
refused to do. The Provincials still continued their work of destruction.

At length when it was ascertained that threats were to no purpose, the party from Cleveland made a desperate rush and commenced
throwing stones and brickbats, which was returned by the opposite
party in a most violent manner. Stones, brickbats, clubs, and axes
were hurled back and forth in a manner that would make an eastern
man shudder to witness the scene. At last a man from Cleveland
received a brickbat in the side of the head. He drew his pistol and
fired. The smell of gunpowder seemed to increase the tiger like disposition that prevailed. The word was given to fire which was obeyed
instantly. Fortunately none were killed, but a number were severely
wounded. As soon as the rifles were discharged the opposite party
made a rush upon their opponents and wrenched their deadly weap-
ons from them, broke them to attoms and threw them into the river
where they must always remain. Eight first rate rifles were thus destroyed in a few minutes besides quite a number of pistols.

One man from Ohio City had a ball pass through his side, another received a ball in the neck, and a number was wounded with
shot. Thus some were wounded, some were knocked over with
stones, others were beaten with clubs in a most savage manner. On
the whole both parties appeared like a bloody set of savages. Both
parties withdrew from the field of battle, the bridge left on its foundation and neither party conquered, but both got most severely

whipped. Two men [on] our side were seized and carried to Cleveland, thrown into jail, remained till next day. I call it our side because I reside in Ohio City, but I took no part on either side whatever.

After more such incidents, including two attempts to blow up the bridge, the town leaders agreed to settle their differences by establishing a ferry service and then building another bridge to serve the people of Ohio City. Eventually, Ohio City merged with Cleveland.

Childhood in Van Wert County: Thaddeus Gilliland's Boyhood, 1835 and After

Thaddeus Gilliland came to Van Wert County with his family in 1835. His father, James G. Gilliland, was one of the area's early settlers. Thaddeus's stories of the early days are ones he heard from his family and neighbors, and later compiled into a history of the county.

Once, while the Wyandot Indians were still here Elmyra Gilliland (now Mrs. M. H. McCoy) and her cousin, Elizabeth Gilliland, were hunting the cows about a mile from home, when they came across an Indian camp and saw smoke coming out of one of the huts. Elizabeth became so frightened that she ran away in terror, lost her bonnet and would not stop to pick it up. Elmyra, who was more inquisitive, went up and threw down one of the slabs of which the huts were constructed, looked in and then drove her cows home. They were not aware that there were any Indians near until then.

Many of the Indians were very friendly and would frequently stay all night at the writer's father's house, and would talk quite freely if there were none but the family present, but if any strangers were about it was difficult to get them to say a word. Of one Indian in particular, whose name was Half John, the writer was quite fond. His hair was so long that it reached down to the seat on which he sat, and the writer used to slip up, pull his hair and then run away. He used to say that he wanted his venison cooked so that when he was eating it the blood would run out of each side of his mouth. . . .

One day in 1839 Sarah Gilliland was teaching school in the McCoy and Beard neighborhood, when a drunken Indian, by the name of Snakehead, came in and scared the teacher and scholars very badly. About half the scholars were red-headed, and the Indians never like red-headed people. Snakehead would pat Daniel Norman on the head and say "Nice Papoose," then he would take M. H. McCoy by the hair and pull him around, give a big whoop and run his knife around and say, "Indian scalp him." Mrs. Beard saw that there was something wrong and arming herself with a handspike drove Snakehead away. He went off muttering "Brave squaw, Brave squaw." He then went to David McCoy's, where he was told that if he would give up his knife and tomahawk he might stay all night. He curled down on the hearth and slept until morning. In the morning he was duly sober and sorry for what he had done. He said, "All Cook whisky." Daniel Cook sold whisky to whoever had money to pay for it, although it was against the law to sell whisky to Indians. . . .

A practical joke that reacted on the originators occurred about this time. Samuel S. Brown carried the mail between Greenville and Van Wert once a week on horseback. Frank Dodds, Frank Mott, S. M. Clark and Bill Parent and one or two others concluded they would have Brown get a pint of good whisky from Greenville as they would not drink Dan Cook's whisky. They decided they would not let Jim Graves have any. But the secret was too good to keep and some one told Graves' wife. Well you know how that goes. The day that Brown was to come, Jim Graves went south along the Greenville road and sat down on a log and waited. When Brown came along, Graves said, "Mr. Brown, the boys are across the creek hunting and wanted me to get that pint of whisky and bring it over to them." Graves got the whisky and when Brown reached town they were all out looking for him, wanting to know if he had brought the whisky. You can imagine their feelings when he said, "I gave it to Jim Graves. He said you were hunting over on the other side of the creek and had sent him over for it."

The following story, told by J.B. Brodnix, is included in Gilliland's history. The Brodnixes were neighbors of the McCoys and Beards. They came from Philadelphia via Cincinnati and Dayton, to Long Prairie, York Township, in 1839.

When we were unloaded on the Long Prairie, father and mother both cried, and offered the man that moved them all that they had—$25— to take them back to Dayton where he lived. This the man refused to do on account of the terrible roads. . . .

In December we moved into the log cabin, half of it floored with puncheons and with a bed quilt serving for a door. There was a fireplace five by seven feet in dimensions, a mud-back wall and a stick chimney. When night would come, the wolves would approach the house and scratch and howl until we could hear nothing else. For 10 years between the months of November and February, from sunset until sunrise, nothing could be heard except the howling of the wolves and the hooting of the owls. . . .

Many and trying were the hardships of those days, much harder for us than for others. Father was a French Huguenot and had never done a day's work; Mother was Scotch and was also raised in the city. Many were the sacks of meal and chunks of pork and other things given us by David W. McCoy, Daniel Beard, Thomas Pollock and others. . . .

With all the hardships, many and dear are the fond recollections of those days.

The great majority of my early associates have crossed the mystic river, a few are waiting to join the mighty throng on the other shore. Time and space would fail me to tell the many thrilling incidents that occurred in the days when this region was being reclaimed.

Ottawa Indians Leave Ohio:
Dresden W.H. Howard's Memoir of the Removal
of Ottawas from the Maumee Valley, 1838

Dresden W.H. Howard grew up in Grand Rapids, Ohio, as a child of the white settlements among the Ottawa Indians, who had long inhabited an area in northwestern Ohio. He grew up to become an Indian agent for the federal government. As an agent, he became involved in arranging for the removal of the Indians from the Maumee Valley to Kansas. His memoirs of these historical events make it clear how much of his sympathies lay with the natives.

No incident in the settlement of the Maumee Valley was fraught with greater interest than the removal of the scattered bands of the last remnant of the Indians in the fall of 1835.

Their original titles to the land had been extinguished by treaty whereby they had conveyed their land to the U.S. Government, although by stipulation they had the right to remain until the settlement of the country by the whites required their removal. That time had now arrived, and the whole country was over run by land speculators more or less since 1832. . . .

As one of the men designated to gather the Indians together and accompany them to Kansas, Howard rode out to meet with the chiefs.

I remember that I was very anxious to take in Chief Ottokee's band, as he had always been from boyhood a particular friend of mine, while Duncan Forsythe was a favorite of the young and intelligent Chief Wauseon, who was a much younger man than his brother, Ottokee. . . .

We were obliged to spend many days, even weeks, in persuading and coaxing them to go; to leave their camp grounds and assemble at the island [Buttonwood]. . . . They had rested so long undisturbed in their quiet camps, that they had begun to think that the day of their removal would never come. But it was now upon them. Many an evening conference was held long into the night, smoking the kinnaknick over this to them important subject. . . . Many weeks were consumed in breaking camp and preparing them to move to the headwaters of the Maumee on an island where many of the Indians were gathered in preparations for the long journey so soon to commence. . . .

It was pitiful sometimes, at these interviews, to observe the silent tear welling from the breaking hearts, steal down the wrinkled dusky cheeks of the old grey haired men, Braves and Warriors in their day, at the painful thought of leaving the graves of their fathers, the old and familiar camping grounds, the springs of sparkling water, the Council fires, never to be revisited, never again to meet in their Council lodge on their native hills and streams. . . .

It was not until the fall of 1838 that the preparations were completed, and the noisy, excited camp of men, women and children, at the island was broken up. . . .

The women, as was the Indian custom, did all the work of packing their limited stock of provisions; beds, blankets, clothing, camp kettles, and other implements of house keeping; catch and bring in the horses from the range; saddle and load them with their goods packed in bundles; lash them upon the horses backs, or, if moving by water, load the canoes, while the men sat in the shade smoking their pipes of tobacco (Kin-nec-ka-neck) as contented and unconcerned as if they had no interest in the noisy confusion about them, until the cavalcade was ready to move, when he shouldered his rifle and lead off on the trail towards their destination and home. . . .

At last all was ready, and on a beautiful morning the 2nd of September A. D. 1838, the long and disorderly wagon train with pack ponies, old women with heavy packs upon their shoulders, young squaws with papoose lashed on boards, slung comfortably upon their backs. The older women were not required to carry heavy burdens, but they had been endured [inured] to it from childhood, and would not at this late day trust their valuables to the white man's wagon or the stumbling pack horse, but they had never started out on such a long journey. . . .

We who had gathered them from their beautiful woods and streams were their friends, and could but sympathize with them, and were not over vigilant or on our guard, and more than once a hint was thrown out, that the tracks through the woods on the trail would be very blind and hard to follow. A few mornings before reaching the waters of the Wabash several small families and individuals, both men and women, were missing from camp, but no great effort was made to follow them. One reason, several hundred still remained in their villages and haunts and it was only a question [of time] when all would bow to the inevitable and seek homes in the west with their friends and neighbors, who had gone before them. All would be removed without reserve. The poor creatures who had deserted our camp, were merely respited for a time from their inevitable doom.

News from Cleveland: Newspaper Stories from a Growing Industrial City, 1839-1841

The following newspaper stories are from the *Cleveland Herald and Gazette*, 1839 to 1841, when Cleveland was a bustling, growing lakeport town, industry was being established, and the railroad was on its way. Finally, Ohio towns were suffering industrial accidents, crime, and all the other ills of modern urban society.

Sept. 20, 1838

TERRIBLE ACCIDENT—Yesterday the cylinder house connected with the Powder Mill of L. B. Austin & Co., about a mile and a half from this place, was blown up, and we are pained to add, caused the death of Mr John L. Ingram, a worthy and industrious young man, who was at the time employed in the mill. Fortunately, there was no other person with Mr Ingram at the time, although there were injured. There was in the building at the time of the accident, about 1000 lbs. powder, and the explosion, as maybe readily imagined, was terrible—scattering the fragments of the house in every direction. Mr Ingram was carried through the air about 30 rods to a bank on the opposite side of the Little Cuyahoga river, against which he was thrown with so much force as to partially bury his body in the earth. His limbs were broken, his body mangled to a shocking degree, and when found, life was extinct. Mr Ingram left a wife and family to mourn his untimely fate.

The cause of the explosion is, of course, unknown; but it is supposed to have proceeded from a spark of fire caused by using an iron sledge hammer in driving some wedges about the machinery, as Mr Ingram had a few moments before taken a hammer from another shop for that purpose and the same hammer was found near his body, and is supposed to have been carried there in his hands.

The loss is estimated at seven or eight hundred dollars.—*Akron Balance.*

June 26, 1839

ROBBERY.—A gentleman from New York city was robbed of about $1800 on one of the canal packets last Saturday night. He had placed his pocket book containing the money in his trunk for safety, and his trunk in the cabin near his berth. On arriving at the Hotel yesterday morning he missed the pocket book.—Fortunately the robber did not find larger packages which were in his trunk, amounting to about $30,000. A person employed on the boat is suspected, and has been arrested.

RAIL ROADS IN THE UNITED STATES—We published a few days ago some account of the railroads in the South either finished or in course of construction. In almost every part of the country this species of internal improvement is advancing with a degree of rapidity which indicates its admirable adaptation to the wants of the age and to the natural character of our territory.

The first railroad constructed in the United States was opened in 1827. This was the Quincy road in Massachusetts, extending from the Quincy quarries to the Neponset river a distance of only four miles. The Mauch Chunk road in Pennsylvania was the next. . . . Such was the extent of railroad in this country twelve years ago. The Baltimore and Ohio Rail Road was begun about the same time—but there was more sagacity displayed at that period in the conception of the design than vigour in the prosecution of it.

The extent of Rail Road in the United States now including all that is in actual operation or in rapid progress to completion, is two thousand two hundred and seventy miles or thereabout. There are other roads in cour[s]e of construction, but not so far advanced, to the extent of two thousand three hundred miles more; making in all upwards of *four thousand five hundred miles* of railroad in this country. . . .

These great iron-bound avenues running through the interior and uniting important points will be as arteries of the system. Connecting with these there are miner ramifications which will go on to multiply, intersecting every portion of the country and giving facilities to a quick and rapid circulation, whereby the inherent energies and resources of the land will be developed to an extent which nothing in the history of the world hitherto has ever equalled. . . . —*Balt. American.*

Nov. 17, 1841

LITTLE MIAMI RAIL ROAD.—The Cincinnatians anticipate travelling from that city to Lake Erie by Rail Road in two or three years from this. A few miles of their end of the Little Miami Rail are completed, and the locomotive "Gov. Morrow" is puffing away upon it. The Chronicle says the road will be ready for use to Milford, 15 miles, in about two weeks. The road to Xenia, 60 miles, will be finished in about a year. Thence to Sandusky city, in connection with the Mad River Rail Road, the work is in progress, and portion completed.

The Last Good-bye: The Xenia Torch-light *Notes the Departure of the Wyandots, 1843*

As Western civilization was stamped firmly onto Ohio, the remaining Indian reservations came under more and more pressure from increasing white settlement around them. Whites squatted on the Indians' lands, sold them liquor, cheated them, and otherwise harassed them. Partly to open their land to white settlement, and partly to move them beyond the depredations of the worst elements of the white community, the government encouraged the Indians to sell out and go west beyond the Mississippi. In March, 1842, the last tribe, the Wyandots of Upper Sandusky, who had been largely Christianized by the work of John Stewart and James Finley, agreed to sell and emigrate. They left on horseback July 11, 1843. The Xenia Torch-light recorded their departure as they passed near the town.

The remains of this once flourishing tribe of Indians passed through our town on Sunday morning last. They encamped about three miles north of town on Saturday evening, where they had intended to remain over the Sabbath, but some person or persons, having injudiciously furnished the intemperate among them with ardent spirits, it was thought best to leave in the morning, for fear that their peace

would be seriously disturbed by those few who had become intoxi-
cated. The general appearance of these Indians was truly prepossess-
ing. Every one of them, we believe, without an exception, was decently dressed, a large proportion of them in the costume of the
whites. Their deportment was quite orderly and respectful. We are
informed that nearly one-half of them make a profession of the Christian religion. They appeared to be well fitted out for their journey,
having a convenient variety of cooking utensils, and provisions in
abundance. The whole number of persons in the company, so far as
we could learn, was about 750. The numbers of wagons, carriages
and buggies owned by the tribe, about 80. Hired wagons 55. Horses
and ponies near 300.

Our citizens seemed to look upon the scene of their departure
from among us with feelings of melancholy interest. To reflect that
the last remnant of a powerful people, once the proud possessors of
the soil we now occupy, were just leaving their beloved hunting
grounds and the graves of their ancestors—that their council fires
had gone out and their wigwams were deserted—was well calculated
to awaken the liveliest sympathies of the human heart. No one, we
are sure, who felt such emotions, could refrain from breathing a de-
vout aspiration to the "Great Spirit," that he would guide and protect them on their journey, and carefully preserve them as a people
after they shall have arrived at their new home in the far, far west.

Thus ended the Native American presence in Ohio, and with it, the last vestiges of the frontier. And yet, not quite. Margaret Grey Eyes left with her family in 1843, but many years later, after the death of her husband, she quietly
returned to Upper Sandusky. She bought a house there, where she was living
when the American government restored the crumbling Wyandot mission
church. And there she died in 1890, the last of her people in Ohio.

Bibliography

Alder, Jonathan. *The Captivity of Jonathan Alder and His Life with the Indians,* prepared for distribution by Orley E. Brown. Alliance, Oh., 1965.

Aldrich, Lewis Cass. "Speech by Otto-wau-kee, 1831." In *History of Henry and Fulton Counties,* edited by Lewis Cass Aldrich, 29-32. Syracuse, N.Y., 1888.

Armstrong, John. "Letter of Ensign John Armstrong to Lt. Col. Josiah Harmar at Ft. McIntosh, April 12, 1785." In *Western Reserve and Northern Ohio Historical Society,* Tracts 1-36 (1870-1877), no. 6:3-4.

Badger, Joseph. *A Memoir of Rev. Joseph Badger. . . .* Hudson, Oh.: Sawyer, Ingersoll & Co., 1851.

Baily, Francis. *Journal of a Tour in Unsettled Parts of North America in 1790 and 1797,* edited by Jack D.L. Holmes. Carbondale: Southern Illinois University and Feffer & Simons, 1969.

Barker, Cynthia. Letter to Julia Buttles, September 19, 1813. In the Julia Buttles Case papers. VFM 1620. From the collections of the Ohio Historical Society, Columbus, Oh.

Barker, Joseph. *Recollections of the First Settlement of Ohio,* edited by George Jordan Blazier. Marietta, Oh.: Marietta College, 1958.

Beatty, Charles. *The Journal of a Two-Months Tour; With a View of Promoting Religion among the Frontier Inhabitants of Pennsylvania, and of Introducing Christianity Among the Indians to the Westward of the Allegheny Mountains.* Edinburgh, 1798.

Bentley, Anna Briggs. "Correspondence of Anna Briggs Bentley from Columbiana County, 1826," edited by Bayly Ellen Marks. *Ohio History* 78 (1969): 38-45.

Böke, Liwwat. *Livvat Böke, 1807-1882, Pioneer. . . ,* compiled and edited by Luke B. Knapke. Minster, Oh.: Minster Historical Society, 1987.

Bradley, Cyrus P. "Journal of Cyrus P. Bradley," edited by George H. Twiss. *Ohio Archaeological and Historical Publications* 15 (1906): 207-70.

Brady, Hugh, John Sprott, and Nancy Stoops. Three accounts of Samuel Brady's rescue of Jane Stoops. In *Frontier Retreat on the Upper Ohio: 1779-1781.* Publications of the State Historical Society of Wisconsin, edited by Louise Phelps Kellogg, vol. 24:203-8. Madison: The State Historical Society of Wisconsin, 1917.

Brown, William Wells. *Narrative of William W. Brown, A Fugitive Slave.* Boston, 1847.

Butler, Richard. "The Journal of Richard Butler, 1775," edited by Edward G. Williams. Second installment. *Western Pennsylvania Historical Magazine 47*, no. 1 (January 1964): 31-46.

Case, Leonard. "Early Settlement of Warren, Trumbull Co., Ohio." *Western Reserve and Northern Ohio Historical Society,* Tracts 1-36 (1870-1877), no. 30:1-13.

Clark, Philothe Case. "Old Esquire Case, J. P., 32 Years in Succession." *The Fire Lands Pioneer 5* (1864): 114-16.

Cleveland Herald & Gazette, September 20, 1838, June 26, 1839, and November 17, 1841.

Cresswell, Nicholas. *The Journal of Nicholas Cresswell, 1774-1777, 2d ed.* New York: Dial Press, 1928.

Croghan, William. Letter to William Davies, July 6, 1782. George Rogers Clark papers, 1781-1784. Virginia Series, vol. 4. Collections of the Illinois State Historical Library 19:71-73. Springfield, Ill., 1926.

Cuming, Fortescue. "Sketches of a Tour to the Western Country." In *Frontier Retreat on the Upper Ohio, 1779-1781,* edited by Reuben Gold Thwaites. Publications of the State Historical Society of Wisconsin 4. Madison: State Historical Society of Wisconsin, 1904.

Curtis, Henry B. "Pioneer Days in Central Ohio." *Ohio Archaeological and Historical Publications* 1 (1887-1888): 240-51.

Cutler, Manasseh. "A Description of the Soil, Productions, etc., of that Portion of the United States Situated between Pennsylvania and the Rivers Ohio and Scioto and Lake Erie," translated by John H. James. *Ohio Archaeological and Historical Society Publications* 3 (1891): 82-108.

Dascomb, Marianne. "Mrs. M.P. Dascomb to Home Friends, Dunbarton, N.H." In appendix to *Oberlin: The Colony and the College, 1833-1883,* by James H. Fairchild. Oberlin, Oh.: E.J. Goodrich, 1883.

Ewing, Thomas. Autobiographical sketch. In *History of Athens County, Ohio,* by Charles M. Walker, 395-96. Cincinnati: Robert Clarke & Co., 1869.

———. "The Autobiography of Thomas Ewing," edited by Clement L. Martzolff. *Ohio Archaeological & Historical Publications* 22 (1913): 147-49.

Faux, William. *Memorable Days in America: Being a Journal of a Tour to the United States . . . and Intended to Shew Men and things as they are in America.* London, 1823.

Finley, James B. *Life Among the Indians; or, Personal Reminiscences and Historical Incidents Illustrative of Indian Life and Character.* Cincinnati, 1857.

Foster, Luke. "Letter of Luke Foster to Thomas Clark." *Quarterly Publication of the Historical & Philosophical Society of Ohio* 18, no. 1 (1923): 102-8.

Fowler, Harvey. "Personal Reminiscences." *Fire Lands Pioneer* 8 (1867): 91-94.

Gilliland, Thaddeus. "Ridge Township." In *History of Van Wert County, Ohio and Representative Citizens,* edited by Thaddeus S. Gilliland, 134-52. Chicago: Richmond & Arnold, 1906.

Gist, Christopher. *Christopher Gist's Journals.* Pittsburgh: J.R. Weldin & Co., 1893.

Grant, Roswell M. "Letter of Roswell M. Grant to the Mahoning Valley Historical Society, September 7, 1875." *Historical Collections of the Mahoning Valley. . . .* 1:74-79. Youngstown, Oh.: Mahoning Valley Historical Society, 1876.

Hawley, Zerah. *A Journal of a Tour Through Connecticut, Massachusetts, New-York, the North Part of Pennsylvania and Ohio, Including a Year's Residence in That Part of the State of Ohio, Styled New Connecticut, or Western Reserve.* New Haven, Oh.: S. Converse, 1822.

Heckewelder, John. "A Canoe Journey from the Big Beaver to the Tuscarawas in 1773: A Travel Diary of John Heckewelder," translated and edited by August C. Mahr. *Ohio State Archaeological & Historical Quarterly* 61:283-98.

———. "First White Child in Ohio," by A.T. Goodman. *Western Reserve and Northern Ohio Historical Society,* Tracts 1-36 (1870-1877), no. 4:1-7.

Henkel, Paul. "Rev. Paul Henkel's Journal," translated by Rev. F.E. Cooper and edited by Clement L. Martzloff. *Ohio Archaeological and Historical Publications* 23 (1914): 162-218.

Hoffman, Charles H. [A New-Yorker, pseud.]. *A Winter in the West.* New York: Harper & Brothers, 1835.

Howard, Dresden W.H. "The Removal of the Indians from the Maumee Valley," edited by Robert F. Bauman. *Northwest Ohio Quarterly* 30 (1958): 10-25.

Howe, Henry. "The Capture and Suicide of a Fugitive Slave." In *Historical Collections of Ohio in Two Volumes,* by Henry Howe, 2:277-78. Cincinnati: C.J. Krehbiel & Co., 1908.

Howells, William Cooper. *Recollections of Life in Ohio, from 1813 to 1840.* Cincinnati: Robert Clarke Co., 1895.

Jolley, Henry. Account of the murder of Logan's family. In "Jefferson County." *Historical Collections of Ohio in Two Volumes,* by Henry Howe, 1:961-62. Cincinnati: C.J. Krehbiel & Co., 1902.

Jones, David. *Journal of Two Visits made to Some Nations of Indians on the West Side of the River Ohio, in the Years 1772 and 1773.* New York, 1865.

Linton, Samuel. "Ancient Correspondence." Letter of Samuel Linton to Abel Saterthwaite, May 5, 1804. *Ohio Archaelogical & Historical Society Publications* 9 (1901): 117-24.

Logan. Speech of 1774. Thomas Jefferson's first version in his Memorandum

Book for 1774. In "Logan's Oration: A Case Study in Ethnographic Authentication," by James H. O'Donnell III. *Quarterly Journal of Speech* 65 (1979): 150-56.

May, John. *Journal and Letters of Col. John May, of Boston Relative to Two Journeys to the Ohio Country in 1788 and '89.* Cincinnati: Robert Clarke & Co., 1873.

Mays, Ruhamah. Letter to Elizabeth Case in Granby, Connecticut, August 23, 1805. In the Julia Buttles Case papers. VFM 1620. From the collections of the Ohio Historical Society, Columbus, Oh.

Melish, John. *Travels in the United States of America in the Years 1806, 1807, and 1809, 1810 and 1811.* Philadelphia: T & G Palmer, 1812.

Morgan, Isham. "A Sketch of Pioneer Life." *Annals of the Early Settlers' Association of Cuyahoga County* 2, no. 7 (1886-1891): 406-11.

Osborn, Charity. Letter to Marcus Mead, March 2, 1864. *Fire Lands Pioneer* 5 (1864): 76-78.

Penn, John, "Letter to the Shawanese Indians Concerning their Difficulties with the People of Virginia." Pennsylvania Archives, 4th ser., vol. 3, *Papers of the Governors, 1759-1785.* Harrisburg, Pa., 1900.

Phittiplace, Job, Dan Thomson, and Eli Thomson. Correspondence. In the Joseph Thomson papers. VFM 2958. From the collections of the Ohio Historical Society, Columbus, Oh.

Pownall, Thomas. *A Topographical Description of the Dominions of the United States of America,* edited by Lois Mulkearn. Pittsburgh: University of Pittsburgh Press, 1949.

Smith, James. *An Account of the Remarkable Occurrences in the Life and Travels of Col. James Smith, During his Captivity with the Indians, in the Years 1755, '56, '57, '58, and '59.* Cincinnati: Robert Clarke & Co., 1870.

————. "Tours into Kentucky and the Northwest Territory." *Ohio Archaelogical & Historical Publications* 26 (1917): 348-401.

Stewart, John. *The Missionary Pioneer, or a Brief Memoir of the Life, Labours, and Death of John Stewart, (man of Colour,) founder, under God of the Mission Among the Wyandotts at Upper Sandusky, Ohio,* collected and arranged by William Walker. New York, 1827.

Stickney, Benjamin. Letter to Major General John S. Gano, Dec., 1813. *Quarterly Publication of the Historical and Philosophical Society of Ohio* 18, no. 1 (1923): 10-11.

Suppiger, Leo. "Swiss Emigrants Seek Home in America," edited by Leo G. Titus. *Bulletin of the Historical and Philosophical Society in Ohio* 14, no. 3 (July 1956): 167-85.

Taylor, Royal. "An Interesting Letter" (to Hon. Harvey Rice, August 25, 1887). *Annals of the Early Settlers' Association of Cuyahoga County* 2, no. 7 (1886-1891): 143-45.

Trent, William. *Journal of Captain William Trent from Logstown to Pickawillany,*
  A.D. 1752, edited by Alfred T. Goodman. Cincinnati, 1871.
Trollope, Frances. *Domestic Manners of the Americans.* New York: Dodd, Mead
  & Co., 1927.
Wiley, Oren. "The Journal of a Vermont Man in Ohio, 1836-1842," edited by
  LeRoy P. Graf. *Ohio State Archaeological and Historical Quarterly* 60 (1951):
  175-99.
Wilson, Henry. "The Account of the Campaign Against the Shawnee Indians
  by Henry Wilson." *George Rogers Clark Papers, 1771-1781.* Virginia Series,
  vol. 3. *Collections of the Illinois State Historical Library* 8:476-84. Springfield,
  Ill., 1912.
Wright, John Stillman. *Letters from the West; or a Caution to Emigrants.* 1819
  Reprint. Ann Arbor, Mich.: University Microfilms, Inc., 1966.
"The Wyandots." *Xenia Torch-light* 5, no. 46 (July 20, 1843): 2.

Further reading

Banta, R.E. *The Ohio.* Rivers of America series, edited by Hervey Allen and
  Carl Carmer. New York: Rinehart & Co., 1949.
Clark, Thomas D. *Frontier America: The Story of the Westward Movement,* 2d ed.
  New York: Charles Scribner's Sons, 1969.
Downes, Randall C. *Council Fires on the Upper Ohio: A Narrative of Indian Af-*
  fairs in the Upper Ohio Valley until 1795. Pittsburgh: University of Pittsburgh
  Press, 1940.
Gilbert, Bil. *God Gave Us This Country: Tekamthi and the First American Civil*
  War. New York: Atheneum, 1989.
Handlin, Oscar, and Lilian Handlin. *Liberty in America: 1600 to the Present.*
  Volume Two, Liberty in Expansion: 1760-1850. New York: Harper & Row,
  1989.
Hill, Leonard U. *John Johnston and the Indians.* Piqua, Oh.,1957.
McConnell, Michael N. *A Country Between: The Upper Ohio Valley and Its Peoples,*
  1724-1774. Lincoln: University of Nebraska Press, 1992.
Michaux, Francois. *Travels to the West of the Alleghany Mountains....* In *Early*
  Western Travels 1748-1846, vol. 3. Edited by Reuben Gold Thwaites. Cleve-
  land: Arthur H. Clark Co., 1904.
Roseboom, Eugene H., and Francis P. Weisenburger. *A History of Ohio.* Colum-
  bus: Ohio Historical Society, 1969.
Schaaf, Gregory. *Wampum Belts and Peace Trees: George Morgan, Native Ameri-*
  cans, and Revolutionary Diplomacy. Golden, Colo.: Fulcrum Publishing, 1990.
Taylor, James. *History of the State of Ohio: First Period. 1630-1787.* Cincinnati,
  1854.

Thomson, Charles. *An Enquiry into the Causes of the Alienation of the Delaware and Shawanese Indians*. London, 1759.

Trigger, Bruce G., ed. *Northeast*, vol. 15 of *Handbook of North American Indians*. William C. Sturtevant, general ed. Washington, D.C.: Smithsonian Institution, 1978.

Wallace, Paul A. *Indians in Pennsylvania. 2d ed.* Harrisburg: Pennsylvania Historical and Museum Commission, 1991.

Index